Laurence Sterne as Satirist

Laurence Sterne as Satirist
A Reading of "Tristram Shandy"

Melvyn New

University of Florida Press
Gainesville
1969

A University of Florida Press Book

Library of Congress
Catalog Card No. 70–79524
SBN 8130–0278–8

PRINTED BY INDIANTOWN PRINTING CO., INC.
INDIANTOWN, FLORIDA

To Joan

and the power of her intense fragility

Acknowledgments

This study of Laurence Sterne's *Tristram Shandy* originated as a doctoral dissertation at Vanderbilt University, under the direction of Professor John M. Aden. For his inspiring teaching of eighteenth-century literature, for his perceptive and careful reading of my work, and for his friendship I am deeply indebted.

It gives me pleasure to acknowledge grants by the University of Florida Humanities Council and the American Philosophical Society during the summer of 1968, which enabled me to further my work on Sterne. Grateful thanks are also due to the staff of the University of Florida Division of Sponsored Research for typing my manuscript.

Reference librarians at Vanderbilt and Florida have been generous with their assistance; in particular, J. Ray Jones of the University of Florida Graduate Research Library has been consistently helpful.

A portion of Chapter I, and a few scattered paragraphs elsewhere, have appeared in somewhat different form, in *Modern Language Quarterly*, XXX (1969). I wish to express my gratitude for permission to use this material here.

While my colleagues at Florida have all been helpful, I shall perhaps be forgiven for singling out three in particular: John Algeo and J. B. Pickard for their patient listening and sound advice; and Aubrey Williams, whose generous assistance and kind encouragement while I turned the dissertation into a book will not be easily repaid.

Contents

Introduction

IN 1767, in a letter to Eliza, Laurence Sterne described a meeting he had had with Lord Bathurst in 1760, after the first four volumes of *Tristram Shandy* had appeared. "I want to know you, Mr. Sterne," Bathurst had said, "but it is fit you should know, also, who it is that wishes this pleasure. You have heard . . . of an old Lord Bathurst, of whom your Popes, and Swifts, have sung and spoken so much: I have lived my life with geniuses of that cast; but have survived them; and, despairing ever to find their equals, it is some years since I have closed my accounts, and shut up my books, with thoughts of never opening them again: but you have kindled a desire in me of opening them once more before I die; which I now do; so go home and dine with me."[1] It is a valuable anecdote—one of those fortunately preserved occurrences which make a literary period more than just a convenient textbook label. Pope had been dead for sixteen years, Swift for fifteen—and though the works of Fielding and Johnson had amply filled the literary scene, they were not Augustans; and so, the old Lord Bathurst, seventy-five years old in 1760, wanted to take Sterne home for dinner because he had found another genius of that cast.

This study argues the validity of Lord Bathurst's observation through a reinterpretation of *Tristram Shandy*. Its claim is basically twofold: *Tristram Shandy* can best be understood by locating it in the mainstream of the conservative, moralistic Augustan tradition;[2] and *Tristram Shandy* can best be understood through the intentions and conventions of the dominant literary form of that

1. *Letters of Laurence Sterne*, ed. Lewis Perry Curtis (Oxford 1935), p. 305.
2. For my concept of what constitutes the Augustan tradition I am particularly indebted to three studies: Paul Fussell, *The Rhetorical World of Augustan Humanism* (Oxford, 1965); Phillip Harth, *Swift and Anglican Rationalism* (Chicago, 1961); Aubrey Williams, *Pope's Dunciad: A Study of Its Meaning* (Baton Rouge, 1955).

1

tradition, satire. The first two chapters are directed toward the first point, through a study of Sterne's relationship to the religious and moral thinking of his day; the third chapter examines those satiric conventions which I believe Sterne borrowed from his Augustan forebears. The major portion of the study, Chapters IV through VII, offers a detailed reading of *Tristram Shandy* as a satire, an answer to the question Christian Pons raises in his review of Henri Fluchère's study of *Tristram Shandy*: "Que signifie donc ce perpétuel coq-à-l'âne? Une satire peut-être? mais de quoi?"[3]

In the halcyon days of critical innocence when I began this study as a doctoral dissertation, it was my intention to base my interpretation of *Tristram Shandy* on a rigidly maintained generic distinction between the novel and satire. The present study makes no such distinction, my critical valor falling victim to my critical discretion. What I have argued here is merely that my approach to *Tristram Shandy* is derived from the approaches of several recent critics to Augustan satire, particularly Swift's; and that, if there are meaningful reasons why the Augustan Age is also the Age of Satire, Sterne shares the Augustan viewpoint underlying the relationship. To have attempted any more in the present study would have necessitated a book twice the length, with two very distinct parts; and, as a result, the reading of *Tristram Shandy*, the primary purpose of this study, would have been overshadowed by a lengthy argument over critical premises.

My analysis of *Tristram Shandy* proceeds chronologically, taking the volumes as they were published. A distinction is maintained throughout between Sterne, the author, and Tristram, the satiric object; and my fundamental contention is that Sterne condemns Tristram's aesthetic and moral codes. The primary organization of *Tristram Shandy* is found in a metaphorical pattern, the satire moving from an opening in birth and creation to a conclusion in dissolution and death. Tristram begins his work in confidence, but he ends in chaos and confusion, lost in the self-created maze of his digressiveness, inclusiveness, and whimsicality. Sterne's attack is ultimately directed against human pride, which creates out of its own barrenness magnificent edifices to its own passions and follies and complex systems bearing no relationship to reason and reality. *Tristram Shandy* joins works like *A Tale of a Tub* and the

3. "Laurence Sterne ou le génie de l'humour," *Cahiers de Sud*, LIII (1962), 433; a review of Fluchère's *Laurence Sterne, de l'homme à l'œuvre* (Paris, 1961).

Dunciad as one further effort to stem the eighteenth century's ever increasing enthusiasm for human self-sufficiency. As an alternative, Sterne offers the more traditional view of man as a limited creature, dependent upon authority and order for a meaningful existence. This is the argument of my interpretation of *Tristram Shandy*.

I

Sterne and the Anglican Church
The source of satiric norms

I have little left to add, but to beg
of GOD, *by the assistance of his holy*
spirit, to . . . enable us to form such
right and worthy apprehensions of our
holy religion,—that it may never suffer,
through the coolness of our conceptions
of it, on one hand—or the immoderate
heat of them, on the other;—but that
we may at all times see it, as it is . . . the
most rational, sober and consistent in-
stitution that could have been given to
the sons of men.

Sterne, "On Enthusiasm"

Sterne and the Anglican Church

THAT STERNE was a clergyman of the Anglican church has proved, more often than not, a source of embarrassment to his critics. If the modern critic is not as apt as the Victorian critic to wax indignant over the imposture, he is, nonetheless, unwilling to give the forty-five sermons which survive a meaningful place in the Sterne canon.[1] John Traugott, for example, refuses to treat them as religious documents; they are rhetorical exercises. He concludes a cursory examination of them with a dismissal of their religious significance: "At any rate it is clear that while Sterne was not perfectly suited for the ministry he nevertheless owed the Church a great debt: it first permitted . . . him to express himself."[2] Traugott argues that the sermons are not to be taken seriously—either as religious doctrine or even as serious attempts at moral persuasion. They present instead, he says, "kittenish mocking of affections . . . ever on the verge of comedy," and his entire discussion is designed to show them in a Shandean light.[3]

Lansing V. D. H. Hammond's account of the sermons is basically a source study, but its findings have far-reaching consequences for a proper understanding of Sterne's Christianity. In the first place, if we accept his well-argued conjecture that most, perhaps all, of the sermons were written prior to 1750, indeed, "in rudimentary form" between 1737 and 1745, we are faced with the

---

1. For the texts of the sermons I have used *The Sermon of Mr Yorick,* vols. I and II (Shakespeare Head ed., 1927), hereafter cited within the text as *Sermons.* I have also adopted Hammond's system of enumeration: Roman numerals indicate the volume; Arabic numerals, the number originally given to a sermon within that volume; and Arabic numerals within parentheses, the cumulative number of the sermon in the complete collection.

2. *Tristram Shandy's World: Sterne's Philosophical Rhetoric* (Berkeley, 1954), p. 106.

3. *Ibid.,* p. 101.

7

interesting proposition that the sermons belong, at least in date, to the Augustan period.[4] Even more significant is Hammond's belief that "with the single exception of Swift's *Sermons*, apparently first published in 1744, Sterne made no use in his own discourses of any writing which had not already appeared in print before 1733."[5] Without discounting the incentives of fame and fortune, it can be inferred that Sterne's willingness to publish his sermons in 1760, and again in 1766, indicates a continued commitment to the religious principles he had worked out twenty years before.[6]

The sources of Sterne's religion are Latitudinarian, Tillotson and Clarke being, according to Hammond, the major sources of the sermons.[7] For Hammond, Sterne's Latitudinarian tendencies suggest the unorthodox cast of his religion, but he is cautious in his final statement of Sterne's position. He is aware, in the first place, of the common rationalistic heritage of Latitudinarianism and deism, citing in evidence Robert Kilburn Root's comment that "except in the heat of controversy, it is not easy to distinguish between the religion of an orthodox divine such as Swift and the free-thinking deists whom he despised."[8] Hammond is also aware, however, of the several attacks on deism in the sermons. Moreover, Sterne's attitudes toward miracles and mysteries "indicate an acceptance of certain fundamental Christian principles to which no advocate of a purely 'natural' religion would be willing to subscribe."[9]

Unfortunately, Hammond saves Sterne from heresy only to

4. *Laurence Sterne's* Sermons of Mr. Yorick (New Haven, 1948), pp. 56–57. For a criticism of this view, see M. R. B. Shaw, *Laurence Sterne: The Making of a Humorist, 1713–1762* (London, 1957), pp. 103–4.

5. Hammond, p. 56.

6. Cf. Arthur Hill Cash's similar defense for his use of the sermons in *Sterne's Comedy of Moral Sentiments: The Ethical Dimension of the* Journey (Pittsburgh, 1966), pp. 25–29.

7. Hammond, pp. 78–81.

8. *Ibid.*, p. 91; Hammond is quoting from Root, *The Poetical Career of Alexander Pope* (Princeton, 1938), p. 181. Cf. G. N. Clark, *The Later Stuarts: 1660–1714* (Oxford, 1934), pp. 30–31: "This insistence on reason was characteristic of English theology from the time of Locke to that of Joseph Butler . . . of the orthodox as well as of the deists, and it was developed by the . . . latitudinarians. . . ." That this is so only increases the importance of distinguishing between the orthodox position and the deistic heresy; cf. Sir Leslie Stephen, *History of English Thought in the Eighteenth Century*, 3rd ed. (New York, 1902), I, 74 ff.

9. Hammond, p. 92. Cf. S. L. Bethell, *The Cultural Revolution of the Seventeenth Century* (London, 1951), p. 17. Bethell corrects Clark's view that the Latitudinarians rejected revelation for reason.

condemn him for superficiality. He notes the indifference to "doctrinal Christianity" and the concern with doctrines not necessarily "peculiar to or distinctive of the Christian religion; his precepts tend to make of Christianity a moral philosophy rather than a religion. . . ." Sterne's failure to marshal authorities and copious quotations and his amazing freedom from the "contemporary language of polemics" are also seen, by Hammond, as indications of Sterne's unorthodox and lukewarm Christian commitment.[10] Hammond, like Traugott, ultimately leaves us with a picture of Sterne as a nominal, Shandean Christian, much like the erstwhile projector of "An Argument Against Abolishing Christianity in England." It is, I believe, a false picture.

A true picture of Sterne's Christianity depends on an understanding of the Latitudinarianism at its roots. The label, it will be recalled, was originally a term of contempt for the Cambridge Platonists, pointing primarily at their advocacy of religious toleration. Insofar as Latitudinarianism implies tolerance, the label is apropos. When, however, it is used to suggest an indifferent sort of Christianity, one at an opposite end from Anglican orthodoxy, then it needs careful qualification. The purpose of the Cambridge Platonists and of their followers, the Latitudinarians, was not the repudiation of orthodoxy but rather its re-establishment after the Interregnum. It was a normalizing and moderating purpose, and its primary instrument was reason. Between the Calvinistic extremism of the Puritans and the politic extremism of Laud, the Cambridge Platonists sought a compromise in the reasonableness of Christianity and of Christian men, hoping to throttle forever the spirit of faction that had dominated seventeenth-century life in England. "The appeal to reason," writes G. R. Cragg, "is the most conspicuous characteristic of the Cambridge school."[11]

The reasonableness of the Cambridge Platonists sought to unite all Christians "on the common ground of the great essentials of religion," while, at the same time, it de-emphasized the finer points of dogma and doctrine which had so disturbed contemporary English Christianity. But it was not the facile reasonableness which would later produce *Christianity Not Mysterious*, not the rationalism which repudiates mysteries simply because they are mys-

10. Hammond, p. 92.
11. *From Puritanism to the Age of Reason* (Cambridge, 1950), p. 42.

teries.[12] Seeking the middle ground, the Cambridge Platonists worked out the compromise between reason, faith, and revelation that served throughout the eighteenth century to unite varying degrees of Christian orthodoxy within the Anglican church. Debates over doctrinal issues would continue and at times would grow vituperative; but the fierce, disruptive struggles of the seventeenth century yielded to the essential governance of one Church, catholic in nature and flexible in doctrine.

On the question of moral conduct, compromise was again the primary concern of the Cambridge Platonists. Moral laws were divinely revealed, but they were also reasonable; and right conduct was based neither on the inexorable authority of the Calvinistic God nor, as in Hobbes, on obedience to a civil ruler, but rather on one's personal response to the right reason within. Eventually this restoration of free will and moral responsibility became the foundation for religious toleration and, in fact, for both deist and Methodist dissent. The essential intent of the Cambridge Platonists, however, was the re-establishment of a Christian's moral responsibility in the face of Calvinist and Hobbist authorities—and the reaffirmation of right reason, hedged by the authority of revelation, as the cornerstone of morality.

In many ways the Latitudinarians are second-generation Cambridge Platonists, although they inherit far more of the rationalism than the mysticism of their teachers. Against the two enemies of the established Church, Catholicism and Puritanism, reason proved the more effective weapon. At times the emphasis on reason was bound to suggest deism, the religion that reason could discover for itself; but the Latitudinarians had a more orthodox view of man's rational capacity: " . . . reason, by recognizing the limitations latent in our knowledge, is the true corrective to dogmatism. So far from making us overconfident, reason encourages diffidence and humility. . . . We are surrounded by such unfathomable mysteries that any form of dogmatism is intolerable arrogance."[13] The continued respect for mystery and the desire to prove reason in accord with revealed Christianity place the Latitudinarians in the center of eighteenth-century Anglicanism.

12. *Ibid.*, pp. 42 ff. That the Cambridge Platonists had a strong mystical strain need not concern us here; as forerunners of the Latitudinarians their fundamental contribution was their belief that reason could not contradict faith; that faith would only support reason; and that reason and revelation were one.
13. *Ibid.*, p. 67.

The Latitudinarian emphasis on reason had far-reaching effects on sermon-writing throughout the eighteenth century. The rejection of "endless debate about theological niceties" freed the sermon from the interminable citation of authorities and extensive quotations of seventeenth-century discourses. The reaction against Calvinism and predestination put renewed emphasis on the Gospel and the Church as guides for moral conduct. The darkness and anger of the Calvinistic God was displaced by a God of light, a God of love and benevolence. This reaction against Calvinism made Latitudinarianism seem more unorthodox than it ever intended to be. Its true direction, however, is conservative: It aims for a reconciliation of reason and revelation, morality and religion. The sermons of the Latitudinarians are moral rather than polemical, temperate rather than fiery, simple rather than intricate. Their aim is not to "liberalize" Anglicanism, but to return it to the center of English religious life after a century of near disaster.[14]

It is of no slight significance to the study of Sterne's Christianity that Locke agrees with the Latitudinarian divines on many major issues. Locke's *The Reasonableness of Christianity* must be considered a document of the Latitudinarian movement, and his *Essay Concerning Human Understanding*, an explanation of the nature of the rationalism which made the movement possible. The rationalistic revolt against dogma, however, is carried further by Locke than by the Latitudinarians; they turned from authority only in reaction to the dogmatism of the seventeenth century, while Locke's revolt was part of his larger struggle against the entire scholastic method. In fact, Locke's revolt against authority and his insistence on an intellectual, almost mathematical, concept of God provide a good illustration of the distance between Latitudinarianism and deism, for Locke is able to find a comfortable middle ground between the two.[15] Similarly Locke's reduction of Christianity to a belief in Jesus as the Messiah is more simplistic than the Latitudinarians would have wished. However, when pressed on the issue, Locke explained that a belief in Christ included a belief in all the doctrines known to come from Christ, thus returning to a fundamentally orthodox position.[16]

14. Cf. Bethell, pp. 17–18. Bethell's essay convincingly demonstrates the orthodoxy of the Latitudinarian position on reason and revelation.

15. See, especially, the discussion of revelation in *Essay Concerning Human Understanding*, IV, xviii–xix. Cf. Cragg, pp. 122–24.

16. Cf. Stephen, pp. 95–97.

Locke also reinforced the Latitudinarian claim that morality was the subject of Christianity, maintaining both theologically and epistemologically that moral conduct is the proper study of mankind. It is on this vital issue that Locke, like the Latitudinarians, shows the essentially orthodox position of his religious views. He had already demonstrated in the *Essay* that reason is a limited faculty; in *The Reasonableness of Christianity* he stresses the weakness of men and the need, except for the relatively few, of a system of rewards and punishments to ensure moral conduct. At times this system is one of calculating prudence; at times it is the promise of immortality; and at yet other times it is a return to the authority of the Bible and tradition. Locke's insistence on the incapacity of men to follow right reason is a view he shares with the Latitudinarians. It contrasts sharply with the deistic and moral-sense schools which brought morality within everyone's capacity.

One of the most significant studies of Swift in recent years, Phillip Harth, *Swift and Anglican Rationalism,* convincingly places the admittedly orthodox Swift within the Latitudinarian tradition. Harth attempts to dull the initial shock of this assertion by using the term "Anglican rationalists" to emphasize "the characteristic which distinguishes them as apologists of the Church of England."[17] Noting first that the older view of Swift as a skeptic in religion has now been replaced by Ricardo Quintana's illustration of his orthodoxy, Harth suggests that this orthodoxy needs a more accurate definition than the fideism now being associated with Swift.[18] The cause of this association is the false dichotomy we have seen in connection with Sterne between "orthodoxy" and "rationalism," which, Harth writes, "misinterprets the religious situation in Restoration England."

I have, to some extent, already indicated that situation. The crucial struggle of Anglicanism was against Puritan and Catholic dissent; deism or freethinking was also an enemy, of course, but the dangers were less immediate. In this struggle the most important single issue was the role of reason and revelation in religion; according to Harth's simplified but valid schematization, it became a question of mediating between "revelation, no reason" dissenters and

17. Chicago, 1961, p. 20.
18. *Ibid.,* pp. 20–21. See Quintana, *The Mind and Art of Jonathan Swift* (New York, 1936) and *Swift: An Introduction* (London, 1955). For Swift as a fideist see Kathleen Williams, *Jonathan Swift and the Age of Compromise* (Lawrence, Kan., 1958).

"reason, no revelation" deists. The fideist position was, of course, common to many Orthodox Anglicans, but, as the century drew to its close, exclusive revelation became more and more associated with the Puritans. The identification of the Catholics as fideists is in part polemical, but the rationalism of the Latitudinarians could well insist that scholastic logic and transubstantiation were unreasonable. At any rate, the linking of dissenters with Catholics on the supposition that they are possessed by essentially the same "unreason" persists even to Sterne's sermons, for example, "On Enthusiasm."[19] The Cambridge Platonists, the Latitudinarians, and Locke all joined to maintain that, in Harth's words, "reason and revelation are not incompatible in religion. On the contrary, reason and revelation together provide the grounds for religion, so that each plays its proper role in the religious sphere and neither can be ignored." Swift, according to Harth, also maintained this position, "historically . . . the mainstream of tradition in the Catholic and Anglican churches."[20]

For Harth, Swift's place in the Latitudinarian tradition is of significance primarily because of the proof it offers that *A Tale of a Tub* makes use of a traditional set of polemical devices. Sterne, too, in his satire against Catholics may possibly be echoing rather faintly these Restoration polemics. My own primary concern, however, is with the set of norms an orthodox position in the Anglican church makes available to the satirist. Apart from its classical and traditional Christian (Catholic) sources, the moral outlook of Augustan satire (the normative values against which man was measured) was provided in large measure by the orthodox stance of Anglicanism on the nature of man and the possibilities and potentialities of his achieving a moral life. At the same time deviations from the orthodox norm provided many of the targets of Augustan satire. It is no accident, as Louis Landa points out in his introduction to Swift's sermons, that "however brief the treatment, his ideas are present extensively [in the sermons]; and we can assess the nature of his mind and define his position in the eighteenth century from the sermons as clearly as we can from his other works."[21]

The relationship between satire and orthodoxy can be seen in

19. Harth, pp. 21–23. Of course, in the heat of polemics, it was just as easy to link Catholicism to deism, as Swift does in "An Argument Against Abolishing Christianity in England."
20. Harth, p. 23.
21. *The Prose Works*, ed. Herbert Davis (Oxford, 1948), IX, 101.

the sermon "On the Trinity," Swift's "most elaborate statement on Christian doctrine" and one which "exhibits clearly the orthodoxy and conventionality of his religious views."[22] The subject is the role of mystery in the Christian scheme; Swift explains why it has a rightful place:

> It would be well, if People would not lay so much Weight on their own Reason in Matters of Religion, as to think every thing impossible and absurd which they cannot conceive. How often do we contradict the right Rules of Reason in the whole Course of our Lives? *Reason* itself is true and just, but the *Reason* of every particular Man is weak and wavering, perpetually swayed and turned by his Interests, his Passions, and his Vices. Let any Man but consider . . . how blinded he is by the Love of himself, to believe that Right is Wrong, and Wrong is Right, when it maketh for his own Advantage. Where is then the right Use of his Reason, which he so much boasteth of, and which he would blasphemously set up to controul the Commands of the Almighty?[23]

That these beliefs in the limits of reason, the power of the passions and self-interest, and the inordinate pride of man operate at the core of Swift's satire is common knowledge. Moreover, Swift makes certain in this sermon on the Trinity that we understand the limits even of right reason: "But because I cannot conceive the Nature of this Union and Distinction in the Divine Nature, am I therefore to reject them as absurd and impossible; as I would, if any one told me that three Men are one, and one Man is three? . . . But the Apostle telleth us, *We see but in part, and we know but in part*; and yet we would comprehend all the secret Ways and Workings of God."[24] Significantly, Landa associates this skepticism with the limitations of reason demonstrated in the *Essay Concerning Human Understanding*. And just as Locke brings skepticism to bear on the systematizing of scholastic philosophers, so Swift uses it to free his sermons from the abstruse speculations of scholastic theologians and those Anglican clergymen who had allowed the spirit of contention to lead them into complex and futile controversies.

Swift's purpose in his sermons is rather bluntly stated at the

22. *Ibid.*, p. 107.
23. *Ibid.*, p. 166.
24. *Ibid.*, pp. 161–62.

opening of "On the Trinity": "This Day being set apart to
acknowledge our Belief in the Eternal TRINITY, I thought it
might be proper to employ my present Discourse entirely upon that
Subject; and, I hope, to handle it in such a Manner, that the most
Ignorant among you may return home better informed of your
Duty in this great Point, than probably you are at present."[25] The
refusal to enter into doctrinal disputes, evident in both Swift's and
Sterne's sermons, has its roots in the insistence that the function of
the clergy is to explain, as simply as possible, the Christian duties
of their communicants. The interest in simplicity dominates the
advice Swift gives in "A Letter to a Young Gentleman, Lately
entered into Holy Orders";[26] the interest in duty is explained in
"On the Trinity": "So, that the great Excellency of Faith, con-
sisteth in the Consequence it hath upon our Actions. . . . Therefore,
let no Man think that he can lead as good a moral Life without
Faith, as with it; for this Reason, Because he who hath no Faith,
cannot, by the Strength of his own Reason or Endeavours, so
easily resist Temptations, as the other who depends upon God's
Assistance in the overcoming his Frailties. . . ."[27] This fast union
of morality and religion is one of the marks of Latitudinarian
Anglicanism which distinguishes it from the deistic assumption of
moral conduct as a possibility quite distinct from religion. Sterne,
I shall demonstrate, also takes this orthodox approach.

Swift's sermon "Upon the Excellence of Christianity" is also of
significance to the present discussion, for here Swift defends the
Christian system of rewards and punishments against the moral
systems of the Greek and Roman philosophers. His discourse returns him to the limits of man as a moral creature and to the necessity of the union between religion and morality: "Now, human
nature is so constituted, that we can never pursue any thing heartily
but upon hopes of a reward. . . . But some of the philosophers gave
all this quite another turn, and pretended to refine so far, as to call
virtue its own reward, and worthy to be followed only for itself:
Whereas, if there be any thing in this more than the sound of the
words, it is at least too abstracted to become an universal influenc-

25. *Ibid.*, p. 159.
26. *Ibid.*, pp. 63–81. See especially his remarks on the proper language for
a sermon, pp. 65–66; on the quoting of learned authorities, pp. 75–76; on the
need to explore the mysteries of the Church, p. 77. Nothing in this advice is
significantly different from Latitudinarian reforms in sermon-writing.
27. *Ibid.*, p. 164.

ing principle in the world, and therefore could not be of general use."[28] Of this attack on the classical philosophers (and modern deists) Landa writes: "Swift follows the traditional line of argument in contending that for the generality of mankind, only Christianity has provided a really effective incentive to reject vice in favour of virtue—the doctrine of future rewards and punishments; effective because it is sensibly attuned to selfish human nature, its appeal being to man's higher self-interest—his eternal welfare."[29] In Augustan satire this union of morality and religion becomes the demand for a recognition of individual insufficiency and the need for acknowledging external controls as a curb to pride and folly. For the rational Christian as for the rational satirist, right reason informs him, above all, of the inadequacy of the very reason he seeks to re-establish.

A third sermon, "On the Testimony of Conscience," explores these problems further and is of particular interest because of Sterne's discourse on the same subject, "The Abuses of Conscience Considered."[30] Swift's sermon is an attack, once again, on a moral system independent of religion, and more particularly, according to Landa, on Shaftesbury's theory of the moral sense. The view that conscience functions independently of the laws of God, that man possesses a "natural sense of right and wrong which exists prior to and independently of the idea of God" was, for Swift, a false and dangerous heresy. Once again, Landa links Swift to Locke, citing Locke's statement from the *Essay* that "the true ground of morality . . . can only be the will and law of a God, who sees men in the dark, has in his hand rewards and punishments, and power enough to call to account the proudest offender."[31] The position, Landa notes, is an orthodox one.

The crux of both Swift's and Sterne's sermons is that the testimony of conscience cannot be trusted; that the conscience is abused by our other interests. Swift writes: ". . . whenever our Conscience accuseth us, we are certainly guilty; but we are not always innocent

28. *Ibid.*, p. 244.
29. *Ibid.*, p. 113.
30. Hammond lists the parallel passages (pp. 151–52), but considers them insignificant (p. 83). Another of Sterne's sermons, "Self-Knowledge" (I, 4), borrows extensively from "The Difficulty of Knowing One's Self," published with Swift's sermons in 1744 or 1745, although considered today of questionable authorship. See Swift, *The Prose Works*, IX, 103–6, 349–62.
31. *The Prose Works*, IX, 115. Landa is quoting from *Essay Concerning Human Understanding*, I, ii, 6.

when it doth not accuse us: For very often, through the Hardness of our Hearts, or the Fondness and Favour we bear to our selves, or through Ignorance, or Neglect, we do not suffer our Conscience to take any Cognizance of several Sins we commit."[32] Sterne's views clearly coincide:

> I own . . . whenever a man's Conscience does accuse him . . . that he is guilty. . . .
> But, the converse of the proposition will not hold true,——namely, That wherever there is guilt, the Conscience must accuse; and, if it does not, that a man is therefore innocent.
> . . . did no such thing ever happen, as that the conscience of a man, by long habits of sin, might . . . insensibly become hard . . . ——Did this never happen:——or was it certain that self-love could never hang the least bias upon the judgment . . . could no such thing as favour and affection enter this sacred court . . . were we assured that INTEREST stood always unconcern'd . . . and that PASSION never got into the judgment seat, and pronounced sentence in the stead of reason, which is supposed always to preside and determine upon the case . . . then, the religious and moral state of a man would be exactly what he himself esteemed it . . . (IV, 12[27]; Sermons, II, 68–69).

It has long been noted that the comment in *Tristram Shandy* "when a man gives himself up to the government of a ruling passion,—or, in other words, when his HOBBY-HORSE grows headstrong,—farewell cool reason and fair discretion!" is an echo of Swift's famous remark in *A Tale of a Tub:* "But when a Man's Fancy gets *astride* on his Reason, when Imagination is at Cuffs with the Senses . . . the first Proselyte he makes, is Himself. . . ." That the same idea appears in the "Abuses of Conscience Considered," with its roots in Swift's "On the Testimony of Conscience," speaks to those critics who slight the echo of *Tale of a Tub*, insisting that Sterne's view of irrational behavior was far different from Swift's, indeed, far more "Christian" than Swift's. On the contrary, it seems evident that both men drew their views from the same source—the orthodox position of the Anglican church on the question of man's ability to find a moral life by himself. Of this morality without religion, Swift says: " . . . those Men who set up for Morality without regard to Religion, are generally but virtuous

32. *The Prose Works*, IX, 150.

in part; they will be just in their Dealings between Man and Man; but if they find themselves disposed to Pride, Lust, Intemperance, or Avarice, they do not think their Morality concerned. . . . "[33] Sterne reaches the same conclusion:

> [The duties of religion and morality] are so inseparably con-
> nected together, that you cannot divide these two *Tables,*
> even in imagination (tho' the attempt is often made in prac-
> tice) without breaking and mutually destroying them both.
>   I said the attempt is often made;——and so it is;——there
> being nothing more common than to see a man, who has no
> sense at all of religion . . . who would yet take it as the bitter-
> est affront, should you but hint at a suspicion of his moral
> character. . . .
>   Let him declaim as pompously as he can . . . it will be
> found at last to rest upon . . . either his interest, his pride,
> his ease . . . (*Sermons,* II, 75–76).

Herbert Read was the first critic to notice that this view of the conscience is essentially a "classical doctrine"; his opinion has been further defended in Arthur H. Cash's article "The Sermon in *Tristram Shandy.*"[34] Working primarily from Lockean psychology, rather than from Latitudinarian theology (whose influence he slights), Cash's conclusions are nevertheless much the same as my own: (1) Sterne's sermons consistently suggest the inability or reluctance of men to judge their own behavior because their passions interfere with their reason; (2) the ethic which results from this view of man is "at bottom . . . conservative," because it reaffirms the orthodox union of religion and morality; and (3) "no one who ever looked into the sermons could doubt Sterne's orthodox view of divine commands." The only serious difference of opinion between Cash and me arises from his distinction between the *parson* who sees the failure of self-governance as "deplorable," and the *novelist* who sees it as "laughable."[35] Cash raises the question of Sterne's apparent faith, revealed here and there in the sermons, in what seems to be a "moral sense," but he is unable to reconcile such faith with a conservative ethic. Nevertheless, he insists that the "soft view" of man is predominant in the "novels"

33. *Ibid.*, pp. 152–53.
34. *The Sense of Glory* (Cambridge, 1929), pp. 144–45; *ELH,* XXXI (1964), 395–417.
35. Cash, pp. 400–404.

which are free from Swiftian satire and written in "the liberal spirit"—thus questioning the significance of his whole study.[36] I shall suggest below that this "soft view" is part of Sterne's Latitudinarian heritage, the survival of polemical arguments against the Puritan view of man, but by no means unorthodox itself.

Cash illustrates very effectively the importance of recognizing Sterne's ethics as conservative. Stressing first Sterne's rationalism, he uses it as an argument against those who regard Sterne as a sentimentalist. He demonstrates, for example, that the famous line from *Tristram Shandy*, "REASON is, half of it, SENSE," is in context not at all an affirmation of sensibility, but rather "that rare instance when Tristram reveals his moral values by telling us that he and his family have been the dupes of their appetites and senses —the very point Sterne makes in *The Abuses of Conscience Considered*. . . ."[37] At the same time, he emphasizes Sterne's allegiance to religion, noting particularly his insistence on the union of religion and morality: "By his admission that moral practice can be effected only through a fear of God's retribution, Sterne acknowledges a fundamental self-concern in man. The concession sets him apart from the more sophisticated rationalists of his own generation, who argued that true morality had to be practiced *for its own sake*."[38] In short, Sterne's rationalism saves him from sensibility, while his religion saves him from "sophisticated" rationalism, that is, from deism. The intimate relationship between deism and sensibility suggests that, polemically, Sterne's position is an orthodox one, diametrically opposed to the liberalizing tendencies in eighteenth-century thought.

This orthodoxy is revealed again and again in the sermons of Sterne; there can be little doubt that Sterne in his sermons not only shares with Swift an orthodox Christianity, but that this conservative position is what provides the moral background of Augustan satire. For example, the very first sermon in Volume I, "Inquiry after Happiness," is a "vanity of human wishes" discourse—a traditional meeting place of sermon and satire.[39] It is surely not

36. *Ibid.*, pp. 414–17.
37. *Ibid.*, p. 410.
38. *Ibid.*, p. 411.
39. In searching for a metaphor for the vanities of dignity, honor, and title, Sterne suggests the "Satyrist's comparison of the chariot wheels,—haste as they will, they must for ever keep the same distance" (I, 1; *Sermons*, I, 10). The satirist is Persius (V, 71–72).

fortuitous that the first sermon written under the *nom de plume,* Yorick, should take man through the stages of life, proving at each stage that all is vanity; Sterne could hardly have been unaware that the serious import of *Hamlet's* Yorick was precisely this. Nor is it fortuitous that this first sermon should contain the following description of a young man's quest for happiness:

> The moment he is got loose from tutors and governors, and is left to judge for himself, and pursue this scheme his own way—his first thoughts are generally full of the mighty happiness which he is going to enter upon. . . .
> In consequence of this—take notice, how his imagination is caught by every glittering appearance that flatters this expectation.—Observe what impressions are made upon his senses, by diversions, music, dress and beauty—and how his spirits are upon the wing, flying in pursuit of them . . . (I, 1; *Sermons,* I, 8).[40]

The uncontrolled and uncontrollable range of Tristram's interests, which the modern critic praises as the desire to capture the diversity of life, assumes in this sermon the far different implications of vanity and naïveté. Sterne's answer to hedonism in general is the traditional answer of Ecclesiastes: fear God and keep His commandments.[41] The union of religion and morality, so fundamental to the meaning of this first discourse, is the most persistent message of Sterne's sermons.[42]

As with Swift, the source of this message is Sterne's view of the limits of man. We have already seen the outlines of this view in the "Abuses of Conscience Considered"; it receives a similar statement in "Self-Knowledge," where Sterne tells us that "we are deceived in judging of ourselves, just as we are in judging of other things, when our passions and inclinations are called in as counsellors, and we suffer ourselves to see and reason just so far and no

40. Cf. "Pride" (IV, 9[24]; *Sermons,* II, 36); Sterne, in discussing the effects of pride on a weak brain, seems again to describe Tristram: The weak mind filled with pride is sure "to become the very fool of the comedy."

41. Five of the fifteen sermons of Volumes I and II deal in a central way with the vanity of this world: in addition to I, 1, see I, 2; II, 8; II, 10; II, 15.

42. See, for example, the strong statements in III, 6(21); IV, 11(26); V, 2(29); V, 3(30); V, 5(32); V, 6(33); VI, 7(34); VII, 16(43). V, 5(32) is of especial interest in that it is a "30th of January" sermon, long an index of political views. Sterne's attack on both "the guilt of our forefathers in staining their hands in blood," and the rebellion of 1745, suggests an essentially conservative position.

farther than they give us leave" (I, 4; *Sermons*, I, 38).[43] Most interesting in this sermon is Sterne's analysis of the possibilities of moral teaching in the face of self-interest; he suggests the moral fable: ". . . as they [moral instructors] had not strength to remove this flattering passion which stood in their way and blocked up all the passages to the heart, they endeavoured by stratagem to get beyond it, and by a skilful address, if possible, to deceive it. This gave rise to the early manner of conveying their instructions in parables, fables, and such sort of indirect applications, which, tho' they could not conquer this principle of self-love, yet often laid it asleep . . . till a just judgment could be procured" (*Sermons*, I, 40). Much has been made by Hammond and others of Sterne's tendency to dramatize his sermons, the implication being that Sterne was more interested in the story he told than in the doctrine he preached. Nothing could be further from the truth, for Sterne's addition of a narrative dimension to several of his sermons is a quite traditional practice in pulpit oratory. Sterne learned much about narrative in writing his sermons; but, above all else, he learned the value of a story as an agreeable vehicle for the often unpleasant task of telling men what they really are. Yorick's comment on preaching, "For my own part . . . I had rather direct five words point blank to the heart," has also been viewed as indicative of Sterne's religious laxity, his "happy-go-lucky disposition."[44] It is clear, however, that Yorick is opposing in this passage the heart to the head as respective seats of truth and hypocrisy. That the heart for Sterne is more closely connected with right reason than with moral sensibility is suggested by the phrase "till a just judgment could be procured" from "Self-Knowledge." When self-deceit is pierced by a story, the heart does not reveal the glory of the naturally moral man, but the truth of the limited man whose reason tells him he must fear God and keep the commandments.[45]

43. Cf. "The Character of Herod" (II, 9), where Sterne suggests that although we are made in God's image, innocent and upright, we are creatures all too easily swayed by our passions, particularly our ruling passion (*Sermons*, I, 101–11).
44. Hammond, pp. 99–101.
45. Cf. "The Prodigal Son" (III, 5[20]; *Sermons*, I, 227): "I know not whether the remark is to our honour or otherwise, that lessons of wisdom have never such power over us, as when they are wrought into the heart, through . . . a story which engages the passions. . . . Is the heart so in love with deceit, that where a true report will not reach it, we must cheat it with a fable, in order to come at truth?"

The strongest attacks on self-deception, however, occur in "Pharisee and Publican in the Temple" and "Pride."[46] In the first, Sterne analyzes the character of the Pharisee as an example of the "worst of human passions;—pride—spiritual pride, the worst of all pride —hypocrisy, self-love. . . ." His dramatization of the Pharisee's prayer in the temple is brilliantly ironic:

> GOD! I thank thee that thou hast formed me of different materials from the rest of my species, whom thou hast created frail and vain by nature, but by choice and disposition utterly corrupt and wicked.
> Me, thou hast fashioned in a different mould. . . . I am raised above the temptations and desires to which flesh and blood are subject—I thank thee that thou hast made me thus —not a frail vessel of clay, like that of other men . . . (I, 6; *Sermons*, I, 73).

Apparent through the irony is Sterne's view of man, "frail and vain by nature." Those critics who expect from an eighteenth-century Anglican clergyman a Calvinistic commitment to unrelieved depravity will, of course, find Sterne quite liberal; but those who understand that eighteenth-century orthodoxy was molded during the Restoration, in reaction to Puritan theology, will see that Sterne's view of man is essentially conservative—man, not irrevocably corrupt, but yet "frail and vain by nature . . . by choice and disposition utterly corrupt and wicked." Sterne's several suggestions of the existence of the innate moral sense must be reconciled with this view and not simply accepted as a deistic glorification of man's moral capability.[47]

The sermon "Pride" offers a more systematic attack on this vice of "little and contracted souls." On the one hand, Sterne argues with those "satyrical pens" that write "all mankind at the bottom were proud alike," for, he says, there are thousands of men of the

46. I, 6, and IV, 9 (24). See also, "Self-Examination" (II, 14; *Sermons*, I, 160–68).

47. Cf. "Vindication of Human Nature" (I, 7). This sermon, often cited as an example of Sterne's "soft view" of man, is no more than an orthodox argument against Hobbes' doctrine of universal selfishness. Sterne argues that although the brightness of God's image has been "sullied greatly" by the fall, and by our "own depraved appetites," yet it is a "laudable pride . . . to cherish a belief, that there is so much of that glorious image still left upon it, as shall restrain him from base and disgraceful actions . . ." (*Sermons*, I, 82–83). The orthodoxy of this "divine residue" and its distance from any sort of deistic or Shaftesburian moral sense should be apparent.

most unaffected humility (IV, 9[24]; *Sermons,* II, 33—34). On the other hand, Sterne supports these same "satyrical pens" insofar as "Pride is a vice which grows up in society so insensibly . . . that upon the whole, there is no one weakness into which the heart of man is more easily betray'd,——or which requires greater helps of good sense and good principles to guard against" (*Sermons,* II, 34). Moreover, in explaining that the origin of pride is in meanness of heart, the vice of "little and contracted souls," Sterne can do no better than to quote "one of our poets . . . in that admirable stroke he has given of this affinity, in his description of a *Pride which licks the dust.*" Sterne's attack on satire in this sermon is often taken out of context as indicative of his negative attitude toward the genre; no recognition is shown that in the same paragraph he gives a qualified assent to the satirists, and in the next quotes Pope's *Epistle to Dr. Arbuthnot* to support his view.[48] The use of satire to attack pride is suggested again in "Job's Account of the Shortness and Troubles of Life Considered" (II, 10). Sterne raises the question at the end of this survey of human misery of what purpose it serves to expose the dark side of human life, and finds it of great importance, since "the holding up this glass to shew him his defects . . ." cures man's pride and gives him humility—"which is a dress that best becomes a short-lived and a wretched creature" (*Sermons,* I, 124). When Sterne criticizes satirists, as he does in "Vindication of Human Nature" (I, 7) where he takes exception to those satirists who have "desperately fallen foul upon the whole species" (*Sermons,* I, 83), he is not necessarily aligning himself with the general attack on satire prevalent in the middle of the century.[49] His obvious taste for the Augustans and our own understanding of them make it at least as possible that he was drawing a distinction between invective and satire; Dryden, Pope, and Swift would do no less.[50]

For Sterne, as for Locke, the Latitudinarians, and the Augustans, excessive pride is inextricably linked to enthusiasm and dissent.

48. "Beauty that shocks you, Parts that none will trust,/Wit that can creep, and Pride that licks the dust." *An Epistle to Dr. Arbuthnot,* 11. 332—33; the lines describe Sporus.

49. See Bertrand A. Goldgar, "Satires on Man and 'The Dignity of Human Nature,' " *PMLA,* LXXX (1965), 535—41.

50. Cf. "Evil-Speaking" (II, 11), and "The Levite and his Concubine" (III, 3[18]). In the latter the attack on satire is actually an attack on the *false* wits of the age who set up as libelers.

The sermon "Humility," for example, becomes strongly polemical, reminding us of the strength of Methodism among the lower classes during the 1740's.[51] Sterne again turns to irony:

> However backwards the world has been in former ages in the discovery of such points as GOD never meant us to know, ——we have been more successful in our own days:—— thousands can trace out now the impressions of this divine intercourse in themselves. . . .
>   It must be owned, that the present age has not altogether the honour of this discovery;—there were too many grounds given to improve on in the religious cant of the last century; . . . when, as they do now, the most illiterate mechanicks, who as a witty divine said of them, were much fitter to *make* a pulpit, than get into one,—were yet able so to frame their nonsense to the nonsense of the times, as to beget an opinion in their followers . . . that the most common actions of their lives were set about in the Spirit of the LORD (IV, 10 [25]; *Sermons*, II, 49–50).

The witty divine is obviously Swift, and Sterne begins to sound more like him with every stroke: "When a poor disconsolated drooping creature is terrified from all enjoyment,—prays without ceasing 'till his imagination is heated,——fasts and mortifies and mopes, till his body is in as bad a plight as his mind; is it a wonder, that the mechanical disturbances and conflicts of an empty belly, interpreted by an empty head, should be mistook for workings of a different kind from what they are . . ." (*Sermons*, II, 51).

It is the sermon "On Enthusiasm," however, which most clearly reveals Sterne's use of Latitudinarian arguments to reject the pride of deism and dissent. Noting the deist's tendency to ignore revelation and the dissenter's contrary tendency to "destroy the reason of the gospel itself,—and render the christian religion, which consists of sober and consistent doctrines,—the most intoxicated,— the most wild and unintelligible institution that ever was . . . ," he defines his purpose to "reduce both the extremes . . . to reason [and] . . . to mark the safe and true doctrine of our church . . ." (VI, 11 [38]; *Sermons*, II, 187). Above all, his theme is to prove the wisdom of "our sufficiency being of God"; his text is John

51. The satiric reaction to Methodism is surveyed in Albert M. Lyles, *Methodism Mocked* (London, 1960). The Jacobite scare in 1745 suggests one reason for the anti-Catholicism of the sermons; in short, Sterne's Anglicanism was facing essentially the same challenges Swift's faced a quarter century before.

15:5: *"For without me, ye can do nothing."* Sterne's arguments for the necessity of revelation are traditional; his arguments against enthusiasm are also traditional, including an interesting linking of enthusiasm with Catholicism: "Already it [enthusiasm] has taught us as much blasphemous language;—and . . . will fill us with as many legendary accounts of visions and revelations, as we have formerly had from the church of Rome. . . . When time shall serve, it may as effectually convert the professors of it, even into popery itself,—consistent with their own principles . . ." (*Sermons,* II, 197). Throughout his attack on the extremes, Sterne persists in arguing the rational middle way, ending with a benediction which defines, exactly and emphatically, his orthodox religious position: ". . . I have little left to add, but to beg of GOD, by the assistance of his holy spirit, to preserve us equally from both extremes, and enable us to form such right and worthy apprehensions of our holy religion,—that it may never suffer, through the coolness of our conceptions of it, on one hand,—or the immoderate heat of them, on the other;—but that we may at all times see it, as it is . . . the most rational, sober and consistent institution that could have been given to the sons of men" (*Sermons,* II, 198).

Article IX of the Thirty-Nine Articles, "Of Original or Birth-Sin," reads in part: "Original Sin standeth not in the following of *Adam* (as the *Pelagians* do vainly talk), but it is the fault and corruption of the Nature of every man, that naturally is engendered of the offspring of *Adam*; whereby man is very far gone from original righteousness, and is of his own nature inclined to evil, so that the flesh lusteth always contrary to the spirit. . . ." As Anglicans, both Swift and Sterne accepted this view of man's nature; it molded their vision of the life they wrote about and the form that that vision took. Article IX, to be sure, rejects the Calvinistic extreme of total depravity, and we search in vain for this view in either Sterne or Swift. Article IX does, however, make absolutely clear that man is not only susceptible, but indeed inclined, to sin; that he possesses, as Ernest Tuveson comments, "a positive tendency to do evil, a mysterious dynamic spirit of perversity for which there is explanation in Genesis and remedy in the Gospel."[52] Such contrariness makes the teachings of the Christian church absolutely

52. "Swift: The Dean as Satirist," *UTQ,* XXII (1952–53), 370. See also, Donald Greene, "Augustinianism and Empiricism: A Note on Eighteenth-Century English Intellectual History," *ECS,* I (1967), 39–51.

vital to man's ethical life; thus, for Sterne and Swift, morality is never to be separated from religion, wisdom never to be divorced from revelation. The faculty of reason is, of course, essential to man, but right reason is never contradictory to revelation. Reason is our most reliable faculty, but it too is rendered imperfect by the perverse tendency to evil which makes revelation our only certain means of salvation.

It is here in the Anglican view of willful and insistent perversity that the Augustan vision of man takes its literary foothold, for in the abuse of reason can be found the root of all religious, social, political, and literary aberrations, all the targets of Augustan satire. If in the religious life the doctrines of the Anglican church provided the norms against which deviations could be measured, the ordered universe suggested that in every other sphere of human endeavor, analogous deviations could be measured by analogous standards. Man's tendency to evil operated in literature as well as in religion, in polite society as well as in the state. It is not at all fortuitous that Swift uses a literary hack to satirize religious enthusiasm, or that the epic action of Pope's *Dunciad* should bring "The Smithfield Muses to the Ear of Kings."[53] For the Augustan satirist, bad writing is a natural symbol for the moral corruption that demands and supplies it, and thus he has, ready at hand, the metaphorical and symbolic patterns which contribute so greatly to the tensions and complexities of his writings. As Geoffrey Tillotson notes, "for Pope, a bad author was to literature what a fool or a knave was to life."[54]

Finally, the relation of the Augustan vision to the Anglican sense of man's perverse inclination to evil suggests the norm by which, ultimately at least, its satire operated. As in religion an acknowledgment of the limitations of man necessarily implies a dependence on the authority of the Church, so in all other realms of conduct authority of some kind is indicated. A rigid codification of that authority—whether it be ecclesiastical, critical, or political —is rarely attempted, the authority more often than not revealing

53. See Aubrey L. Williams, *Pope's* Dunciad: *A Study of Its Meaning* (Baton Rouge, 1955). Of this "analogy," Williams writes: "The inundation of England by purveyors of bad art, and the untutored or degenerate taste which hailed their literary efforts, was a 'conjuncture' of events suggesting a general slackening in the moral and social fibre of the nation." Artistic deterioration, he adds, is the "metaphor by which bigger deteriorations are revealed" (p. 14).

54. *On the Poetry of Pope* (Oxford, 1938), p. 35.

itself by its expressed sensitivity to deviations from its spirit rather than by a crystalization of its law. This may, in fact, prove the ultimate virtue of Augustan authority, at its best—that it refuses to be categorical, that it resists the systematic fallacy, to which Puritans and projectors alike were so prone. Augustan authority rather tends to invite man to look for the operation of reason or common sense or nature; to look for generality, moderation, and compromise; and to acknowledge his inherent weakness, limitation, and need for discipline, tradition, and control. The authority or norm, in other words, is not so much abstractly defined as it is pragmatically revealed or exposed: In each sphere of human activity it emerges, characteristically, from the satiric consideration of deviations. In short, more important to an understanding of the moral world of Augustan satire than any precise measure of its norm is the simple fact of the norm itself. The ultimate field of that norm is Anglicanism; not, however, some specific doctrine of Anglicanism violated, say, by Puritan enthusiasm, but the acceptance by the satirist (and his audience) of an orthodox Christian position, catholic enough to include Pope, as normative.

Similarly, I would suggest that deviations from the norm, while as various as man's contrary imagination, all spring essentially from the same source: man's prideful rebellion against his own limited nature and the authority placed over him to discipline his waywardness. I have already shown how Swift and Sterne agree in finding excessive pride at the root of both deism and dissent. If we turn to *Gulliver's Travels*, we note that pride is still the central concern. Edward Rosenheim, for example, writes: "I do not think the crucial concepts in *Gulliver's Travels* are 'man' or 'animal' or 'rational,' for all the obvious importance of these terms. In the *Travels*, as in the *Tale*, Swift's most profound intellectual commitments hinge, I believe, upon his conception of knowledge and of pride. . . ."[55] Kathleen M. Williams recognizes the same problem: "Swift frequently comments on man's strange inability, shared with no other animal, to know his own capacities, and the form which this inability most often takes . . . is a refusal to realise how narrowly we are bounded by our bodies, by senses and passions and by all the accidents of our physical presence in a material world."[56]

55. *Swift and the Satirist's Art* (Chicago, 1963), p. 220.
56. "'Animal Rationis Capax.' A Study of Certain Aspects of Swift's Imagery," *ELH*, XXI (1954), 196.

And we need not agree completely with Tuveson's reading of Book
IV, to accept the validity of this view of Gulliver among the
Houyhnhnms: "The dilemma and despair . . . [of Gulliver], in
his inevitable failure to be able to emulate the patterns of perfection,
in his failure to understand the whole situation, would be those of
anyone who attempts to account for human nature without original
sin."[57] The refusal to recognize, because of pride, one's own limited
nature; the refusal to accept, because of pride, the authority of what
has been: These are the essential vices of Augustan satire. And con-
versely, the use of the reason to control pride and acknowledge one's
limitations; the use of the reason to argue against pride the necessity
for authority: These are the essential virtues by which these vices are
measured and condemned. In the tense interplay of authority,
pride, and reason, the Augustans defined their satiric vision; it is as
well, I believe, the vision Sterne accepted and upheld in his satire,
Tristram Shandy.

57. Tuveson, p. 369. See also Samuel H. Monk, "The Pride of Lemuel
Gulliver," *Sewanee Review*, LXIII (1955), 48–71; Edward Wasiolek, "Relativity in *Gulliver's Travels*," PQ, XXXVII (1958), 110–16; James Brown,
"Swift as Moralist," PQ, XXXIII (1954), 368–87. Brown comments at one
point: ". . . the fault is that of pride, the condition ignored is Original Sin, the
final result is vicious action—moral chaos" (p. 381).

Sterne and Sentiment
The source of satiric targets

But for Sterne, virtue is never sanctioned by a sensation or feeling or moral sense; it is sanctioned only by reason. When Sterne's characters (or he himself) forget this ideal, they lose their autonomy and become the objects of his laughter.

Arthur Hill Cash, *Sterne's Comedy of Moral Sentiments: The Ethical Dimension of the* Journey

Sterne and Sentiment

HEN IN 1704 Swift published *A Tale of a Tub,* he included an ironical salute to anyone who would undertake the rescue of human complacency:

... whatever Philosopher or Projector can find out an Art to sodder and patch up the Flaws and Imperfections of Nature, will deserve much better of Mankind, and teach us a more useful Science, than that so much in present Esteem, of widening and exposing them. ... And he, whose Fortunes and Dispositions have placed him in a convenient Station to enjoy the Fruits of this noble Art; He that can with *Epicurus* content his Ideas with the *Films* and *Images* that fly off upon his Senses from the *Superficies* of Things; Such a Man truly wise, creams off Nature, leaving the Sower and the Dregs, for Philosophy and Reason to lap up. This is the sublime and refined Point of Felicity, called, *the Possession of being well deceived;* The Serene Peaceful State of being a Fool among Knaves.[1]

Seven years later such a philosopher appeared on the scene and quickly won the acclaim and the following Swift had predicted. I quote from *Spectator,* No. 10: "Since I have raised to my self so great an Audience, I shall spare no Pains to make their Instruction agreeable, and their Diversion useful. For which Reasons I shall endeavour to enliven Morality with Wit, and to temper Wit with Morality. ... It was said of *Socrates,* that he brought Philosophy down from Heaven, to inhabit among Men; and I shall be ambitious to have it said of me, that I have brought Philosophy out of Closets and Libraries, Schools and Colleges, to dwell in Clubs and Assemblies, at Tea-Tables, and in Coffee-Houses."[2] Thus quite unconsciously was joined, early in the century, the debate which

1. *A Tale of a Tub,* eds. A. C. Guthkelch and D. Nichol Smith, 2nd ed. (Oxford, 1958), p. 174.
2. *The Spectator,* ed. Donald F. Bond (Oxford, 1965), I, 44.

raged throughout, for behind the *Spectator* venture lay a view of human nature and human activity radically opposed to Swift's view—the view defined in Chapter I. Upon an infinite variety of fronts the battle was joined in the eighteenth century; but of most significance to this study is that engagement which can be called the Battle of Satire and Sentiment, or, less metaphorically, the satiric/sentimental dichotomy. The disadvantages inherent in any such simplification of the thought of an age are many. For one, the question seems begged by the use of "sentimental (-ist)" since the word, to the twentieth century, is pejorative. Second, while dichotomy is an effective argumentative device, it obviously functions less well as an explanatory one. Finally, too many of the century's great figures, Shaftesbury, Fielding, Goldsmith, to span the century, are reduced to one side or the other only by misrepresentation of their total achievement.[3] Nonetheless, the distinction between satirist and sentimentalist is a useful one for much of the intellectual life of the century, and of especial pertinence to the problem at hand.

The source of sentimentalism was, for many years, traced to Shaftesbury's *Characteristics* and no further. In an important article in 1934, however, R. S. Crane convincingly demonstrated its beginnings in the same movement which provided the origins of eighteenth-century Anglican orthodoxy—the activity of the Cambridge Platonists immediately following the Interregnum.[4] In discussing the essential orthodoxy of this movement, and of the Latitudinarianism which followed, I set aside, momentarily, this aspect of their thought, although it is as much a part of their orthodoxy as their commitment to the union of religion and morality. Reacting against the Calvinistic view of God as cruel and implacable, and against its dismissal of all human endeavor—of "good works" or "Christian virtues"—as inconsequential, the Cambridge Platonists *returned* to a more Christian (and, to them, more reasonable) concept of the infinite goodness of God and to "the identi-

3. Cf. R. L. Brett, *The Third Earl of Shaftesbury* (London, 1951), p. 59: "He has been called in turn a Stoic, a Deist, a sceptic, a Platonist and a disciple of Spinoza. He has been assigned to both of the opposed schools of eighteenth-century moral philosophy; those who made reason and those who made feeling the faculty of moral judgment."

4. "Suggestions toward a Genealogy of the 'Man of Feeling,'" *ELH*, I (1934), 205–30. Significantly, Brett begins his study of Shaftesbury with a chapter on the Cambridge Platonists.

fication of virtue with acts of benevolence."[5] In no way, however, should these views be confused with unorthodoxy or with a turning away from the view of man defined in Chapter I. As Louis I. Bredvold concludes of the Cambridge Platonists: "They had pleasant things to say about both virtue and human nature. As good Anglicans they did not deny that man is sinful and in a fallen state, but they insisted that he still retains something of the image of God in which he was made. . . . They were not moral relativists; they were not saying that man is the measure of all things. They were profoundly convinced that the moral law is eternal and immutable, that goodness is an attribute of God and must be forever the same."[6]

No single aspect of this renewed concern with God's benevolence was more emphasized by the Latitudinarian divines than the exhortation of Christian men to emulate that benevolence; "charity was one of their favorite themes: not the charity which was primarily love of God; not charity merely to the parish poor or to fellow Christians, but a 'general kindness' to all men because they are men, an active desire to relieve their sufferings, if not to alter the social conditions in which they live. . . . "[7] In the orthodox tradition, it is important to note, benevolence and the associated virtues are reflections of God in man. Far from removing God from His place in a moral universe, the Latitudinarians returned Him to its center, making morality a religious duty, a fulfillment of God's revelation; and, because reason and revelation are one, benevolence becomes the mark of the *reasonable* man. The recognition was strong, at the same time, that men were not reasonable, that they were not inclined to benevolence but to malevolence, not to good but to evil. At times, under the pressures of pulpit oratory, the Latitudinarian divine would place special emphasis on the divine residue in man, particularly, as Landa notes in his introduction to Swift's sermons, in Charity sermons "on the duty and pleasure of doing good."[8] This was no more than to say that, in the good Christian, right reason can, with effort and faith, exercise sway over the passions and their natural tendency toward corruption. To have insisted, as many in the eighteenth century did, on man's

5. Crane, p. 206.
6. *The Natural History of Sensibility* (Detroit, 1962), pp. 8–9.
7. Crane, p. 211.
8. *The Prose Works,* ed. Herbert Davis (Oxford, 1948), IX, 125.

instinctive propensity to benevolence, independent of the laws of God, would have been contradictory to the entire moral position of Latitudinarianism. Crane expresses surprise, in the face of the century's overwhelming endorsement of benevolence, that the modern critic can call the moral ideal of the Augustan period "cold intellectuality."[9] The term does seem too stark, but it also reminds us of the reasonable nature of benevolence to the Augustan mind; "cold intellectuality" serves as a useful contrast to the "warmth" and "wetness" which sought to expel it. That the "Age of Reason" is in many ways a misnomer for the Augustan age is a truism often repeated in recent years. However, in spite of the Augustan concern with the awful powers of passion, and the vital necessity for religious faith, there is too much truth in the label "Age of Reason" for it to be readily dismissed. And nowhere is that truth better revealed than in the continuing debate throughout the century over the role of benevolent feelings in the moral structure of the universe.

Swift's sermon most concerned with the question of benevolence, "On Mutual Subjection," makes clear the orthodoxy within which a reasonable benevolence operated. Using as his text, I Peter 5:5: *"Yea, all of you be subject one to another,"* Swift first defends, as God-ordained, the hierarchical structure of society, and then argues the mutual dependence of each order upon the other, since all orders, from king to tradesman, are insufficient by themselves. Benevolence, then, is a direct result of man's imperfections: "God Almighty hath been pleased to put us into an imperfect State, where we have perpetual Occasion of each other's Assistance. There is none so low, as not to be in a Capacity of assisting the Highest; nor so high, as not to want the Assistance of the Lowest."[10] At the same time, Swift acknowledges clearly and precisely the conflict which the divine imperative to benevolence (of which Christ is the primary example) raises within the nature of man: "And, although this Doctrine of subjecting ourselves to one another may seem to grate upon the Pride and Vanity of Mankind, and may therefore be hard to be digested by those who value themselves upon their Greatness or their Wealth; yet, is it really no more than what most Men practise upon other Occasions."[11] Finally, one of

9. Crane, pp. 215–16.   10. *The Prose Works,* IX, 143.
11. *Ibid.,* p. 145. The "other Occasions" are the practices of good manners and civility.

the primary rewards of benevolence, "of subjecting ourselves to the Wants and Infirmities of each other," is the extinguishing in ourselves of "the Vice of Pride." Swift explains: "For, if God hath pleased to entrust me with a Talent, not for my own Sake, but for the Service of others, and at the same time hath left me full of Wants and Necessities which others must supply; I can then have no Cause to set any extraordinary Value upon myself, or to despise my Brother, because he hath not the same Talents which were lent to me. His Being may probably be as useful to the Publick as mine; and therefore, by the Rule of right Reason, I am in no sort preferable to him."[12]

Swift's reliance on reason to explain the operation of benevolence, coupled with his suggestion of a psychomachy between benevolence and pride, illustrates the method by which Anglican orthodoxy absorbed the renewed interest in a benevolent God. There can be no question that Swift was far less optimistic than many of the Latitudinarians over man's inclinations toward benevolent action, but both Swift's reserve and the Latitudinarians' optimism operate within the framework of an orthodox moral scheme which makes God, not man, the measure of virtue. Given the orthodox frame of the interdependence of religion and morality due to the limits of man, no amount of optimism within that frame can be anything less than orthodox; and even as "sentimental" an idea as the "pleasures of pity" can be adapted by Swift to his own orthodoxy: "What is there, that can give a generous Spirit more Pleasure and Complacency of Mind, than to consider, that he is an Instrument of doing much Good? . . . The wickedest Man upon Earth taketh a Pleasure in doing Good. . . . "[13] In short, as is really quite obvious, orthodox Christianity cannot help but be involved with questions of benevolence, of charity, good humor, love, and pity—concepts expressive of the new dispensation. That these words become part of the vocabulary of a quite unorthodox movement in the eighteenth century should not confuse this fundamental fact, just as the deistic takeover of "reason" must not be allowed to blind us to the rational dimension of Anglican orthodoxy.

Several of Sterne's sermons address themselves to the problem of charity, most significantly the so-called "Charity Sermon," printed

12. *Ibid.*, pp. 145–46.
13. *Ibid.*, p. 148.

in York in 1747. Using the story of Elijah and the widow, Sterne pictures benevolence as a function of humility, and joins Swift in finding it at war with pride: ". . . GOD certainly interwove that friendly softness in our nature to be a check upon too great a propensity toward self-love . . ." (I, 5; *Sermons,* I, 55). In addition, Sterne uses the argument of self-interest, citing "reason and scripture" to the effect that "a charitable and good action is seldom cast away"; and, indeed, charity becomes a measure against the vanity of the world, for "the great instability of temporal affairs" makes it certain that "many a man has lived to enjoy the benefit of that charity which his own piety projected" (*Sermons,* I, 60–61). It is above all, however, the example of Christ that exhorts us to benevolence, though the appeal of that example is to reasonableness: "The consideration of this stupendous instance of compassion [the Passion], in the Son of GOD, is the most unanswerable appeal that can be made to the heart of man, for the reasonableness of it in himself.—It is the great argument which the apostles use in almost all their exhortations to good works . . ." (*Sermons,* I, 66). One does good in order to follow the "amiable pattern" of Christ and to discharge, as best one can, the "immense debt" His sacrifice entailed; nothing could be more Christian and less touched with the cant of sensibility than this.

As for the "pleasures of pity," Sterne cites the Preacher of Ecclesiastes when he declares, "that he knew of no good there was in any of the riches or honours of this world, *but for a man to do good with them in his life,"* and comments: "Nor was it without reason he had made this judgment.——Doubtless he had found and seen the insufficiency of all sensual pleasures; how unable to furnish either a rational or a lasting scheme of happiness . . ." (*Sermons,* I, 62). Like Swift, Sterne labors first to establish a reasonable basis for benevolence. Only then does he suggest the possibility of other rewards, though at first his appeal is to physical rather than emotional well-being: " . . . I cannot conceive, but that the very *mechanical motions* which maintain life, must be performed with more equal vigour and freedom in that man whom a great and good soul perpetually inclines to shew mercy to the miserable, than they can be in a poor, sordid, selfish wretch . . ." (*Sermons,* I, 63). Even when Sterne recognizes that he is praising charity only by condemning its opposite, his consideration continues in an orthodox vein. Asking whether anything could be "more lovely and engaging" than charity, he answers by having his congregation draw "the most perfect and amiable character, such, as according to our conceptions of the Deity, we should think most acceptable to him . . ." (*Sermons*, I, 65). Benevolence is, of course, the attribute most favored, but God, not man, is the measure and the demonstration of this fact. Sterne's other sermons devoted to benevolence in no way contradict this essential orthodoxy.

By beginning and ending their argument for benevolence in a direct confrontation with the Calvinistic conception of God, the Cambridge Platonists and those orthodox Anglican divines who followed them were able to re-establish good humor, love, and charity at the center of an orthodox Christian scheme.[14] Needless to say, however, Puritanism was replaced by the challenge of Hobbes as the Restoration drew on, and Hobbes, by centering his attention not on God's nature but on man's, dramatically changed the entire course of eighteenth-century thought on benevolence. The secularization of the question of benevolence flows through Shaftesbury and Hutcheson, Hume and Adam Smith, to its popularization in the movement now pejoratively labeled "sentimentalism." Because it posited an absolute faith in man's capacity to lead, by himself, a moral life, this secular tradition very soon found itself under fire from the orthodox tradition; and the satiric/sentimental dichotomy began to emerge.

To be sure, the religious and secular arguments against Hobbes were often one and the same. Hobbes was as dangerous an enemy to the Cambridge Platonists as the Puritans, and they directed many arguments to him; at the same time, a secular philosopher like Shaftesbury could make much use of the existing Anglican stance on benevolence in his own attack on Hobbes. It is precisely this possibility for confusion, however, that necessitates the distinction I am suggesting, for between a benevolence based on God and a benevolence based on man, in spite of the similarities of vocabulary, lies the crucial division of a century of English thought. In a word, when the moral philosophers decided, as Crane says they did, "that even without government they [men] can be trusted to live together peacefully in sympathetic and helpful mutual rela-

14. This may seem a curious assertion in view of the central position of *caritas* and *agape* in the Christian religion. That there was a displacement of these values in seventeenth-century Christianity is perhaps indicated by Crane's linking the Latitudinarian emphasis upon them to Shaftesbury's secular morality, rather than seeing such emphasis as central to the Christian scheme.

tions," they found themselves in sudden and direct opposition to the Anglican church.[15]

Concomitant with this shift in emphasis from God to man is a similar shift from the importance of reason to the importance of emotion in the moral life. Here again the Latitudinarian influence can be felt, for in the reaction against Calvinism, Anglican orthodoxy had moved away from the stoical condemnation of all emotions to a more moderate recognition of their place in any valid system of Christian ethics. That such a recognition also forms the basis of the Augustan satirist's position on the passions was pointed out by Professor Lovejoy: "Pope devotes many lines of versified argumentation to showing that the motive-power and the principal directive force in man's life is—and should be—not reason, but the complex of instincts and passions which make up our 'natural' constitution."[16] There is, needless to say, a vast difference between this concern with the passions and the "glorification" of emotion which becomes the hallmark of the "sentimentalists." And yet, in a writer like Shaftesbury, it is easy to see how the two views become confused; in spite of his great enthusiasm for an instinctive "moral sense," Shaftesbury was never far removed from the orthodox ideal of reason and revelation as the ultimate tests of moral action. Insisting first that our ideas of good and evil are completely divorced from divine revelation, and, second, that any system of enforcement must be equally removed from the rewards of religion, he posits instead the "moral sense" which inheres in each individual, independent man. The precise nature of this faculty is elusive, but R. L. Brett is not very far off when he suggests that it is the "reason": "The use of the phrase 'moral sense' does not betoken a wish to set up a separate faculty, but simply a desire to describe accurately the nature of the moral judgment. . . . At times he seems to suggest that it is the reason which is the faculty and this is in keeping with the rest of his theory; for what he objects to is the idea that we make moral judgments by a process of *reasoning*."[17] Shaftesbury objected to *reasoning* as a process because he wanted to keep the intuitiveness and immediacy of the moral sense paramount. Because the moral sense was analogous to the aesthetic sense, the

15. Crane, p. 222.

16. A. O. Lovejoy, " 'Pride' in Eighteenth-Century Thought," *MLN*, XXXVI (1921), 36.

17. Brett, p. 81.

recognition and approval of the morally harmonious and proportionate had to have the same instinctive surety as it did in the aesthetic experience. But Shaftesbury never reduces morality entirely to sentiment as his followers were soon to do. In his scheme, the moral sense functions too much like the conscience or even the divine residue of right reason for Shaftesbury to be labeled a sentimentalist pure and simple, and his constant reliance on taste and good breeding suggests an ever present awareness that without "grace" the individual moral sense is incomplete.

All this in no way ameliorates, of course, the extreme danger in which Shaftesbury put orthodoxy. His attack on religion's place in morality; his insistence that our knowledge of good and evil is "antecedent to, and independent of, any religious beliefs";[18] and his refusal to accept any system of rewards and punishments, virtue being its own best reward, all threatened the tenuous alliance between revelation, reason, and morality so carefully worked out by the Cambridge Platonists and Latitudinarians. Moreover, his repeated emphasis on the pleasurable effects of doing good, on the "naturalness" of virtue to the human creature, quickly loses any orthodox ring it might have when we realize that the analogy drawn is constantly to aesthetics and never to the divine model. Finally, as William E. Alderman points out, the stress on the moral sense as an individual possession was replete with potential havoc: "In reality the theory if applied in full would tend to make the ethical norm a variable rather than a constant standard. . . . Were morality made to depend wholly upon passing intuitions, conscience would no longer be the rational force that we conceive it to be. If we accept the doctrine that an instinctive reaction is as infallible as a studied judgment, we hereby deny the need of any restraint and struggle."[19]

However innocuous Shaftesbury's original intentions (and it must be granted, as Bredvold points out, that Shaftesbury was "no relativist"), there cannot be any doubt that his philosophy of the moral sense stands squarely behind the phenomenal growth of emotionalism and individualism in the eighteenth century. Willey accurately summarizes this development from the seeds Shaftesbury planted:

18. B. Willey, *The Eighteenth Century Background* (London, 1940), p. 71.
19. "Shaftesbury and the Doctrine of Moral Sense in the Eighteenth Century," *PMLA*, XLVI (1931), 1093.

> As the eighteenth century wore on, it was discovered that the 'Nature' of man was not his 'reason' at all, but his instincts, emotions, and 'sensibilities,' and what was more, people began to glory in this discovery, and to regard reason itself as an aberration from 'Nature'. . . . Shaftesbury, Hutcheson, and Hume had prepared the way by proclaiming that our moral judgments, like our aesthetic judgments, are not the offspring of Reason at all; but proceed from an inner sentiment or feeling which is unanalysable. . . . Wesley and Whitefield range the world, converting their ten thousands, not by rational ethical suasion, but by impassioned appeals to the heart. When we reach this phase satire declines, and ceases to be the normal reaction of representative minds to existence. It survives mainly in minds . . . which retain an affinity with the early eighteenth century.[20]

Willey is certainly justified in using the fate of satire to help demarcate the progress of sentimentalism, for, from its beginnings in Shaftesbury, the sentimental had always found itself in opposition to the satiric; and the success of the former could only mean, metaphorically speaking, the death of the latter.[21] In describing the several reactions to the *Characteristics*, Shaftesbury's editor, J. M. Robertson, suggests that Mandeville represents the satiric school that answered Shaftesbury by insisting on the "enormous force of egoism in human affairs," while John Brown's *Essays on the Characteristics* (1751) might be taken as representative of the theological answer which re-emphasized the real existence of evil and insisted on the necessary role of religion in morality. Such "theological utilitarianism," he writes, "dignified by Butler and confused by Paley, became the ruling English orthodoxy." Most significant, as Robertson notes, "a curious sympathy" grew up between Mandevillism and the Church—the same sympathy I have already suggested between satire and orthodoxy, for both

20. Willey, pp. 108–9. Cf. W. J. Bate, *From Classic to Romantic* (New York, 1961 [1946]), pp. 163 ff.

21. Cf.: "The decline of Satire was not . . . due to any criticism or opposition it encountered; rather was it the result of that revised estimate of human nature which is at the root of what we customarily term 'sentimentalism' " (Andrew M. Wilkinson, "The Decline of English Verse Satire," *RES*, n.s. III [1952], 223). Wilkinson goes on to say that the sentimental assumption that man was without sin was by far the "most important" factor in the decline of satire since it "obviates the necessity for it" (p. 225). See also Ronald Paulson, *Satire and the Novel in Eighteenth-Century England* (New Haven, 1967).

were arguing the same belief in the limits of man and the dangers of setting his moral life free from external controls.[22]

The debate between satirist and sentimentalist over the nature of man was often profound, touching, as we have seen, the deepest roots of eighteenth-century theology and philosophy. By concentrating on the theological origins of the dichotomy, I have been using the evidence at hand, Sterne's sermons, to suggest his clerical role as an orthodox Anglican, and, by inference, his literary role as a satirist. Such an inference can be misleading, however. Sterne's orthodoxy *suggests* a satiric outlook, but does not *necessitate* one; the proof of his position on the satirist's side of the dichotomy must be found in *Tristram Shandy* and not in his sermons.

The translation of theological or philosophical conviction into literary symbols is, of course, one of the conspicuous phenomena of literary history. The quarrel of the ancients and the moderns— to illustrate near our own period of interest—issued at last in a Swiftian *Battle of the Books* that embraced symbolically the most divisive forces of the Restoration. In the same way, the eighteenth-century debate between satire and sentiment finds a literary embodiment in the tale of ingénu quest or misadventure, such as we find in *Rasselas* and *Candide*. The debate is also embodied in the emerging literary struggle between the *humorist* and the *satirist*. Other literary conventions, needless to say, are at work in *Tristram Shandy*: the sentimental vignette, the various devices of learned wit, the Rabelaisian use of bawdy—these and many more "conventions" answer Sterne's need to make literary the nonliterary issues which surrounded him. None is as central to the work, however, as that of "amiable humor," for the seriousness with which we take Tristram's "humor" determines our view of the entire work. Tristram is so obviously a humorist that if the work is indeed a satire, then he must be its target.

In his study of eighteenth-century humor, Stuart Tave begins by examining the century-long reaction against satire by those forces I have designated sentimental; his analysis makes clear the larger considerations which were embodied in the satire/humor debate:

> The reaction against satire, a powerful force within the most vigorously satirical period of English literature, was a rejection of the basic satirical assumptions of clear and fixed standards, cosmic, social, and moral, against which the aberra-

22. *Characteristics* (London, 1900), I, xxxix-xli.

tions of man are measured with a just severity. The reaction was, on its strong side, the substitution of a more historical interpretation of life, one in which particular persons, motives and circumstances, explanations, light and shade, were valid and necessary considerations that preceded judgment; and when all these were weighed in the balance, the result was more often forgiveness than condemnation, Christian mercy than strict justice, or even loving acceptance of human weakness and irrationality as an element of the universal scheme. Less happily, the reaction was a blurring of standards, the reduction of vice to folly, the avoidance of moral responsibility, facile charity.[23]

Tave is working, rather obviously, toward a view of this reaction which can keep separated those works which were artistically successful from those which were not. There is, to be sure, value in distinguishing between the humorist and the sentimentalist, particularly in view of the pejorative connotations of the latter term, but the distinction is not as significant as their mutual opposition to the satirist. This becomes clearer when, late in his study, in discussing *Tristram Shandy,* Tave makes the following distinction: " . . . amiable humor measured reality not, as the satirist tends, by an ideal against which reality is terribly wanting, nor did it, in the manner of the sentimentalist, deny or falsify the gap between the real and the ideal. It accepted the difference with a liberal tolerance, or unlike both satirist and sentimentalist, it found the ideal in the varied fulness of the real with all its imperfections."[24] Certainly romantic irony (which is what Tave has defined) offers a deeper insight into reality than does facile sentimentalism—but the difference is finally one of degree, not of kind. The refusal of amiable humor to measure man by an absolute standard places it in opposition to satire. When Tave argues, however, that, for the satirist, "reality is terribly wanting," he prejudices the case with the word "terrible." A satirist like Horace or Erasmus or even Pope in *Rape of the Lock* certainly establishes an attitude toward the discrepancies he perceives that is short of the bitterness or despair suggested by "terrible"; and yet it is an attitude far different from the "liberal tolerance" of the humorist. In several ways, both *Tristram Shandy* and *A Sentimental Journey* can be seen as efforts to define that difference, efforts which are complicated by Sterne's use in both

23. *The Amiable Humorist* (Chicago, 1960), pp. 24–25.
24. *Ibid.,* pp. 166–67.

of narrators who embody precisely that "liberal tolerance" which is the cornerstone of the humorist's attitude toward experience.

For example, Tave would like us to see Sterne combining "a warm enthusiasm with a cool awareness of its inevitable incongruity," or perceiving clearly that "oddity is irreducible," while still recognizing "its demand of love."[25] Tave finds "warm enthusiasm" in Tristram's humor and "cool awareness" in the organization of the work (that is, in Sterne's art), but he seems unaware that his sources are distinct. Thus, in the following comparison to Pope, Tave shifts without warning from Sterne to Toby, forgetting that Tristram is between them: "Unlike Pope, to whom the difference between human and divine vision was absolute, Sterne tries to see with both the human eye and with the divine; the dangers are manifest, but he is at home in digressive chaos, confident of his path. . . . Under the pressure of human foolishness Pope had the apocalyptic vision of the uncreating word, chaos, universal darkness. Toby pities the devil himself, making the completest reconciliation. There is an ultimate grandeur thus revealed in Toby; and a total absurdity, as he tries humanly to reconcile incommensurables."[26] The "grandeur" in Toby is revealed by the same Tristram who is at home in "digressive chaos." But Tristram never sees Toby as an absurdity, for he is too much a Toby himself. This view of Toby is the reader's, and it is shaped by his vision of Toby and Tristram and the Shandy world from a vantage point established by Sterne—the vantage point of a normality against which deviations can be measured and found absurd. Without this vantage point the world of the hack writer in A Tale of a Tub and the world of the Laureate in the Dunciad become Swift's and Pope's worlds, and we would be swept along by the "grandeur" of the dunces' Procession. Indeed, it is perhaps the greatest absurdity of all that Tristram believes the Shandy folly has a "grandeur" to it.

The difference between humor and satire is well illustrated in Arthur Cash's fine study of A Sentimental Journey. That Sterne's position in the Journey is neither sentimental nor simplistically satiric is made clear in the first chapter.[27] Less clear, perhaps, is

25. Ibid., p. 166.   26. Ibid., pp. 173–74.

27. Arthur Hill Cash, Sterne's Comedy of Moral Sentiments: The Ethical Dimension of the Journey (Pittsburgh, 1966), pp. 17–24. Cash rejects the idea put forth by Rufus Putney and Ernest N. Dilworth that Sterne is simply burlesquing sentimentalism in A Sentimental Journey. I think we can also reject the idea for Tristram Shandy: Sterne's treatment of Uncle Toby, while not

where this leaves Sterne. Cash calls him a humorist, but his convincing reading of the *Journey*, in which he uses the sermons as a key, seems to me to argue instead that Sterne is a satirist—and that Yorick is the humorist who is measured by Sterne's moral yardstick and found wanting. This is not a mere quibble over labels. Cash cites Herbert Read's definition of "humorist" in his opening chapter: "All real humorists are classicists, because it is the nature of a classicist to see things finite, and see things infinite, but not to confuse these two categories. The classicist, like the humorist, acknowledges the 'hollowness and farce of the world, and its disproportion to the godlike within us'—and that is Coleridge's definition of humor."[28] Indeed, Read goes so far as to say that Coleridge's definition of humor "might just as well be a definition of classicism."[29] If by "humorist" we mean, then, the "classical" capacity to see that bawdiness and sentiment, good and evil, the godlike and the hollowness are all part of the human experience, I would have no disagreement with calling Sterne—or Swift or Pope—a humorist.[30]

It seems to me, however, that Read's definition stops short of

---

favorable to my mind, is more complex than a burlesque. See Putney, "The Evolution of *A Sentimental Journey*," *PQ*, XIX (1940), 349–69; and "Laurence Sterne, Apostle of Laughter," in *The Age of Johnson: Essays Presented to C. B. Tinker* (New Haven, 1949), pp. 159–70; and Dilworth, *The Unsentimental Journey of Laurence Sterne* (New York, 1948).

28. Cash, p. 21. Cash is quoting from *Collected Essays in Literary Criticism* (London, 1938), p. 260; the essay appeared first in *TLS*, May 26, 1927, and was reprinted in *The Sense of Glory* (Cambridge, 1929). Read refers to a lecture by Coleridge surveying Sterne, Swift, and Rabelais under the general rubric of "The Nature and Constituents of Humour"; see *The Literary Remains*, ed. H. N. Coleridge (London, 1836), I, 131–48. Much of Coleridge's lecture is derived from Jean Paul Richter, *Vorschule der Aesthetik* (1804), Section 31 in *Sämtliche Werke*, Part I, Vol. XI, 111–12.

29. *The Sense of Glory*, p. 145. Coleridge's definition of humor is: ". . . a certain reference to the general and the universal, by which the finite great is brought into identity with the little, or the little with the finite great, so as to make both nothing in comparison with the infinite. The little is made great, and the great little, in order to destroy both; because all is equal in contrast with the infinite" (Coleridge, p. 136).

30. Gardner D. Stout, in the introduction to his edition of *A Sentimental Journey* (Berkeley, 1967), argues skillfully that Sterne (Yorick) is a humorist because he keeps the roles of quixotic benevolist and benevolent jester constantly if paradoxically balanced (pp. 44–45). My own view, derived from Cash's analysis, is that the "jester" in the *Journey* (and in *Tristram Shandy*, where the same dichotomy exists) does not balance the "benevolist," but rather measures him, challenges him, undercuts him, and corrects him; in brief, that the "jester" fulfills a satiric function by measuring the "benevolist" and finding him wanting.

what Jean Paul and Coleridge recognized as the unique element of humor: Good and evil, the godlike and the hollowness become indistinguishable when measured against the infinite; and this is profoundly unclassical. The difference is in the source of values which make distinctions possible. For the humorist, the Infinite, to use Coleridge's terms, does not permeate the Finite world, and hence the values of the Finite, all man-made, are equal and nothing. But for the classicist (or satirist) the Infinite world does indeed permeate the Finite, by reason, by Scripture, by the tried and tested; hence, the classicist is provided with a set of values which enables him to give sanction to certain actions and to withhold it from others. Most significantly, Cash demonstrates over and over again that just such a set of values is consistently operative in *A Sentimental Journey*. For example, he says of Yorick that "although he is a clergyman, Yorick has no adequate notion of true moral virtue. In fact, he is positively mistaken. He thinks that by finding benevolent affections in their most simple form he will find moral virtue."[31] The "humorist" does not talk about what is "true moral virtue" and what is "positively mistaken," since for him "everything is equal and nothing before the Infinite." But Cash is being led by his sensitive reading of the text to make the moral judgments that Sterne wished for the reader to make, judgments which result from weighing the actions of Yorick against the orthodox Christian morality that Sterne preached as a clergyman and endorsed as an author: "When he speaks, in the sermons, of good or vicious passions, he means only to indicate their general tendency toward virtuous or evil *acts*; but the moral worth of the act is determined by some standard outside the emotional constitution—by the law of God or the pronouncements of reason."[32] And again: "Significantly, he does not conclude his argument for the naturalness of benevolence . . . with the advice that we should all relax and be natural. Instead Sterne emphasizes man's relation to God, begging his listeners to think upon the 'just God overlooking, and the terror of an after-reckoning' which should lead to the sacrifice of many appetites and passions."[33] As Cash notes, this is a

31. Cash, p. 55. Cf. his chapter "Sentimental Commerce," pp. 31–53, where this interpretation of Yorick is put forth and defended.
32. *Ibid.*, p. 64.
33. *Ibid.*, p. 70. Cash is talking about the sermon "Vindication of Human Nature" (I, 7), but his point is that the doctrine therein underlies all the sermons and *A Sentimental Journey* as well.

"very orthodox doctrine," evident "upon almost every page of Sterne's sermons." It argues, above all, a willingness on Sterne's part (and hence on the reader's part) to judge human conduct by a pre-established, external standard, and, when necessary, to find it wanting. Indeed, the existence of such standards, the fact that for Sterne, "the moral ideal lies outside the moral agent," is the central meaning of "The Abuses of Conscience Considered," the central Christian statement of *Tristram Shandy*.[34] In terms of the dichotomy between satire and sentiment, Sterne's willingness to measure men against absolute norms places him, with men like Swift and Johnson, on the side of the satirists; to quote Cash again: " . . . Sterne had a moral and religious perspective much like theirs, for he too was an eighteenth-century rationalist."[35]

All this is not to say that Sterne is anti-benevolent or is ridiculing charity or kindness in *A Sentimental Journey*. Rather, he is seeking a *proper* charity, one in accord with the laws of reason and the laws of God; and he is weighing this proper charity against what might be called Shaftesburian charity, a charity that is sanctioned by man, not by God, by the heart, not the head; a benevolence that Cash calls "mechanical."[36] One would be in error to assume that either the orthodoxy of Sterne's religion or his position on the satirist side of the dichotomy militates against benevolence per se. Sterne's attack is against that kind of benevolence which undermines religion and reason by freeing men's moral judgments from them. Sterne defends the laws of reason and the laws of God (and certainly charity and love had rational and divine sanction in the eighteenth century) and in so doing allows the Infinite to permeate the Finite with a set of absolute values. This is what the satirist persistently does, and what the humorist, with equal persistence, must avoid doing.

That Sterne shared a classical or orthodox or satiric attitude with men like Swift and Johnson does not, of course, absolutely lead to the conclusion that *Tristram Shandy* is a satire; the proof of that assertion, as I cannot reiterate too often, must be found in a convincing reading of the work itself. Sterne's orthodoxy does encourage one, however, to approach his work as a satire rather than

34. *Ibid.*, p. 109. Cf. Cash, "The Sermon in *Tristram Shandy*," ELH, XXXI (1964), 395–417.

35. *Sterne's Comedy*, p. 104.

36. *Ibid.*, pp. 56–57 and *passim*.

a novel or as *sui generis*. It suggests that a certain set of conventions, collectively known as "satire," may be operative in *Tristram Shandy* and that the reader may best understand the work by approaching it through those conventions. The reading of *Tristram Shandy* which comprises the bulk of this study is based on the assumption that just such a set of conventions is operative and that a critical understanding of them produces a valid and satisfying reading of the work. While it is possible that the successful application of the genre of satire to *Tristram Shandy* will contribute toward proving the validity of that generic distinction, let me emphasize that the only concern at present is to reach a valid critical understanding of Sterne's masterpiece. The question of how to define satire, or even whether it is a viable generic distinction, is not the issue here, although obviously the successful application of a generic distinction strongly argues both its viability and its definition. Indeed, it has been a primary assumption throughout the conduct of this study that any generic classification of a literary work can only be justified by the significance of the insights which such classification makes possible.

It is broadly assumed that genre by definition has to do with the common taxonomic characteristics of many works, and this, of course, is fundamentally correct. At times, however, this inductive process can prove self-defeating, insofar as it suggests that generic distinctions are merely identifying labels for the use of critics and libraries, pigeonholes external to and independent of both the creative and critical processes. On the one hand, this view of generic distinctions leads to a formalistic approach, the reduction of numerous distinctive works of art to their lowest common denominator.[37] On the other hand, as a reaction against formalism, the inductive process may lead to a refusal to take generic distinctions seriously, as in Arnold Kettle's definition of the novel: "The novel . . . is a realistic prose fiction, complete in itself and of a certain length. Any such definition of a term so loosely and variously used over a long period is bound to be somewhat arbitrary."[38] Kettle's definition inadvertently demonstrates what the Augustan, for one, long knew: that ignoring generic considerations is more truly arbitrary than recognizing them. For the Augustan, as for any artist, genre

37. An illustration of the dangers of this approach to generic questions may be Ronald Paulson's *The Fictions of Satire* (Baltimore, 1967).
38. *An Introduction to the English Novel* (London, 1951), I, 28.

provides a set of conventions, "institutional imperatives," which help give shape to his work, but which are also shaped by him.[39] Most significantly genre prevents the artist from relying solely on his own whims—the real meaning of literary arbitrariness. Similarly, a knowledge of the genre of a particular work provides an insight for the critic into those conventions and assumptions which give form and meaning to that work—again preventing the arbitrariness of critical judgment which condemns an author for failing to accomplish what he never attempted.[40]

When generic differences are erroneously considered as narrow and arbitrary pigeonholes, the tendency of the critic is quite naturally to demand a definition of each genre equally narrow and equally arbitrary. He demands to know the precise formal distinctions of the novel; he wants a list of what the novel must contain, what it cannot contain; what it must do, and what it must never do. No approach to the problems of genre can be more futile. Genre can, in other words, be over-defined as well as under-defined: "The seventeenth and eighteenth centuries are centuries which take genres seriously; their critics are men for whom genres exist, are real. That genres are distinct—and also should be kept distinct—is a general article of Neo-Classical faith. But if we look to Neo-Classical criticism for definition of genre or method of distinguishing genre from genre, we find little consistency or even awareness of the need for a rationale."[41] One feels that what is being looked for in these critics is a rigidity of generic distinction, which they, with their perhaps instinctive insight into the nature of genre, would have found impossible to provide. With all their obvious attention to genre, it is nevertheless a fact that the neo-classical critics felt free to label *Hudibras, MacFlecknoe, The Rape*

39. Cf. Norman Holmes Pearson, "Literary Forms and Types; or, A Defense of Polonius," *English Institute Annual*, 1940 (New York, 1941), p. 70: "Thus, forms may be regarded as institutional imperatives which both coerce and are in turn coerced by the writer." Pearson uses an anthropological analogy whereby genre is to literature what institution is to culture (pp. 67–68). See also J. M. Stedmond, *The Comic Art of Laurence Sterne* (Toronto, 1967), p. 161 and *passim*.

40. Cf. Northrop Frye, *Anatomy of Criticism* (New York, 1966 [Princeton, 1957]), pp. 303–4; and E. M. W. Tillyard, *The Epic Strain in the English Novel* (London, 1958). Tillyard defends generic distinctions by saying that "a right classification puts the mind in a right direction and reduces the danger of a wrong one" (p. 23).

41. René Wellek and Austin Warren, *Theory of Literature* (New York, 1942), p. 239.

of the Lock, and *The Vanity of Human Wishes* as satires. They did so, I would suggest, not because satire had no meaning for them, but because they saw genre as a complex of intentions, styles, forms, conventions, decorums, and tendencies which defined not the final form of any artistic work, but rather the possibilities and potentialities that governed the artistic process.[42] Similarly, when I call *Tristram Shandy* a satire I do not intend to substitute a generic label for a critical analysis; rather, the label helps to define what critical approaches, what possibilities and potentialities, are governing my critical process. In the following chapter I shall briefly explore the sources of my approach to *Tristram Shandy*— several recent investigations of satire in general and of Swiftian satire in particular. But I have no intention of defining satire in the course of this study; at best, I shall attempt to show, through the critical approaches I take (and also by those I reject), the conventions and designs which I believe governed the creation of this one particular work. In this manner, the genre is defined not by a rigid enumeration of points of similarity between *Tristram Shandy* and works commonly accepted as satire, but rather through the success or failure of a critical approach based on generic assumptions. And this I feel is as it should be.

42. See Ian Jack, *Augustan Satire: Intention and Idiom in English Poetry: 1660–1750* (Oxford, 1942), pp. 146–47 and *passim*.

Sterne and Swiftian Satire
The source of satiric conventions

The task we face, then, in trying seriously to investigate the relationship between a writer's moral beliefs and the literary works he has created is not limited to answering the questions that puzzle us; like Pamela's, our most serious problem is first to get the question asked in a legitimate manner so that our answers will testify to something more than the sincerity and respectability of our desires.

Sheldon Sacks, *Fiction and the Shape of Belief: A Study of Henry Fielding*

Sterne and Swiftian Satire

HE EPIGRAPH of this chapter, from Sheldon Sacks' *Fiction and the Shape of Belief: A Study of Henry Fielding,* echoes my purpose in it: to define what seems to me to be the "legitimate manner" of asking questions about *Tristram Shandy.* I am not attempting in this chapter to define satire or to prove that *Tristram Shandy* is one; my aim is simply to enumerate a quite selective catalogue of the critical approaches I think are most pertinent to a valid interpretation of Sterne's work. Since the evidence of my first two chapters points to a close correspondence between Sterne and the Augustan view, I have depended rather heavily on several recent critics of Swift, the great exemplar of the union between that view and the form of satire. The questions they have asked about Swift's satires will be the questions I shall ask about *Tristram Shandy.*

There has been some hesitation among Sterne's critics to compare him to Swift or, in the face of Sterne's *"viva la joia,"* to call *Tristram Shandy* a satire. John Traugott's hesitation is particularly interesting, since his is one of the most influential studies of Sterne's work. Traugott discusses his failure to call *Tristram Shandy* a satire in his closing pages, immediately after deciding that Sterne created "his own genre." He then goes on to speak of Sterne's "true cultural and intellectual climate" as that of the Augustans and their search "through the agency of satire for the true aspects of man's place in his society." But, although Sterne was indeed the "true heir of Swift and Pope," he is today so vile in "certain critical circles" (and satirists are so vilified by "critics who cant about love") that Traugott would not endanger his reputation by "associating him with the . . . eighteenth-century satirists." The fallacy of Traugott's position, catering to "critics who cant," emphasizes his failure throughout his study to consider the question of satire as an integral part of his investigation: "I have not spoken primarily of his satire; but now, looking back over his forms of persuasion, can we see them as any other than the most radical techniques of the true satirist?"[1] This is indeed true. Traugott's analysis of Sterne's "rhetorical snares," the *argumentum ad hominem* directed against the reader, defines a traditional weapon of satire.[2] Similarly, his belief that Sterne was dramatizing the failures of rational communication is easily converted into a satiric theme, as Traugott admits.[3] And finally, Traugott suggests that " . . . large portions of *A Tale of a Tub* and *Tristram Shandy* seem almost interchangeable, so exact is Sterne's feeling for certain aspects of Swift's style and tone."[4]

This last suggestion was anticipated in at least one significant instance: D. W. Jefferson's essay "*Tristram Shandy* and the Tradition of Learned Wit," published three years before Traugott's study. Jefferson maintains that Sterne's wit is the same as that found in "Augustan comic and satirical writing. . . . " *A Tale of a Tub, Peri Bathous,* and *Martinus Scriblerus* are cited as examples, and Jefferson calls Sterne "perhaps the last great writer in the tradition."[5] Among the traits which distinguish its continuity, Jefferson mentions these: (1) "The power to use logic to give a show of plausibility to an absurd or unreasonable argument . . ."; (2) the bold treatment of religion, comparing Sterne in this to Rabelais and Swift; (3) satire on scholasticism, particularly on abstract speculation and consultation of learned authorities; (4) the realistic, schematized portrayal of absurdities by which "the precision . . . of the description serves simply to give heightening to gross absurdity"; and (5) a classical respect for order which is often manifested, for satiric contrast, in an apparent delight in disorder.[6] On the foundations thus laid will be built much of my own reading of *Tristram Shandy*.

J. M. Stedmond is another critic who has linked the form of *Tristram Shandy* to Augustan satire. In his article "Satire and

1. *Tristram Shandy's World: Sterne's Philosophical Rhetoric* (Berkeley, 1954), p. 149.

2. *Ibid.*, p. xi. See also pp. xii–xiii, 147–50.

3. *Ibid.*, p. 9.

4. *Ibid.*, p. 15. See also pp. 16–17, 19, 124, 149 for further statements of Swift's influence on Sterne. Yet Sterne is *not* like Swift because "*Tristram Shandy* is a comedy, not a nerve-jangling satire on the human situation . . ." (p. 19). I think Professor Traugott begs the question.

5. *EinC*, I (1951), 227.

6. *Ibid.*, pp. 229–39.

Tristram Shandy," Professor Stedmond cites *Martinus Scriblerus, A Tale of a Tub,* and the *Dunciad* as the tradition to which *Tristram Shandy* belongs and adds, significantly, "Walter, Toby, Tristram, all are manifestations of the dunce." Moreover, Stedmond finds *Tristram Shandy,* "in its way," an extension of the *Dunciad;* and, like Swift's *Tale,* it is a Grub Street production, a "graphic description of the times": "Swift attacked the Grub Street hack by parodying his style; Pope sallied against the pedantic dunce by burlesquing his method; and Sterne, in his turn, donned cap and bells in order to show up foolishness by playing the fool."[7] Ronald Paulson suggests much the same thing: "*Tristram Shandy* is constructed like a satire rather than a novel and presents within the first volume all the elements of the Tory fiction as composed by Swift. The plot is, as with Swift, the book itself, and the form closely resembles Swift's epitome (in *A Tale of a Tub*) of the seventeenth-century literature that can be called wit-writing or wit-as-process and the hack-writing that derived from it. These forms of expression disdained all tradition, authority, or rules, and their only virtue was the reflection of the writer's own eccentric mind. In both cases the object ridiculed is the same self-sufficiency of mind. . . ."[8] My own reading of *Tristram Shandy* grows out of suggestions such as these,[9] reinforced by a detailed reading of the entire work.

The meeting place of the Augustan viewpoint and satiric form is perhaps indicated in the first point that Northrop Frye makes concerning the genre of satire: ". . . satire is militant irony: its moral norms are relatively clear, and it assumes standards against which the grotesque and absurd are measured."[10] The Augustan's insistence on moral and artistic standards, as well as his reaction against moral and aesthetic relativism, helps explain why satire became his predominant mode of expression. At the same time, the

7. *SEL,* I, 3 (1961), 53–55, 62; reprinted in *The Comic Art of Laurence Sterne* (Toronto, 1967). Cf. Martin Price, *To the Palace of Wisdom* (New York, 1964), pp. 325–26.

8. *Satire and the Novel in Eighteenth-Century England* (New Haven, 1967), p. 249. Cf. Ernest Tuveson, "Locke and Sterne" in *Reason and the Imagination: Studies in the History of Ideas, 1600–1800* (New York, 1962), pp. 265–66, 272–74.

9. In actuality, my unpublished doctoral dissertation (Vanderbilt University, 1966), containing much the same reading offered here, was completed before Paulson's work appeared.

10. *The Anatomy of Criticism* (Princeton, 1957), p. 223.

presence of a clear standard against which deviations are measured plays a large part in determining the form satire takes, from the bipartite structure of formal verse satire to the activity of normative characters and ironic personae in prose satire. The norm need not be explicitly stated, but Frye seems correct in maintaining that "satire demands . . . at least an implicit moral standard . . . [this] being essential in a militant attitude to experience."[11] *Militant*, of course, does not refer only to the tone of the satire or the intensity of the attack, but also to the commitment the satirist makes to a measurement of human behavior and achievement by a constant yardstick. Frye is quick to note that "wit or humor" is essential to satire, and his discussion of the several "phases" of the genre indicates that the entire satiric tradition belongs to what he defines, in terms of its mythos, as a comic experience rather than a tragic one.[12]

Frye's discussion of the formal characteristics of prose satire is also of interest to our present purposes. For example, he notes that satire "deals less with people as such than with mental attitudes." A list of such attitudes, he adds, would include "pedants, bigots, cranks, parvenus, virtuosi, enthusiasts," all handled in terms of their "humor" or ruling passion, "their occupational approach to life as distinct from their social behavior."[13] In addition, Frye finds a constant theme of satire, "the ridicule of the *philosophus gloriosus*," and suggests in explanation that, while "the novelist sees evil and folly as social diseases . . . the . . . satirist sees them as diseases of the intellect, as a kind of maddened pedantry which the *philosophus gloriosus* at once symbolizes and defines."[14] My approach to Walter, Toby, and Tristram is governed by the idea that the mental (and moral) attitudes they represent are the raison d'être of their creation.

Frye also notes the loose-jointed narrative form common to satire, its unity arising from a "single intellectual pattern" rather than from a connected plot. Disorderliness, digressiveness, and even "violent dislocations in the customary logic of narrative" are to be expected; but he warns us against considering these appearances of

11. *Ibid.*, p. 224.
12. See *ibid.*, pp. 223–39.
13. *Ibid.*, p. 309.
14. *Ibid.* Frye notes the erudition which marks prose satire, its tendency to expand into an "encyclopaedic farrago," its overwhelming of pedantic targets with "an avalanche of their own jargon" (p. 311).

carelessness as indicative of any actual haphazardness on the part of the author. Satire, he argues, does not use its narrative and characters as the novel does; concern for the orderly outcome of the story or the fate of the characters, so vital to the novelist, is of secondary consideration to the satirist.[15]

Sheldon Sacks has accepted this distinction as the basis for a very rigorous division between satire and the novel. Satires, for Sacks, are "works which ridicule particular men, the institutions of men, traits presumed to be in all men, or any combination of the three." This is sufficiently commonplace; what follows is not:

> But they do not do this incidentally; all their parts are designed to this end and, indeed, can only be understood *as* parts of a whole to the extent that they contribute to such ridicule. In other words, this is the principle that actually informs the work. . . . If we assume also that *Gulliver's Travels* is a coherent satire, then all the elements of fiction it contains— the traits ascribed to the created characters, the actions portrayed, the point of view from which the tale is told—will have been selected, whether consciously or intuitively, to maximize the ridicule of some combination of the three objects of satire.[16]

The same insistence upon unity of purpose is seen in Sacks' definition of the novel:

> In any work which belongs to this class, characters about whose fates we are made to care are introduced in unstable relationships which are then further complicated until the complications are finally resolved by the complete removal of the represented instability.
>   . . . it is crucial to insist that a work is a represented action [a novel] only if every element—including any formulated ethical statement or ridiculed object—is subordinate to the artistic end just described.[17]

Sacks defines yet another mutually exclusive form, the apologue, "a fictional example of the truth of a formulable statement." It seems to me, however, that the distinction between apologue and satire is predicated on the doubtful assumption that the nature of

15. *Ibid.*, pp. 310–11.
16. Sheldon Sacks, *Fiction and the Shape of Belief: A Study of Henry Fielding* (Berkeley, 1964), p. 7.
17. *Ibid.*, p. 15.

satire excludes any statement of its norms.[18] I would instead group satires and apologues together as similar forms of prose fiction, at least insofar as both tend to subordinate their fiction to the ideas which it is created to serve; both are, in other words, fictions dominated by what Arnold Kettle calls "pattern": "In this kind of novel it is not unfair to say that the author starts with his pattern, his moral vision, and that the various elements of the novel, character and plot in particular, are continuously subordinated to . . . the pattern."[19] This form, whether we call it satire or the novel of pattern (and all three critics, Frye, Sacks, and Kettle, use *Gulliver's Travels* as an example), was most readily adaptable to the Augustan vision. I say "adaptable," because the Augustans did not pour their eighteenth-century issues into an iron-cast mold; Swift's satires offer ample evidence that the tradition of prose satire, as it came to the eighteenth century, was shaped by the Augustans to answer their own peculiar needs, just as Sterne, arriving a generation later, would have to reshape his Augustan inheritance. Nevertheless, the satiric form served the Augustan vision at almost every turn, and we may agree with Paulson's observation that "the novel and satire are convenient poles from which to chart the patterns of change in eighteenth-century literature and criticism."[20] Above all, while the novel provided a form for the ever increasing interest in "human experience for its own sake,"[21] satire provided a traditional vehicle for the defense of absolute standards and a means by which art and morality could be brought to bear simultaneously on aberrations from those standards, aberrations which everywhere threatened to overwhelm civilized life.

Without doubt, the Augustans could speak with some skill of the standards they championed, but W. K. Wimsatt is correct in maintaining that their special skill was reserved for presenting the aberrations: "My view is that the English Augustans were, at their best and their most characteristic, laughing poets of a heightened unreality. The world which the Augustan wit found most amusing and into which he had his deepest visions was an inverted, chaotic reality, the unreality of the 'uncreating word'—the 'true

18. *Ibid.*, p. 11n13. Cf. "Norms in Satire: A Symposium," *Satire News Letter*, II (1964), 2–25.

19. *An Introduction to the English Novel* (London, 1951), I, 17.

20. Paulson, *Satire and the Novel*, p. 3. See his discussion of this polarity, pp. 3–8.

21. *Ibid.*, p. 3.

No-meaning' which 'puzzles more than Wit.' The peculiar feat of the Augustan poet was the art of teasing unreality with the redeeming force of wit—of casting upon a welter of unreal materials a light of order and a perspective vision."[22] This need not imply, however, that the satirist admits the unreality of his created world; as Alvin B. Kernan notes, satire, of all the major literary genres, "has traditionally made most pretense of being realistic."[23] One predominant tension in Augustan satire, for example, is that between "heightened unreality" on the one hand, and strict realism on the other. The satirist repudiates the Muse, repudiates form and decorum, repudiates his own claims as a serious artist; but his insistence on so doing suggests, says Kernan, the conventional nature of these repudiations. Long before Sterne, satirists had found it convenient to make the claim that it was not they but their pens that wrote. While the prevalence of irony in the satiric form is a complex phenomenon, it is perhaps not totally misleading to suggest that the essential irony of satire is just this continued insistence of the satirist that he is not an artist, that the highly stylized language and grotesque world of his work are not the results of art, but of his slavish imitation of life and his heroic devotion to truth.

On the one hand, the irony can be quite simple, fulfilling the rhetorical demands of the satiric situation. The necessary sympathy between reader and author is established by the latter's claim to "plain dealing," or his more dramatic claim that "Fools rush into my head, and so I write." On the other hand, the irony can become quite involved when tied to the favorite Augustan practice of the ironic persona. Here the putative author may tell us he is a skilled and brilliant craftsman, but the chaotic disorder of his work gives him the lie; or, like the satirist, he may tell us he writes without art—and we, reading his book, are inclined to agree with him and condemn him for it. But this, of course, is only the first level of the irony: Behind the lie is the truth that the satirist has carefully and deliberately shaped the disorder of his work, and the reader relishes this irony as well; behind our condemnation of the persona's artlessness is the awareness that the author has purposefully and expertly made him the artless dunce he is. It is essential, for example, that we feel the chaotic nature

22. "The Augustan Mode in English Poetry," *ELH*, XX (1953), 9.
23. *The Cankered Muse: Satire of the English Renaissance* (New Haven, 1959), pp. 2–3. Cf. Paulson, pp. 11–23.

of Tristram's attempt to tell his life; at the same time, however, we must also feel that the chaos is Sterne's deliberate, highly organized, and quite conventional means of satirizing the mind capable of producing chaos. Kernan speaks at length to this point:

> The dunces always begin by constructing outsize, heroic images of themselves and building colossal monuments to their self-importance. At the same time . . . they drive all spirit down to matter and reduce the vital to mere mechanics. As this work goes forward, the ideas which provide the organizational forms for the material world are inevitably destroyed, and the world ceases to be arranged in meaningful patterns. . . . But it has become obvious that these actions of dullness are all self-defeating . . . because they always achieve the exact opposite of what is intended. The more the dunces speak to show their learning, the more they reveal their ignorance. . . .[24]

The root meaning of satire in "hodgepodge" is at work here, with the basic irony of a conventional disorder; at the same time, however, there is the sophistication of several simultaneous ironies resulting from the separation of author and speaker. The Augustans inherited from the satiric tradition the chaotic world of satire; they passed the tradition on to Sterne with the addition of an ironic persona who glories in it.

It is thus important for the understanding of Augustan prose satire to insist that a distinction be maintained between the author and his ironic persona. Ricardo Quintana, talking about Swift's satire in particular, is urgent in his insistence that the two be distinguished. Swift, he suggests, creates in his satires, "a fully realized character and a fully realized world for him to move in." At times, as in *Gulliver's Travels,* the satiric action is developed simply in terms of the "character's reactions to this world"; at other times, as in *Tale of a Tub,* the action derives "from the crazy assurance with which the character makes himself at home in his cloud-cuckoo-land, tidies the place up, and proceeds to enlarge the bounds of his estate."[25] There can be little doubt of the value and validity of Quintana's thesis; it is necessary, however, that a word of caution be added before its application to *Tristram Shandy.* Too often, the insistence that persona and author are distinct has led to an insup-

24. *The Plot of Satire* (New Haven, 1965), p. 81.
25. "Situational Satire: A Commentary on the Method of Swift," *UTQ,* XVII (1947–48), 130–31. Cf. William Bragg Ewald, Jr., *The Masks of Jonathan Swift* (Oxford, 1954), p. 29.

portable corollary that the persona must demonstrate the same consistency of character we seek in the central intelligence of a novel. But the satirist has no interest in the consistency of his characters, and thus he often allows his persona an improbable range of intellectual and emotional reactions—from the obtuse and unfeeling to the keenly perceptive.[26] At the same time, again drawing an analogy to the novel, the critic is prone to feel that any rent in the mask, any authorial intrusion, is, by necessity, a weakening of the narrative fabric. To be sure, it is; but the satirist is not interested in his narrative as is the novelist, and a most effective way to show this lack of concern is to interrupt the story at every turn. No novel could be written with this total disregard for consistency of character and authorial inviolability. The very nature of satire, however, seems to demand that the use of a persona be subject to the same conventional disregard for order, consistency, and unity as are the other formal elements. As with the literary hack in *A Tale of a Tub*, Tristram can often be expected to speak with his author's voice, to have an insight into his own folly, or the folly of his family, which is quite beyond the perception normally assigned to him. When Sterne wants to speak, he does; when he wants to identify himself with Tristram, he does; and, when he wants to demonstrate a particular folly through his persona, he does that also.[27] Such maneuverability would be damaging to the novel; it is conventional in satire.

Yet another aspect of Augustan satire which should be mentioned is its exuberance, what John M. Bullitt calls its "sparkling and bubbling vitality." Wimsatt, we remember, calls the Augustans "laughing poets" and, indeed, it is difficult to find an eighteenth-century writer who seems to enjoy himself more than Swift—

26. Cf. Edward W. Rosenheim, Jr., *Swift and the Satirist's Art* (Chicago 1963), pp. 153–54. Rosenheim defends the idea that the persona of a satire can present a constantly shifting point of view.

27. Alan D. McKillop links Sterne's handling of Tristram to the conception of the satirist as "the *naïf*, the *ingénu*, the simple heart," and notes his debt to Maynard Mack's article "The Muse of Satire," *Yale Review*, XLI (1951), 80–92, from which he is quoting ("The Reinterpretation of Laurence Sterne," *Etudes Anglaises*, VII [1954], 39–40; later reprinted, with minor changes, in *The Early Masters of English Fiction* [Lawrence, Kan., 1956]). See also Lawrance Thompson, "A Comic Principle in Sterne-Meredith-Joyce" (Oslo, 1954). Thompson treats the persona as a device of irony, quite within the limits suggested for its legitimate use by Irvin Ehrenpreis, "Personae," in *Restoration and Eighteenth-Century Literature* (Chicago, 1963), pp. 25–37. My own treatment is similar.

unless it be Sterne. A. E. Dyson notes this facet of Swift's work: ". . . Swift, writing for gentlemen, intended to give pleasure by what he wrote. . . . Sooner or later most writers about *Gulliver* hit upon the word 'exuberance', and then pause doubtfully, wondering whether . . . such a word can have any place in describing him. Yet 'exuberant' he certainly is, even in Book IV of *Gulliver*. . . . Clearly, Swift enjoyed his control of irony: enjoyed its flexibility, its complex destructiveness, his own easy mastery of it. Clearly, too, he expects his readers to enjoy it."[28] Ian Watt has pointed out that satire, by its very nature, insists upon a sharp dichotomy between an elite which upholds its standards and the mob which does not; "a small band, a righteous minority, ever battling for truth against every kind of deviation from the norm. . . ."[29] Speaking to a chosen few, the satirist can engage in the most complex ironies with the assurance that, within his group, his meaning is secure. This is not to suggest that satire is "coterie" literature, for from a rhetorical viewpoint, "a chosen few" are all those who side with the satirist against the "mob," that is, all his readers, if the satire is effective. Nevertheless, there is in Augustan satire a strong sense of communal effort and communal appreciation which seems to play a significant role in shaping its form. This is particularly evident in the exuberance of Augustan satire, which depends, above all, on confidence in one's capacity to delight one's audience, a knowledge that dazzling virtuosity, so integral a part of the satiric tradition, will be taken in the right spirit. The Scriblerians provided this appreciative reception for Augustan satire; for *Tristram Shandy* it is quite possible that, at least in the beginning, the "Demoniacs" provided the same type of delighted audience.

Of this group which met at John Hall-Stevenson's Crazy Castle, we know only that they enjoyed their cups, their library of Rabelaisian satires, and their bawdy jokes—a traditional enough trinity.[30] Even this scanty evidence makes it difficult to believe that the

28. "Swift: The Metamorphosis of Irony," *Essays and Studies*, n.s., XI (1958), 66. Edgar Johnson's belief that the satirist's "high spirits" are one way of overcoming the "Censor" also has its validity; see *A Treasury of Satire* (New York, 1945), pp. 9–16.

29. "The Ironic Tradition in Augustan Prose from Swift to Johnson," in *Restoration and Augustan Prose* (Los Angeles, 1956), p. 21.

30. See Wilbur L. Cross, *The Life and Times of Laurence Sterne* (New Haven, 1929), pp. 130–37.

"Demoniacs" would find entertainment in a sentimental tale; and, on the contrary, quite easy to believe that they, as an inner circle, would enjoy an ironic attack on the York personalities they detested in common, and, more generally, on everything else which Sterne found "laugh-at-able in my way."[31] Like the Augustan satirists, Sterne appears to have conceived his satire for the amusement of a congenial male audience; and like Augustan satire, *Tristram Shandy,* in spite of apostrophes to "Madam," strikes the reader as essentially attuned to the masculine ear—quite unlike the eighteenth-century novel.

Although I shall follow the method of Swift's critics and consider Sterne's use of the bawdy and scatological as primarily a rhetorical device, some note should be made of its appeal to a group like the "Demoniacs," who surely enjoyed this aspect of *Tristram Shandy* as much as the Scriblerians must have enjoyed putting together "The Double Mistress." Northrop Frye points out that Swift, in his use of scatology, "is simply following where his genius leads him," and he adds the observation that every great satirist has been "what the world calls obscene."[32] That the satirist uses the scatological to remind men of themselves is not to be gainsaid; that he also uses it because he enjoys sexual innuendo and knows his readers will also is merely to remind ourselves of the prevalence of the obscene in literature, from Aristophanes to Shakespeare, from Lucian to Rabelais. The scatological has always been one of the most traditional of exuberant subjects; and one of satire's traditional targets, significantly, has been the hypocritical gravity which would deny that fact.

Because a genre is not a die-casting, any listing of its formal characteristics will necessarily be incomplete. What I have attempted to do in these opening pages is to suggest several prominent aspects of prose satire which find significant echoes in *Tristram Shandy,* and, by doing so, to suggest as well some of the approaches I shall take in reading the work as a satire. Before I turn to *Tristram Shandy,* however, one final aspect of prose satire demands attention

31. Lewis Perry Curtis, ed., *Letters of Laurence Sterne* (Oxford, 1935), p. 74: "The Plan, as you [may] well percieve, is a most extensive one,—taking in, not only the Weak part of the Sciences, in wch the true point of Ridicule lies—but every Thing else, which I find Laugh-at-able in my way—" (Letter to Robert Dodsley, dtd. May 23, 1759, offering the first volume of *Tristram Shandy* for publication).
32. Frye, p. 235.

—its rhetoric. The intimate union of satire and rhetoric is now a commonplace among critics of satire; of particular interest to the study of *Tristram Shandy* is the frequent juncture of the two in the ironic persona. The ironic persona was considered above in its organizational role, but it is apparent that such a device is fundamentally rhetorical. Norman Knox sees irony, satire, and rhetoric all coming together in the eighteenth century to produce a rhetorical stance which he labels the "grave manner."[33] An offspring of the age's reawakening to Cervantes and of the popularity of burlesque, the "grave manner" is quite simply Swift's "Vein, ironically grave"; what Pope called, in describing Swift's style, "Cervantes' serious air." Richard Owen Cambridge, in his preface to the *Scribleriad*, defines this attitude in terms of the mock-heroic: "It should, throughout, be serious, because the originals are serious; therefore the author should never be seen to laugh, but constantly wear that grave irony which *Cervantes* only has inviolably preserv'd."[34] Knox maintains that by mid-century Swift had joined Cervantes as a model of "grave irony," and had established it as the dominant weapon of satire. Moreover, "a small body of theory had been evolved. It came not fully formed from the forehead of an Aristotle but arose out of the nature of the thing and the trials and errors of the Augustan ironists and their readers."[35] The rhetorical trope of irony, which at one time referred almost solely to the "blame-by-praise" figure, had come to define for the Augustan satirists the fundamental organizing principle of their work—an ironic persona whose intensely serious engagement in the bathetic, the trivial, and the absurd was the starting point of an attack on human folly and perversity. In *The Life and Opinions of Tristram Shandy, Gentleman*, the serious attempt of Tristram to be an artist, to recite his "life," is the "grave manner" which controls the work, and in his "opinions," the rhetoric of mock-encomium is everywhere operative. Indeed, the word "opinion," itself, suggests this, for it had not lost its Baconian sense of notions based on mistaken impressions as opposed to the conceptions of right reason.

Alvin Kernan has remarked that because the style of satire so

33. *The Word Irony and Its Context, 1500–1755* (Durham, N.C., 1961), pp. 162–73. Cf. Paulson, *The Fictions of Satire* (Baltimore, 1967), pp. 39, 97–98.
34. Quoted in Knox, p. 170.
35. *Ibid.*, p. 184.

often calls attention to itself, it is regularly referred to as rhetorical, and he cites as examples, "the set piece, the verbal device, the outrageous appeal to the emotions, the tricky arrangement of the argument, the enormously inflated or deflated image" which seem always to be a part of the satiric style.[36] At times, the rhetoric of satire is a persuasive and argumentative style, quite removed from the style of *Tristram Shandy*. At other times, however, the rhetoric of satire is designed, to quote Kernan, as "an attack on the false styles and elaborate rhetoric of other writers and other kinds of poetry"—and this rhetoric is central to *Tristram Shandy*. To be sure, such an attack carries its own argument and its own persuasiveness, for behind the attack on false rhetoric is Swift's conviction that "there are solecisms in morals as well as in language." Pope, too, never allows us to forget that false rhetoric "is an expression of some fundamental human failing." Kernan's reading of *Peri Bathous* has this in mind: "The variegating, confusing, or reversing tropes and figures are the products of minds which have lost all sense of order and proportion. They have given themselves over to fancy and vanity, and in their striving to show themselves unique and clever 'say nothing in the usual way, but (if possible) in the direct contrary.'"[37] The satirist creates a world in which an inflated, fragmented, and jumbled rhetoric feels completely at home; "he shows us men whose language is indecorous and whose pretensions to decency and honor are as much a sham as their speech." The primary vehicle for this false rhetoric is, of course, the ironic persona, whose grave obtuseness allows the rhetorical solecism to merge with the moral; his "insensitivity to meanings," says Martin Price, "serves to characterize a moral blindness."[38]

Fundamental, then, to the rhetoric of satire is the device of inversion—the simplest form of irony, by which "the satirist pretends *to praise what he means to condemn* or he pretends *to condemn what he means to praise*."[39] Irony of this nature is a trap, for the reader must constantly supply the good sense that the persona

36. *The Plot of Satire*, pp. 16–17.
37. *Ibid.*, pp. 30–31. Cf. Philip Pinkus, "Satire and St. George," *Queen's Quarterly*, LXX (1963), p. 37: "Ultimately every satire creates a world of madness, an upsidedown world where evil is good and the traditional principles of order, harmony and reason are overturned, where there is no centre, no abiding values. . . . "
38. *Swift's Rhetorical Art* (New Haven, 1953), p. 58.
39. John M. Bullitt, *Jonathan Swift and the Anatomy of Satire* (Cambridge, Mass., 1953), pp. 50–51.

lacks. Moreover, since the forcefulness of the satire often depends on the satirist's success in trapping the unwary reader, we cannot always expect the type of overt "signaling" that frequently accompanies comic wit. In a work like *A Tale of a Tub*, for example, Swift consistently signals for us the ironic inversion which informs the Hack's praise of skimming the surface of things; he does so, however, only to draw our attention away from the equally ironic inversion which praises the "deep" investigation—and when he finally shuts the trap with "Last Week I saw a Woman *flay'd*, and you will hardly believe, how much it altered her Person for the worse," all but the most initiated of readers discover the truth of Swift's "Go, go, you're bit." Martin Price perceptively describes the interaction between persona and reader in a satire of this nature: "The common dupe Swift invents, like his counterpart in the reader, is not clear sighted in selfishness; he is neither a rebel nor a Machiavel. A man of middling virtue, he would recoil from an accurate recognition of the ends he is promoting, and Swift, of course, never allows him that recognition but demands it instead of the reader. Rather, the fool among knaves is somewhat vain, somewhat proud, and very gullible. . . . This kind of man is both too dense to be morally alert and too naïve to disguise his folly."[40] In reading *Tristram Shandy* as a satire, I shall suggest that Tristram functions in the same way, constantly offering to his readers a vast range of folly in a most grave and panegyric manner; our function is to recognize, in that manner, the rhetoric of satiric inversion.[41]

Eugene Hnatko, in an important article, *"Tristram Shandy's Wit,"* has suggested that Sterne employed four basic rhetorical devices; I have numbered them for clarity: "(1) a deliberate confounding of a conventional means of representing a mode of reality with the reality itself; (2) an extensive use of what would have been to neoclassic critics heterogeneous terms engaged in similitude; (3) a peculiar irony growing out of an adopted 'blind spot'; and, finally . . . (4) a displacement of emphasis on some aspect of discourse."[42] Hnatko considers all four devices examples of false wit and concludes that, although Sterne "was well aware of the

40. *Swift's Rhetorical Art*, pp. 87–88.
41. I am paraphrasing Price, p. 93: "The most important function of the Tale Teller . . . is his gradual absorption of a vast range of folly in his panegyric and imitation."
42. *JEGP*, LXV (1966), 47.

critical repute of false wit," he nevertheless "seems to have had a deliberate joy" in using it. Significantly, Hnatko defends Sterne's "bad taste" by suggesting that "these examples of 'false' wit are, of course, not without precedent among the Augustans. Although the pejorative 'false,' applied by Addison, did much to render them suspect, much of the best eighteenth-century satire incorporates them."[43]

The truth of this statement can be easily demonstrated in all four devices. The deliberate confounding of reality with its conventional representations, for example, is defined by Bullitt as a typical operation of the "converting imagination," the mechanical operation of mind best illustrated by the literary hack of *A Tale of a Tub*: "The imagination which interprets words as exact and accurate descriptions of things, suffers, too, from mechanical inelasticity. . . . The words men use are merely artificial and arbitrary labels . . . and words have in themselves no necessary connection with the facts they describe. One frequent fallacy of the converting imagination, then, is to expect, by tagging a name to a thing, to influence the essential nature of the thing itself."[44] *A Tale of a Tub*, as the product of such a mind, is filled with examples of this "false" wit—indeed, this operation of the converting imagination is Swift's primary weapon against the claims of projectors and system-makers.

Similarly, the "conceited" style of the second device is tied by Hnatko to what Martin Price calls Swift's method of extension: The comparison is made ludicrous and tasteless by its application to first one, then another, and yet another, heterogeneous situation. Again, Hnatko compares the third device, the "irony growing out of a blind spot," to Swift's use of the persona, and comments, ". . . there is a naïveté in Tristram which involves Sterne's most extensive use of irony."[45] Finally, the device of displacement is used by Swift as an important satiric device. Paulson describes it thus: "The usual practice in the *Tale* is for a respectable context to be set up, and one word placed in it which, reasserting its normal

43. *Ibid.*, p. 52.
44. Bullitt, p. 141.
45. Hnatko, p. 57. Hnatko insists upon a difference in both rigor and attitude between Swift and Sterne; he suggests that Swift's personae are blind to a "common humanity or sympathy" while Tristram is blind simply to sexual decency. I would suggest that Hnatko is using one aspect, albeit a glaring one, to stand for the whole of Tristram's blindness.

meaning, completely alters the significance of the context. . . ."[46]

For Hnatko, Sterne's "false" wit is primarily an indication of his own peculiar taste and his unclassical indifference to the values of "true" wit. That the Augustans also practiced "false" wit in their satires does not alter this basic premise for Hnatko; neither does the fact that the third device, the ironic persona, suggests the raison d'être of the other three. It is not Sterne, but Tristram, who is characterized by his "false" wit. Without denying that Sterne (like Swift and Pope) enjoys parodying the style of the dunces, I believe we must also recognize that the false wit of *Tristram Shandy* is being constantly reflected in a satiric mirror.

Alvin Kernan's study *The Plot of Satire*, published in the same year as Hnatko's article, might have guided Hnatko to the satiric function of *Tristram Shandy*'s "false" wit. Kernan's thesis, that satire uses the style of the knaves as part of its attack on them, suggests the parodic function of that "false" wit which Hnatko would simply lay at Sterne's door. The accuracy with which selections from *Peri Bathous* define the style of *Tristram Shandy* attests to the validity of Kernan's approach, though he does not himself consider Sterne's work a satire.[47] The following, for example, is quite suggestive of Tristram's artistic credo:

> . . . whoever would excell therein must studiously avoid, detest, and turn his Head from all the Ideas, Ways, and Workings of that pestilent Foe to Wit and Destroyer of fine Figures, which is known by the Name of *Common Sense*. His Business must be to contract the true *Góut de travers*; and to acquire a most *happy, uncommon, unaccountable Way of Thinking*.
>
> He is to consider himself as a *Grotesque* Painter, whose Works would be spoil'd by an Imitation of Nature, or Uniformity of Design. . . .
>
> His Design ought to be like a Labyrinth, out of which no body can get you clear but himself.[48]

Kernan finds in this passage a gloss on the hodgepodge nature of satire; the "mob tendency" which encompasses the detailed, en-

46. Paulson, *Theme and Structure in Swift's* Tale of a Tub (New Haven, 1960), p. 60.

47. Kernan discusses *Tristram Shandy* only briefly, and only in terms of a "comic" or "tragic" vision. He finds the work a "perfect confrontation" of the two—Tristram desperately trying to achieve the dignity of tragedy, while his life and opinions always return us to comedy (*The Plot of Satire*, p. 96).

48. Ed. Edna Leake Steeves (New York, 1952), pp. 17–18.

cyclopedic, and exuberant nature of prose satire: "Whatever particular form dullness may take in a given satire, it moves always toward the creation of messes, discordancies, mobs, on all levels and in all areas of life."[49]

The passage Kernan cites as suggestive of satire's "magnifying tendency" also seems pertinent to *Tristram Shandy*: ". . . but above all, preserve a laudable *Prolixity*; presenting the Whole and every Side at once of the Image to view. For Choice and Distinction are not only a Curb to the Spirit, and limit the Descriptive Faculty, but also lessen the Book, which is frequently of the worst consequence of all to our Author."[50] Tristram, absolutely certain of the importance of his task and of our interest in it, persistently refuses to exercise any manner of restraint or selectivity in his writing; everything is included, not because Sterne strives for novelistic realism, but because Tristram has convinced himself that the promulgation of his life and opinions is of universal concern.

Finally, the style of *Tristram Shandy* exhibits the "diminishing tendency" of satire, which, Kernan suggests, is taught on every page of *Peri Bathous*, since bathos is its essence. The rhetoric of diminution, so common in Swift, reduces life to its "grossest constituents"; in particular, it diminishes "the vital to the mechanical and the spiritual to the vulgarly material."[51] One obvious offshoot of the "diminishing tendency" is the scatology common to the entire satiric tradition; in *Tristram Shandy*, the back-yard wars of Uncle Toby, the associational thought processes of the Shandy family, and the minute explanations of poses and gestures, all seem to partake of this tradition as well.

These suggestions concerning the form and rhetoric of prose satire, combined with the Augustan viewpoint defined in Chapters I and II, are the pegs on which depend a reading of *Tristram Shandy* as a satire. In order to focus attention on the shifting pattern of the satire in the later volumes, I shall consider the work as it was published, volume by volume. Let it be emphasized at the outset that the important work of this study still lies before us: A valid reading of *Tristram Shandy* is my primary concern. This is what I now intend to provide with an approach to *Tristram Shandy* as a satire.

49. *The Plot of Satire*, p. 68.
50. *Peri Bathous*, p. 33.
51. *The Plot of Satire*, p. 53.

IV

"Tristram Shandy" as a Satire
Volumes I and II

*WHEN a man gives himself up to
the government of a ruling passion,—
or, in other words, when his* HOBBY-
HORSE *grows head-strong,—farewell
cool reason and fair discretion!*

The Life and Opinions of
Tristram Shandy, Gentleman, II.v.93

Volumes I and II

HE GESTATION of *Tristram Shandy* is a mystery and is likely to remain one. Having allowed his friends to convince him to suppress *A Political Romance* in January, 1759, Sterne quite surprises the critic with his first mention of *Tristram Shandy* in a letter dated May 23, 1759. It is a covering letter for the first volume, and is addressed to Robert Dodsley; the second volume is promised by Christmas. Sterne characterizes the work briefly: "The Plan, as you . . . will percieve, is a most extensive one,—taking in, not only, the Weak part of the Sciences, in wch the true point of Ridicule lies—but every Thing else, which I find Laugh-at-able in my way. . . ."[1] Certainly this sounds more like the prospectus to a satire than to a novel; and when Sterne suggests, in a postscript, that the work may be published "cum Notis Variorum" we feel even more secure in that judgment. Moreover, Sterne's correspondence during 1759–60 continually suggests that he was encountering the tribulations of a satirist. To a friend who had urged caution, he writes:

> I will use all reasonable caution—Only with this caution along with it, not to spoil My Book;—that is the air and originality of it, which must resemble the Author—& I fear 'tis a Number of these slighter touches which Mark this resemblance & Identify it from all Others of the [same] Stamp —Which this understrapping Virtue of Prudence woud Oblige Me to strike out. . . . Still I promise to be Cautious— but I deny I have gone as farr as Swift—He keeps a due distance from Rabelais—& I keep a due distance from him— Swift has said a hundred things I durst Not Say—Unless I was Dean of St. Patricks. . . .[2]

1. Lewis Perry Curtis, ed., *Letters of Laurence Sterne* (Oxford, 1935), p. 74.
2. *Ibid.*, p. 76. Sterne seems to suggest in the first sentence that the author of the work (i.e., Tristram) must be distinguished from the man of caution (i.e., Sterne). Cf. a second draft of this letter, p. 78: " . . . I concluded . . .

Again, in answer to a criticism of Slop's fall, Sterne offers in defense his version of that "grave irony" which Cervantes had come to represent to the century: "I will reconsider Slops fall & my too Minute Account of it—but in general I am perswaded that the happiness of the Cervantic humour arises from this very thing—of describing silly and trifling Events, with the Circumstantial Pomp of great Ones. . . ."³ This seems to me a precise statement of the "magnifying" tendency Kernan finds characteristic of all satire. In addition, Sterne had written in a second draft of this letter: "As for Slop's fall . . . that very thing should constitute the humour, which consists in treating the most insignificant Things with such *Ornamenta ambitiosa,* as would make one sick in another place." In the original draft, interestingly enough, Sterne promises to erase all defects of "*Ambitiosa ricidet ornamenta.*"⁴ Sterne seems aware, then, of the dangers he faces in *imitating* dullness, and he tells us, for example, that he has "burned more wit" than he has published. Between the decorum urged by Horace and the need to use excessive (false) wit to characterize his persona, lies one of the major tensions of *Tristram Shandy*—as of burlesque in general.

The most important evidence of Sterne's satiric intentions appears in a letter dated January 30, 1760. Of it, Curtis writes: "The laboured formality of this letter suggests that Sterne may have intended it as a public defence of his book, should the necessity arise."⁵ How real the protests were over Sterne's satire on Dr. Richard Mead, the Kunastrokius of Volume I, is a moot point; Sterne's defense of himself is in the tradition of satiric apologia. His "adversarius" has urged upon him the dictum *De mortuis nil nisi bonum.* The reply is lengthy, but it is valuable evidence of Sterne's satiric bent:

> I declare I have considered the wisdom, and foundation of it over and over again, as dispassionately and charitably as a good Christian can, and, after all, I can find nothing in it, or make more of it, than a nonsensical lullaby of some nurse, put into Latin by some pedant, to be chanted by some hypocrite to the end of the world, for the consolation of departing lechers.—'Tis, I own, Latin; and I think that is all the weight

that you really thought . . . the vein of humour too light for the colour of my Cassock—a Meditation upon the four last things had suited it better—I own—but then it must not have been wrote by me."
3. *Ibid.,* p. 77.
4. *Ibid.,* pp. 76–79.
5. *Ibid.,* p. 91.

it has—for, in plain English, 'tis a loose and futile position below a dispute—*"you are not to speak any thing of the dead, but what is good."* Why so?—Who says so?—neither reason or scripture.—Inspired authors have done otherwise—and reason and common sense tell me, that if the characters of past ages and men are to be drawn at all, they are to be drawn like themselves. . . . However, if like the poor devil of a painter, we must conform to this pious canon, *de mortuis, &c.* which I own has a spice of piety in the *sound* of it, and be obliged to paint both our angels and our devils out of the same pot— I then infer that our Sydenhams, and Sangrados, our Lucretias,—and Massalinas, our Sommers, and our Bolingbrokes —are alike entitled to statues, and all the historians, or satirists who have said otherwise since they departed this life, from Sallust, to S[tern]e, are guilty of the crimes you charge me with, "cowardice and injustice."[6]

In addition, Sterne twice maintains that his purpose in writing is moral correction: "But why do you doctors of the faculty attack such a one [a dead man] with your incision knife? Oh! for the good of the living.—'Tis my plea"; and again, he speaks of his "hopes of doing the world good by ridiculing what I thought deserving of it—or of disservice to sound learning, &c." The nature of satire is such that a tradition of defense early established itself as a necessary accompaniment; Sterne's letter differs in no significant way from the arguments of this tradition.

The incipient drama which emerges in Sterne's correspondence at this time, between the satirist who must write and his friends (and superiors) who advise caution and tolerance, had received an earlier, more ample, treatment in the opening pages of *Tristram Shandy* itself. The exchange between Yorick, the satirist, and Eugenius, his friend, can trace its origins from Horace and Trebatius to Pope and Arbuthnot, the tradition of the apologia satire. The juxtaposition, in the opening chapters, of Tristram's conception with Yorick's death serves a twofold purpose vital to the satiric organization of the work. In the first place, Sterne seems to suggest the replacement of Yorick by Tristram, signaling, I believe, the important shift of authorial duties to an ironic persona. Second,

6. *Ibid.*, pp. 88–89. That personal satire was proving a problem to Sterne is suggested by a letter he wrote to Robert Dodsley in the autumn of 1759, assuring him that "all locality is taken out of the book—the satire general" (Curtis, p. 81).

the contiguity of the death and conception (in Tristram's relation of them, but not, of course, in time) suggests, perhaps, the incompatibility of Yorick's satiric spirit with the story Tristram is preparing to tell. To be sure, in the jumbled Shandy world, Yorick is able to return several times in the course of the work, for he is dead when Tristram begins to write of his conception, but chronologically he dies in Tristram's thirtieth year. Yorick's black page is a dramatic sign of our entrance into the chaotic world of Tristram's mind, where the satiric spirit, with its measuring of human folly by absolute standards, lies dead and buried. And yet, Yorick is very much alive during the years that Tristram is able to cover in nine volumes. His function, I suggest, is a normative one, reminding us of the values which governed the world before his death set Tristram free from all values; it operates most profoundly at the end of the second volume where Sterne inserts the entire "Abuses of Conscience Considered" sermon, identified as Yorick's, as a normative gloss on the Shandy world we have been exposed to.

Both his dramatic retirement from the scene before a dozen chapters are over and his several reappearances in a normative role mark Yorick as a vital figure to the reading of *Tristram Shandy* as a satire, a figure to be studied with more care than critics have hitherto afforded him. It becomes necessary, for example, to recall that Yorick's function in *Hamlet* is not that of a jester, but rather of a *memento mori*:

> Alas! poor Yorick. I knew him Horatio; a fellow of infinite jest, of most excellent fancy. . . . Where be your gibes now? your gambols? your songs? your flashes of merriment, that were wont to set the table on a roar? . . . Now get you to my lady's chamber, and tell her, let her paint an inch thick, to this favour she must come; make her laugh at that.

One need not claim tragic implications for *Tristram Shandy* in order to acknowledge the pervasive presence of death throughout the work. Hamlet, learning to temper his idealism with the knowledge that "the noble dust of Alexander" now stops a bunghole, is able to embrace his fate, accepting the inevitable destruction which marks the tragic experience. In satire, however, the mortal nature of man serves as a mirror to reflect his extraordinary follies, his blindness to the frailty and temporality of human existence. Tristram's narrative is about his birth, and we never really proceed beyond his infancy. Yet from beginning to end, death finds its way into the Shandy world: the deaths of Yorick, of Bobby, of Le Fever, and, most significantly, the personification of Death as it pursues Tristram across the continent in Volume VII, demonstrating in doing so the absurdity of Tristram's lifelong project to chronicle his life. Yorick, rising from the dead, so to speak, is the gentle yet insistent reminder throughout *Tristram Shandy* that, do what he will, a man's life is a fragile and limited experience, accompanied by death even in the midst of procreation.

Sterne's Yorick is more than a reminder of death; he is a parson and satirist as well. Like the other characters in *Tristram Shandy*, Yorick makes his appearance mounted—"a lean, sorry, jack-ass of a horse, value about one pound fifteen shillings; who, to shorten all description of him, was full brother to *Rosinante*. . . . "[7] Tristram's use of the hobby-horse, or ruling passion, to define character is at work here, although the theory is not fully delineated until chapter xxiv. Thus Tristram tells us that, "as he never carried one single ounce of flesh upon his own bones, being altogether as spare a figure as his beast,—he would sometimes insist upon it, that the horse was as good as the rider deserved;—that they were, centaur-like,—both of a piece" (I.x.19). Most noteworthy about Yorick's mount, particularly when contrasted to the others we encounter, is its modesty: ". . . for he was as lean . . . and as sorry a jade, as HUMILITY herself could have bestrided." Yorick refuses to embellish the horse with a magnificent saddle in his possession; rather, "not caring to banter his beast . . . [he] had seriously befitted him with just such a bridle and such a saddle, as the figure and value of such a steed might well and truly deserve" (I.x.18–19). Here, then, is an important clue to the values Yorick embodies, the normative role which demands humility rather than pride, and a sense of propriety in presenting one's self to the world. In the Shandy world, where galloping hobby-horses make collisions the rule, and where each man is constantly at work embellishing and ornamenting his mount, Yorick's simplicity, humility, and inability to gallop assume a significant moral dimension.

Yorick's relationship to the *memento mori* tradition is twice suggested by Tristram in his discussion of the various reasons Yorick gave for riding such a "meek-spirited jade of a broken-winded horse." In the first place, "he would say, he found himself

7. *The Life and Opinions of Tristram Shandy, Gentleman*, James Aiken Work, ed. (New York, 1940), I.x.18. Hereafter cited in text.

going off fast in a consumption; and, with great gravity, would pretend, he could not bear the sight of a fat horse without a dejection of heart, and a sensible alteration in his pulse . . . " and again, "for on such a one he could sit mechanically, and meditate as delightfully *de vanitate mundi et fugâ sæculi,* as with the advantage of a death's head before him . . ." (I.x.20). Behind the humility of Yorick is an important awareness of his own fragile existence, an awareness absent in the other characters. At the same time, and closely related to this awareness, Yorick senses his own foolish figure as a human being: "His character was,—he loved a jest in his heart—and as he saw himself in the true point of ridicule, he would say, he could not be angry with others for seeing him in a light, in which he so strongly saw himself . . . " (I.x.19). Yorick is by no means the *vir bonus;* like the Shandys, he is often guilty of the follies which trap all mankind, and indeed, if we may believe Tristram, he is a victim of his own naïveté. But Yorick, unlike the Shandys, sees the errors and weaknesses his flesh is heir to, and thus serves as a foil to the blindness which surrounds him. It is significant that the story Tristram offers as the "true" cause of Yorick's broken-winded horse suggests that the parson at one time galloped around the countryside on the fastest horses the villagers had ever seen. Benevolence was his hobby-horse, a benevolence which he eventually came to see as useless. Tristram tries to consider Yorick's dismounting as an extension of his benevolence, but Yorick's words signal the ironic inversion the reader must make: " . . . Besides this he considered, that with half the sum thus galloped away, he could do ten times as much good;—and what still weighed more with him than all other considerations put together, was this, that it confined all his charity into one particular channel, and where, as he fancied, it was the least wanted, namely, to the child-bearing and child-getting part of his parish; reserving nothing for the impotent,—nothing for the aged,—nothing for the many comfortless scenes he was hourly called forth to visit, where poverty, and sickness, and affliction dwelt together" (I.x.21). As will happen time and again throughout the work, Tristram's sentimental flight is grounded by the gravity with which he accepts both the serious and the ludicrous, without distinction. Tristram sees nothing wrong with what he has just said; for the alert reader, "the impotent" renders the sentimental passage somewhat less than convincing.

Experience had taught Yorick that benevolence could just as effectively be dispensed from a slow-moving nag as from a hard-charger. To be sure, since it lacked the glitter of his cross-country jaunts, it was not a benevolence that would win Yorick public favor, and he suffers at the hands of "public opinion." Tristram hopes to restore Yorick's image with a panegyric to his "noble heart"; the comparison to Don Quixote looks two ways, however: "I have the highest idea of the spiritual and refined sentiments of this reverend gentleman, from this single stroke in his character, which I think comes up to any of the honest refinements of the peerless knight of *La Mancha*, whom, by the bye, with all his follies, I love more, and would actually have gone further to have paid a visit to, than the greatest hero of antiquity" (I.x.22). Don Quixote, astride his Rosinante, is unconscious of the reality of the beast; Yorick, on the contrary, astride his own Rosinante, is quite aware of the horse he rides, and the figure he makes as a rider. Between the blindness of the one and the awareness of the other lies the essential difference between Tristram's panegyric and Sterne's satire, between Tristram's love of the knight and Sterne's love of the "grave manner" with which Cervantes presents him. It is not that Yorick should not be praised, but simply that Tristram praises him for the wrong thing.

The gravity of Tristram, which dupes him into accepting Yorick's benevolence to the impotent as indicative of "refined sentiments," is, significantly enough, the prime target of Yorick's satire: "For, to speak the truth, *Yorick* had an invincible dislike and opposition in his nature to gravity;—not to gravity as such;—for where gravity was wanted, he would be the most grave or serious of mortal men for days and weeks together;—but he was an enemy to the affectation of it, and declared open war against it, only as it appeared a cloak for ignorance, or for folly; and then, whenever it fell in his way, however sheltered and protected, he seldom gave it much quarter" (I.xi.26). Tristram would like to attribute Yorick's attitude to his naïveté and *gaité de cœur*, and it is rather obvious that he does not share the parson's convictions. Yorick's comment that "the very essence of gravity was design, and consequently deceit;—'twas a taught trick to gain credit of the world for more sense and knowledge than a man was worth . . . " is prefaced by "Sometimes, in his wild way of talking, he would say. . . . " And again, when Yorick adds that gravity "was no better, but often worse, than what a *French* wit [Rochefoucauld] had long ago defined it,—*viz. A mysterious carriage of the body to cover the defects of the mind . . .* " Tristram thinks it is "great imprudence" on his part to say so. In "plain truth," says Tristram, "he was a man unhackneyed and unpractised in the world, and was altogether as indiscreet and foolish on every other subject of discourse where policy is wont to impress restraint. *Yorick* had no impression but one, and that was what arose from the nature of the deed spoken of; which impression he would usually translate into plain *English* without any periphrasis,—and too oft without much distinction of either personage, time, or place; . . . if it was a dirty action,—without more ado,—The man was a dirty fellow . . ." (I.xi.26–27). The rhetoric of inversion is at work here, signaled perhaps by Tristram's assertion that this is the "plain truth." What Tristram calls a lack of policy in Yorick is, in reality, the satiric attitude which underlies *Tristram Shandy*. By commenting on Yorick's lack of restraint, Tristram ironically mirrors his own unrestrained outpourings. By suggesting the directness of Yorick's style, he calls attention to his own periphrastic one. And finally, by appearing to condemn Yorick for judging people by their actions rather than allowing opinion or interest to sway his judgments, Tristram inadvertently establishes the norm by which we may judge his entire work, written under the motto, as translated by Work, "It is not actions, but opinions concerning actions, which disturb men."

Having suggested Yorick's role as the satirist of the work, Sterne places him, in chapter xii, in the traditional situation of having to defend his satire against the cautions of a well-meaning friend, the adversarius of formal verse satire. Eugenius, probably John Hall-Stevenson, issues the traditional warning: "In these sallies, too oft, I see, it happens, that a person laugh'd at, considers himself in the light of a person injured . . . and reckons up his friends, his family, his kindred and allies,—and musters up with them the many recruits which will list under him from a sense of common danger;—'tis no extravagant arithmetic to say, that for every ten jokes,—thou hast got a hundred enemies . . . " (I.xii.28–29). Yorick, like all satirists, disclaims any spleen or malice in his satires; and Eugenius supplies the usual rejoinder: "I believe and know them to be truly honest and sportive:—But consider, my dear lad, that fools cannot distinguish this,—and that knaves will not. . . . " Finally, Yorick promises to reform, again a traditional gesture; the tear in his eye, however, seems more than balanced by the irony in his words: "*Yorick* scarce ever heard this sad vaticination of his destiny read over to him, but with a tear stealing from his eye, and a promissory look attending it, that he was resolved, for the time to come, to ride his tit with more sobriety" (I.xii.30). As before, Tristram's attempt to create the pathetic vignette is transformed into bathos by his insensitivity to the meaning of his own words. Yorick, too, seems almost aware of Tristram's blindness, at least to the point of defeating his intentions: "*Yorick's* last breath was hanging upon his trembling lips ready to depart as he uttered this;—yet still it was utter'd with something of a *cervantick* tone" (I.xii.31). Work annotates *cervantick* as "satirical"; I would suggest instead that Sterne is thinking of the "grave manner" which had come to characterize Cervantes' style. Because this is Yorick's final speech before we turn his black page and enter the Shandy world, it is just possible that Sterne is trying to suggest the satiric stance with which it is to be presented. Certainly the sense of a new world is made dramatically apparent by the black page—and when we turn it, in memory of Yorick, we are at once immersed in the Shandy folly: "It is so long since the reader of this rhapsodical work has been parted from the midwife, that it is high time to mention her again to him, merely to put him in mind that there is such a body still in the world, and whom, upon the best judgment I can form upon my own plan at present,—I am going to introduce to him for good and all . . . " (I.xiii.35).

The Shandy world can perhaps best be approached as satire by recognizing a distinction between the worlds of Tristram's past and present, the Shandy household and the author's study. The two worlds, years apart, exist simultaneously throughout *Tristram Shandy,* and their frequent crisscrossings and collisions provide much of the hodgepodge effect we associate with prose satire. In part, the two worlds are unified by Tristram himself, though it is worthwhile to note that in the Shandy household Tristram is never more than a child, acted upon but not acting, while in the author's world, the Shandy family is apparently dead, Tristram alone surviving to tell the story. That is to say, we never see Tristram physically interacting with the Shandy family (except in Volume VII), and, although there is little question that he is its spiritual and intellectual heir, he is ultimately disengaged from the "history" he chronicles. In almost every event he records, Tristram is not remembering the past but simply setting it down, playing the role of historian rather than of biographer. The disorderly account we receive of the Shandy family is not a result of Tristram's psychological involvement in the events he presents, but of the theory of writing he embraces. To speak of Tristram's consciousness pervading the Shandy world, as many critics have done, is somewhat misleading because it suggests an involvement beyond Tristram's interests. I would suggest, instead, that we speak of Tristram's "art" pervading the Shandy world: Tristram is not wrestling with his past, but with his theory of writing which allows neither discrimination nor selection. In brief, *Tristram Shandy* is not a psychological novel, but a satire, and thus it finds its coherence not in human consciousness, but in satiric target and satiric attack.

Rather obviously, there are many similarities between the follies of the Shandy household and those of the author's study. In essence, both worlds are centered upon the same activity, creation. The concern of the Shandy household, setting aside Toby's amours, is the birth of Tristram; the concern of Tristram, the family historian, is to create for Sir and Madam the Shandy family, ostensibly as a prelude to his own life. This concern over creativity, apparent from the first scene to the last, becomes, I believe, the most pervasive metaphor of the work, and provides *Tristram Shandy* with the unity we seek in vain if we treat it as a novel. Operating in an ever widening circle of reference, the metaphor moves from the work's obvious interest in procreation and writing to encompass the whole of man's physical and intellectual efforts to propagate himself and his ideas. Whether it be the insemination of Mrs. Shandy or of a new "scientific" system, the creating of volumes or of miniature battlefields, the Shandy body and mind are in a constant state of begetting. At the same time, impotence and ignorance, clumsiness and folly block the Shandy efforts at almost every turn—the physical insufficiency, more readily characterized, becomes metaphorically one with the intellectual. Uppermost in the Shandy world is the desire to perpetuate itself and its ideas, to share its experiences and its theories with a world which is at best indifferent and, more frequently, hostile. Sterne's satiric attack is twofold. In the first place, he satirizes the creative urge in man, insofar as it results in "creations" wholly inadequate to the purposes they were intended to serve. Second, Sterne attacks the desire to promulgate these follies and failures, the insistence upon converting one's neighbors to one's own point of view: in short, the riding of hobby-horses. Ultimately, both attacks return to the "gravity" Yorick condemns, for Sterne is not attacking creativity as such (or procreativity for that matter), but rather the attitude of pride and self-sufficiency with which men offer, from their frail bodies and pitiable minds, solutions to the universe. The final sin is taking oneself and one's ideas more seriously than either warrants. The final virtue is humility.

That Tristram in his study opens his work with his unfortunate conception in the Shandy bed suggests immediately the metaphorical unity underlying the two worlds of *Tristram Shandy*. In part, Sterne is perhaps parodying the novel, with its pretense of accuracy and completeness; in part, the situation enables him to satirize the learned debate waged during the century on the function of the homunculus (sperm) in human reproduction. Tristram's attitude toward the debate is more revealing than the debate itself: "The HOMUNCULUS, Sir, in how-ever low and ludicrous a light he may appear, in this age of levity, to the eye of folly or prejudice:—to the eye of reason in scientifick research, he stands confess'd—a BEING guarded and circumscribed with rights:—The minutest philosophers, who, by the bye, have the most enlarged understandings, (their souls being inversely as their enquiries) shew us incontestably . . . " (I.ii.5).[8] The gravity with which Tristram accepts the findings of "scientifick research" suggests his sympathy with their minute investigations, a sympathy which mirrors Walter Shandy's personality and indicates a fundamental similarity between father and son.[9] At the same time, by insisting that the homunculus, having as we do "skin, hair, fat, flesh, veins, arteries, ligaments, nerves, cartilages, bones, marrow, brains, glands, genitals, humours, and articulations," is as much a person as the Lord Chancellor of England, Tristram inadvertently reveals the essential nature of Sterne's ironic persona: "Now, dear Sir, what if any accident had befallen him [the homunculus] in his way alone?—or that, thro' terror of it, natural to so young a traveller, my little gentleman had got to

8. See Louis A. Landa, "The Shandean Homunculus," in *Restoration and Eighteenth-Century Literature* (Chicago, 1963), pp. 49–68. That Sterne is also parodying the novel's quest for particularity is strongly suggested in I.iv.
9. Cf. Tristram's view of his father, I.iii.6: " . . . an excellent natural philosopher, and much given to close reasoning upon the smallest matters."

his journey's end miserably spent;—his muscular strength and virility worn down to a thread . . . —I tremble to think what a foundation had been laid for a thousand weaknesses both of body and mind, which no skill of the physician or the philosopher could ever afterwards have set thoroughly to rights" (I.ii.6). It is worth noting that this first Shandean theory, although in reality belonging to Walter, is presented by Tristram as his own. The theory allows Sterne to begin his work with an elemental diminution of man, who, in spite of his various poses and profundities, can never rise above the constituent elements he shares with his homunculus. In asserting the importance of the "little man" Tristram reduces to naught the significance of the "great man."

The procreative act in the Shandy bed is thwarted by the association of ideas which Locke labeled as most dangerous to rational thought. In essence, association reduces the mind to a machine, producing arbitrary and irrational connections of ideas rather than the rational links which Locke maintains are essential to valid reasoning. Significantly, Tristram, in explaining the importance of the "animal spirits," praises the process immediately before his mother's unfortunate question:

> . . . you have all, I dare say, heard of the animal spirits, as how they are transfused from father to son, &c. &c.—and a great deal to that purpose:—Well, you may take my word, that nine parts in ten of a man's sense or his nonsense, his successes and miscarriages in this world depend upon their motions and activity, and the different tracks and trains you put them into, so that when they are once set a-going, whether right or wrong, 'tis not a halfpenny matter,—away they go cluttering like hey-go-mad; and by treading the same steps over and over again, they presently make a road of it, as plain and as smooth as a garden-walk, which, when they are once used to, the Devil himself sometimes shall not be able to drive them off it (I.i.4–5).[10]

The image of the "mad" rider here is a dominant one in *Tristram Shandy,* and is ultimately connected to the hobby-horse. Tristram,

10. Cf. I.iv.9: " . . . from an unhappy association of ideas which have no connection in nature, it so fell out at length, that my poor mother could never hear the said clock wound up,—but the thoughts of some other things unavoidably popp'd into her head,—& *vice versâ:*—which strange combination of ideas, the sagacious *Locke* . . . affirms to have produced more wry actions than all other sources of prejudice whatsoever."

typically enough, is interested only in the speed of the "animal spirits"—their direction and their goal are alike inconsequential. The mechanical image of the mind as a series of grooves, each worn into a fixed habit of mind by a madcap horseman, appeals to Tristram, perhaps because of his own inconsistent nature, his inability to keep to the track. By having his animal spirits dispersed, Tristram avoids the mechanical nature of mind which characterizes the Shandy household. In its place, however, is the disorganized, uncontrolled, and undisciplined mind which writes *Tristram Shandy*. In both instances, the mind is arbitrary and insufficient, the extremes of mechanization and disorganization meeting in irrational juxtaposition to the rational mind. Tristram, writing in his study forty-one years after Mrs. Shandy's question, is besieged by a "thousand weaknesses both of mind and body . . . "—the work he writes begins its career, like the homunculus, with no hope of success, though, to be sure, Tristram is blind to the implications of the theory he here supports.

Indeed, one of the dominant characteristics of Tristram as an author is his abundant confidence. We receive a good taste of this self-assurance in I.iv; the sense of an ironic persona is particularly strong in passages of this nature: "As my life and opinions are likely to make some noise in the world, and, if I conjecture right, will take in all ranks, professions, and denominations of men whatever,—be no less read than the *Pilgrim's Progress* itself—and, in the end, prove the very thing which *Montaigne* dreaded his essays should turn out, that is, a book for a parlour-window; I find it necessary to consult every one a little in his turn . . . " (I.iv.7). Such assurance enables Tristram to dismiss Horace handily, and with him the classical notion that literature functions within a tradition and decorum accepted alike by writer, reader, and critic. Tristram's rejection of Horace is by no means the result of a study of classical principles, however; indeed, Tristram's knowledge of Horace is admittedly imperfect:

> . . . right glad I am, that I have begun the history of myself in the way I have done; and that I am able to go on tracing every thing in it, as *Horace* says, *ab Ovo*.
>
> *Horace*, I know, does not recommend this fashion altogether: But that gentleman is speaking only of an epic poem or a tragedy;—(I forget which)—besides, if it was not so, I should beg Mr. *Horace*'s pardon;—for in writing what I

have set about, I shall confine myself neither to his rules, nor to any man's rules that ever lived (I.iv.7–8).

Tristram's rebellion is not against Horace, but against the idea of restraint or rule. He writes, he says, for the "curious and inquisitive," and to please them—his primary concern—requires neither decorum nor logic, but, on the contrary, novelty and surprise. Tristram puts all his hopes on these two effects, producing them by going "deeper" than any author had ever gone and "insinuating" more than any had ever insinuated: "What these perplexities of my uncle *Toby* were,—'tis impossible for you to guess;—if you could,—I should blush . . . as an author; inasmuch as I set no small store by myself upon this very account, that my reader has never yet been able to guess at any thing. And in this, Sir, I am of so nice and singular a humour, that if I thought you was able to form the least judgment or probable conjecture to yourself, of what was to come in the next page,—I would tear it out of my book" (I.xxv.80). The satire is directed not only at those mid-eighteenth-century authors who, like Tristram, wrote specifically to please the demand for novelty and surprise but at the reading public as well. Tristram's entire creative effort is guided by public accommodation, and the lively manner in which he involves us in the creative process ultimately serves Sterne's satiric ends. This is, to be sure, a commonplace conclusion of satire: The literature of a society is a precise reflection of what that society deserves. I doubt whether Sterne meant to compliment the mid-eighteenth century by giving it Tristram.

Sterne's efforts to implicate us, as readers, in this satiric attack are numerous. The questions of "Sir" and "Madam," for example, are a rather direct means of suggesting our spellbound absorption in the narrative as it unfolds. Somewhat more subtle is the implication of our salacious nature by a suggestive insinuation which Tristram quickly abandons while we draw conclusions. To illustrate, we are set to counting months by the insinuation of this remark: "On the fifth day of *November*, 1718, which . . . was as near nine kalendar months as any husband could in reason have expected. . . . " The page before, Tristram had insisted, with a display of scientific finality, that he was conceived the first Sunday night in March, eight not nine months before. And yet, when we have finished our calculations and drawn the obvious conclusion, we discover that Tristram has dropped the issue completely. Tristram's incessant use of detail here encourages us to betray our interest in anything that hints of the salacious; and while he blithely continues his narrative, proving on every page that no father ever had a truer son, we remain behind, distracted by our persistent regard for sexual innuendo.

A more elaborate trap is set for us in I.xviii, where Tristram mentions "my dear, dear *Jenny*," in trying to explain by analogy Mrs. Shandy's decision to have the midwife. Four pages later, he tacks a caveat to the reader onto the chapter which warns him that he has mistaken the reference to "Jenny." He is not, Tristram says, to take the author for a married man, in spite of the "tender appellation of my dear, dear *Jenny*,—with some other strokes of conjugal knowledge. . . . " The point is, of course, that no one would ever have assumed "dear, dear *Jenny*" to be his wife, precisely because of the "tender appellation." Tristram's second warning is far closer to our original idea: "Not that I can be so vain or unreasonable, Madam, as to desire you should therefore think, that my dear, dear *Jenny* is my kept mistress;—no,—that would be flattering my character in the other extream . . . " (I.xviii.49). The willingness with which our minds move to the licentious bears the brunt of the playful satiric attack; but the idea that calling Jenny a kept mistress would flatter Tristram also suggests that he is a target as well. It is, however, the suggestion that Jenny "may be my friend" which conclusively implicates both the reader and Tristram in Sterne's satire: "—Friend!—My friend.—Surely, Madam, a friendship between the two sexes may subsist, and be supported without—Fy! Mr. *Shandy*:—Without any thing, Madam, but that tender and delicious sentiment, which ever mixes in friendship, where there is a difference of sex. Let me intreat you to study the pure and sentimental parts of the best *French* Romances;—it will really, Madam, astonish you to see with what a variety of chaste expression this delicious sentiment, which I have the honour to speak of, is dress'd out" (I.xviii.49). Surely this is a passage where not Sterne but an ironic persona is speaking; the praise of the "expression" of sentiment strikes at the core of sentimentalism—its substitution of words for deeds, appearance for reality. The satiric device of allowing words the significance of reality itself is to be a primary weapon in Sterne's attack against sentimentalism.

The implication of the reader into Tristram's study is furthered by two recurring devices—the suggestion that author and reader should be friends, and the insistence that we may learn a great deal from *Tristram Shandy*. The former is made an excuse for Tristram's love of trivia: "As you proceed further with me, the slight acquaintance which is now beginning betwixt us, will grow into familiarity; and that, unless one of us is in fault, will terminate in friendship.—*O diem præclarum!*—then nothing which has touched me will be thought trifling in its nature, or tedious in its telling" (I.vi.11). Friendship enables Tristram to divulge to the reader plans for his book that must be kept secret from the critics. The "anatomical" nature of satire is clearly in Sterne's mind when he has Tristram promise that

> all this will be more exactly delineated and explain'd in a map, now in the hands of the engraver, which, with many other pieces and developments to this work, will be added to the end of the twentieth volume,—not to swell the work,—I detest the thought of such a thing;—but by way of commentary, scholium, illustration, and key to such passages, incidents, or inuendos as shall be thought to be either of private interpretation, or of dark or doubtful meaning after my life and my opinions shall have been read over . . . ;—which, betwixt you and me, and in spight of all the gentlemen reviewers in *Great-Britain* . . . I am determined shall be the case.—I need not tell your worship, that all this is spoke in confidence (I.xiii. 35–36).

The satiric hodgepodge, insofar as it serves as a satiric reflection of bad writing and bad thinking, is foisted upon the reader as something essential and desirable; the sense of a whispered conspiracy makes him almost as responsible as the author himself for the chaotic nature of *Tristram Shandy*. Having thus gained the reader's support, Tristram can now abandon all pretense of getting on with the work. He has, he writes,

> Accounts to reconcile:
> Anecdotes to pick up:
> Inscriptions to make out:
> Stories to weave in:
> Traditions to sift:
> Personages to call upon:
> Panegyricks to paste up at this door:
> Pasquinades at that . . . (I.xiv.37).

"In short, there is no end of it . . . " and Tristram states his intention to "go on leisurely, writing and publishing two volumes of my life every year;—which, if I am suffered to go on quietly, and can make a tolerable bargain with my bookseller, I shall continue to do as long as I live." The classical values of selectivity and proportion are replaced by Tristram's values of inclusiveness and longevity. Art is uprooted by economics, and, most significantly, we are implicated in the blame for this unfortunate state of affairs.

At times, Tristram abandons the pose of friend to become teacher instead. An extension of his self-assurance, the device is often no more than a brief assertion that he is "writing this book for the edification of the world" (I.xviii.44). Then again, it can be a more extensive claim, as when he rebukes Madam for missing the clue that *my mother was not a papist*: " . . . 'Tis to rebuke a vicious taste which has crept into thousands besides herself,—of reading straight forwards, more in quest of the adventures, than of the deep erudition and knowledge which a book of this cast, if read over as it should be, would infallibly impart with them" (I.xx.56). Sterne's satire here makes use of a favorite device of Swift's; by attacking directly what needs to be attacked, the other extreme, though equally unacceptable, is made to appear of some worth. The trap is sprung when the reader agrees to reject one extreme only to accept another. The following, I believe, could just as easily have been written by Swift, so skillfully does Sterne capture Swift's idiom:

> It is a terrible misfortune for this same book of mine, but more so to the Republick of Letters;—so that my own is quite swallowed up in the consideration of it,—that this self-same vile pruriency for fresh adventures in all things, has got so strongly into our habit and humours,—and so wholly intent are we upon satisfying the impatience of our concupiscence that way,—that nothing but the gross and more carnal parts of a composition will go down:—The subtle hints and sly communications of science fly off, like spirits, upwards;—the heavy moral escapes downwards; and both the one and the other are as much lost to the world, as if they were still left in the bottom of the ink-horn (I.xx.57).

The sexual terms used to describe the quest for new adventures recall Tristram's several attempts to involve the reader's pruriency in his creative act; certainly his appeal to novelty and surprise suggests that, whatever Tristram may say to the contrary, his work is designed to please an audience whose primary concern is for "fresh adventures."

At the same time, the irony of inversion is quite strong in the alternative: "subtle" and "heavy," "upwards" and "downwards" are used, as in Swift, to suggest unsatisfying extremes of intangible spirituality and gross materialism. The "deep erudition" that Tristram offers us is of appeal primarily to our concupiscence—that is, it drops downwards; the subtleties of science that we do not grasp have so little relation to the material world they are supposed to explain that they do indeed fly upwards: What better example of grossness and subtlety than the document which immediately follows this passage, the "MEMOIRE presenté à Messieurs les Docteurs de SORBONNE"?

The self-assurance that enables Tristram to recommend the erudition of his own work is one aspect of a more general pride he exhibits in the intellectual achievements of his own day. His rejection of the past is balanced by a complete absorption with the present. One manifestation of this absorption is the panegyric on modern learning which follows a survey of "modern" theories of English humor: "Thus,—thus my fellow labourers and associates in this great harvest of our learning, now ripening before our eyes; thus it is, by slow steps of casual increase, that our knowledge physical, metaphysical, physiological, polemical . . . and obstetrical, with fifty other branches of it, (most of 'em ending, as these do, in *ical*) have, for these two last centuries and more, gradually been creeping upwards towards that Aκμη of their perfections, from which, if we may form a conjecture from the advances of these last seven years, we cannot possibly be far off" (I.xxi.64). It is hardly conceivable that Sterne shares this enthusiasm with Tristram— clearly we are to distinguish the author from his ironic persona. Like his optimism concerning the future fame and importance of his work, this enthusiasm for modern science is strongly suggestive of the "modern" who authors *A Tale of a Tub*. Sterne complicates the character of his persona, however, by having Tristram, in spite of his assurance, and even arrogance, troubled as well by a sense of his own inadequacies. In the present passage, for example, Tristram concludes that he was not only conceived in an unfortunate manner, but that the time of his birth was unpropitious as well. He reasons that when his age reaches the acme of learning (and it is only a matter of days and weeks), it will mean the end of writing; the end of writing will end reading; and the end of reading will "put an end to all kind of knowledge,—and then—we shall have all to begin over again . . . " (I.xxi.64). That would be the "thrice happy Times" to have been born into, a time "when a man in the literary world might have stood some chance." This is the reasoning of a Grub-Street hack.

Tristram's feeling that he was born at the wrong time is the echo of a larger regret, voiced earlier:

> ON the fifth day of *November*, 1718 . . . was I . . . brought forth into this scurvy and disasterous world of ours.—I wish I had been born in the Moon, or in any of the planets . . . for it could not well have fared worse with me in any of them . . . than it has in this vile, dirty planet of ours; . . . not but the planet is well enough, provided a man could be born in it to a great title or to a great estate; . . . but that is not my case; . . . for which cause I affirm it over again to be one of the vilest worlds that ever was made;—for I can truly say, that from the first hour I drew my breath in it . . . I have been the continual sport of what the world calls fortune . . . (I.v.9–10).

On the one hand, the mingling of Tristram's outrageous optimism in himself and modern man with this pessimistic attack on fortune and the world can be seen as an exercise of satire's freedom in presenting character: Consistency is not a desideratum as it is in the novel. On the other hand, the two attitudes may be seen as the necessary effects of a single cause: Tristram's total involvement with the material, the present. Because he measures life only by his physical condition at any given moment, Tristram necessarily feels himself the sport of fortune. At the same time, because he values the gifts of fortune so highly, he is easily betrayed into excessive optimism by any temporal success, by every turn of the wheel. Tristram's diatribe against the world is a ludicrous inversion of the Christian tradition of *contemptus mundi*. For the Christian, the "things" of the world are contemptible; for Tristram, the world itself is scurvy because he has not been given its "things." As with his acknowledgment of his dispersed homunculus, Tristram tells us that he is the sport of fortune without considering this information's effect on our opinion of his book. In every way, *Tristram Shandy* reflects an author who "in every stage" of his life has been pelted "with a set of as pitiful misadventures and cross accidents as ever small HERO sustained." Indeed, the more Tristram pursues worldly fame and fortune through his writing, the more we recognize that Fortune is not yet finished with Tristram.

We receive a last look at Tristram in his study in chapter xxii, where many of the elements of his character meld. The chapter begins by quoting Bishop Hall, "That it is an abominable thing for a man to commend himself." Tristram agrees; "And yet, on the other hand, when a thing is executed in a masterly kind of a fashion, which thing is not likely to be found out;—I think it is full as abominable, that a man should lose the honour of it, and go out of the world with the conceit of it rotting in his head" (I.xxii.72). The play on "conceit" and the use of "rotting" undercut Tristram's self-glorification, but he is insensitive to this fact and blithely continues to praise his own digressive skill: "By this contrivance the machinery of my work is of a species by itself; two contrary motions are introduced into it, and reconciled, which were thought to be at variance with each other. In a word, my work is digressive, and it is progressive too,—and at the same time" (I.xxii.73).[11] The word "machinery" is suggestive of Tristram's mechanical approach to writing; and, while it is true that the digressions do not really interrupt the narrative, it is only because the narrative is of slight intrinsic interest. Certainly Tristram's digressive style would be foolhardy were we actually concerned with Tristram's biography. As it is, we quite willingly allow our attention to be diverted—an indication, perhaps, that we are not reading *Tristram Shandy* as a novel. The digressive style has a long and honorable tradition in classical writing, and Sterne is no more satirizing the use of the digression than did Swift in his "Digression in Praise of Digressions." What he is satirizing is the perversity which finds digressions the "sunshine" and the "soul" of the work, making them so important to the book that "take them out . . . —you might as well take the book along with them." Like the classical author, Tristram uses the digression for variety, but since he and his audience desire constant variety, the digression in his hands loses its raison d'être. Order, proportion, and direction

11. Tristram further explains his method by reference to planetary movements: " . . . that of the earth's moving round her axis, in her diurnal rotation, with her progress in her elliptick orbit. . . . " In this manner, he says, "the greatest of our boasted improvements and discoveries have come from some such trifling hints" (I.xxii.73). The "magnifying" tendency of satire is displayed with cutting irony.

give way to whim—and Tristram inadvertently comments on his abuse of the digression when he begins the very next chapter: "I Have a strong propensity in me to begin this chapter very non-sensically, and I will not balk my fancy" (I.xxiii.74).

If the fundamental concern of the Shandy household and Tristram's study is creation, the fundamental device which links the two worlds is the hobby-horse. Tristram's first mention of hobby-horses is significant and often overlooked:

> . . . But every man to his own taste.—Did not Dr. *Kunastrok-ius*, that great man, at his leisure hours, take the greatest delight imaginable in combing of asses tails, and plucking the dead hairs out with his teeth, though he had tweezers always in his pocket? Nay, if you come to that, Sir, have not the wisest of men in all ages . . . had their HOBBY-HORSES;—their running horses,—their coins and their cockle-shells, their drums and their trumpets, . . . —their maggots and their butter-flies?—and so long as a man rides his HOBBY-HORSE peace-ably and quietly along the King's highway, and neither com-pels you or me to get up behind him,—pray, Sir, what have either you or I to do with it? (I.vii.13)

It was, we remember, this attack on Dr. Mead that Sterne defended in his unpublished apologia. That the hobby-horse, a quaint and playful device in Tristram's hands, should be first introduced as the central device of the most biting personal satire in the work is perhaps not accidental. Tristram, to be sure, allows Dr. Kuna-strokius his particular vice; Sterne, on the contrary, defends his obligation to satirize Dr. Mead, intimating by doing so the satirist's belief in moral absolutes. Tristram's system of universal tolerance fails because Tristram is unable to distinguish between a Dr. Kun-astrokius and a numismatist, between a collector of butterflies and a collector of maggots.[12] In addition, Tristram suggests at the out-set that particular aspect of the hobby-horse which poses the most danger to civilized society: its pervasive, persistent urge to proselyt-

---

12. The annotation of maggots as "whimsical fancies" in Ian Watt's edition of *Tristram Shandy* (Boston, 1965), p. 10, seems at best only partially ade-quate. Sterne would not have broken the unity of his series of specific "whimsical fancies" by including a generic term. See his further use of "maggots," I.xxiii.74. It is worth recalling, perhaps, in reading this passage, Pope's condemnation of numismatists and butterfly collectors in the *Dunciad*, IV. Sterne's use of both as "innocent" hobby-horses may suggest a softening of attitude on his part; or, if there is an allusion to the *Dunciad*, it may warn us of the insidious nature of even the most innocent hobby-horse—it begins in jest and ends in earnest.

ize. Were the hobby-horse a quiet and peaceful beast, were the rider at peace with himself and the world, we could perhaps endorse, as Tristram does, the aphorism *de gustibus non est disputandum*. Time and again, however, the hobby-horse and its rider reveal a far different nature, metaphorically represented by the speed with which the various horses of the Shandy world race about the countryside, at times colliding with one another, and by the consideration of horse and rider as one and the same beast.

It is this second aspect of the hobby-horse, that horse and rider become one, which lends itself to the drawing of character:

> A man and his HOBBY-HORSE, tho' I cannot say that they act and re-act exactly after the same manner in which the soul and body do upon each other: Yet doubtless there is a communication between them of some kind, and my opinion rather is, that there is something in it more of the manner of electrified bodies,—and that by means of the heated parts of the rider, which come immediately into contact with the back of the HOBBY-HORSE.—By long journies and much friction, it so happens that the body of the rider is at length fill'd as full of HOBBY-HORSICAL matter as it can hold;—so that if you are able to give but a clear description of the nature of the one, you may form a pretty exact notion of the genius and character of the other (I.xxiv.77).

Tristram has just rejected the method of those who would draw a man's character "merely from his evacuations," the system smelling "too strongly of the lamp." Sterne's intentions, however, will not allow Tristram to ignore the physical nature of man; and the hobby-horse, as this passage demonstrates, provides an abundance of scatological implications. Nor is Tristram wholly unaware of these implications. In his discussion of the various methods of describing character, his sense of the physical man is clearly evident; the mechanical nature of his view through a *Momus'* glass is worth noting: " . . . view'd the soul stark naked;—observ'd all her motions,—her machinations;—traced all her maggots from their first engendering to their crawling forth;—watched her loose in her frisks, her gambols, her capricios . . . " (I.xxiii.74). Equally significant is Tristram's rejection of this method of character study: "But this . . . is not the case of the inhabitants of this earth;—our minds shine not through the body, but are wrapt up here in a dark covering of uncrystalized flesh and blood . . . " (I.xxiii.75). Still in the same vein, Tristram rejects "wind instruments" (with a glance at the Italian *castrati*), evacuations, and the *Non-Naturals* as means of describing character, posing, in regard to the last, the question, "Why the most natural actions of a man's life should be call'd his Non-Naturals . . . " (I.xxiii.74–76). There is in all this bawdiness the desire of the satirist to keep a man's character closely tied to his body.

Speaking of his own inclinations to mount, Tristram writes: ". . . for happening, at certain intervals and changes of the Moon, to be both fiddler and painter, according as the fly stings:—Be it known to you, that I keep a couple of pads myself, upon which . . . I frequently ride out and take the air;—tho' sometimes, to my shame be it spoken, I take somewhat longer journies than what a wise man would think altogether right" (I.viii.13–14). Tristram is also aware of this reluctance to dismount in other men, even in those Lords to whom he offers his Dedication: ". . . when I behold such a one, my Lord, like yourself, whose principles and conduct are as generous and noble as his blood, and whom, for that reason, a corrupt world cannot spare one moment;—when I see such a one, my Lord, mounted, though it is but for a minute beyond the time which my love to my country has prescribed to him, and my zeal for his glory wishes,—then, my Lord, I cease to be a philosopher, and in the first transport of an honest impatience, I wish the HOBBY-HORSE, with all his fraternity, at the Devil" (I.viii.14–15). In short, the danger Tristram sees is that a man becomes so enamoured of his beast that he forgets he is mounted, forgets the world on foot around him, forgets, indeed, everything which makes him a contributor to, and partaker of, civilized society. While, on the one hand, horse and rider become one, on the other, they enter into a romantic affair, significantly colored by the Elizabethan use of "hobby-horse" for a harlot. In either case, the implications are the same: The hobby-horse tends to turn a man into a beast—at worst, a Dr. Kunastrokius; at best, an ass. In the Shandy world, where every figure is mounted and galloping, and where no effort is made to check the horses, much less to dismount, the chaotic world of satire is the result.

That Walter's hobby-horse is projection and disputation and that Toby's is military science is obvious enough. Only slightly less evident, perhaps, is the observation that Tristram's hobby-horse is *Tristram Shandy*. As a writer, Tristram never really dismounts;

he becomes one with his hobby-horse, falling into the very danger of which he warns "my Lord." Chapter vi, for example, ends with a metaphorical passage comparing his work to a journey, a pervasive comparison in all nine volumes. Chapter ix ends with a dedication to the Moon, "who, by the bye, of all the PATRONS or MATRONS I can think of, has most power to set my book a-going, and make the world run mad after it."[13] Not only is *Tristram Shandy* Tristram's hobby-horse, but Tristram reveals, time and again, his desire to have the reader mounted with him. As Tristram describes the Shandy household through each member's hobby-horse, the irony of his own position astride the most runaway of the Shandy steeds becomes more and more evident.

The Shandy household constitutes a world of "four *English* miles diameter, or thereabouts, of which the cottage [of the midwife] . . . is supposed to be the centre" (I.vii.11). By thus narrowing his satiric world, Sterne is better able to create, with his fast-moving horses, the sense of confusion and cross-purposes essential to the satiric scene. At the same time, the little world of the Shandys is part of the "diminishing" tendency of satire; Sterne had achieved the same effect in the *Political Romance*.[14] The crowning accomplishment in this regard is Sterne's creation within this little world of a garden where the great battles of King William's and Queen Anne's reigns are reduced to Toby and Trim's playthings. Walter's theories and Toby's maneuvers are both employed on a field which reflects satirically the vanity of human efforts when measured with a due regard for divine proportions.

Within the Shandy world, Walter Shandy, as husband, elder brother, and father, is the theoretical master; and it is perhaps significant that one of the foremost of his many theories is concerned with the justification of this mastery. Typically enough, Walter turns Sir Robert Filmer's defense of the divine right of kings by analogy to the patriarchal family into a defense of the rights of husbands by analogy to the success of monarchies (I.xviii). Walter

13. The actual dedication reads, significantly: "*Bright Goddess*, If thou art not too busy with CANDID and Miss CUNEGUND's affairs,—take *Tristram Shandy*'s under thy protection also" (I.ix.17).

14. A Swiftian effect is achieved by Sterne in a later discussion of the size of the "world": " . . . whenever 'tis said that such a one is of great weight and importance in the *world*,—I desire [his "circle of importance"] may be enlarged or contracted in your worship's fancy, in a compound-ratio of the station, profession, knowledge, abilities, height and depth (measuring both ways) of the personage brought before you" (I.xiii.35).

loses the argument: Mrs. Shandy will have the midwife, and her husband may open a bottle of wine with Dr. Slop in the back parlor. In a small way, Mrs. Shandy's victory signals the complex pattern of defeat which marks Walter Shandy's life from the bedroom scene which opens Volume I to the final failure of the prize bull in Volume IX. The most traditional target of satire in *Tristram Shandy*, Walter, the *philosophus gloriosus*, like the many projectors and scientists and philosophers who precede him, faces a continual series of rebuffs from the reality which his theories do not begin to explain.

Walter suffers similar defeat at the hands of his brother. Representative of their arguments is the one over Aunt Dinah's indiscretion, which concludes with Walter arguing that thousands of lives are "cast away, (in all civilized countries at least)—and consider'd as nothing but common air, in competition of an hypothesis." This, replies Toby, is "downright MURDER":

> —There lies your mistake, my father would reply;—for, in *Foro Scientiæ* there is no such thing as MURDER,—'tis only DEATH, brother.
> My uncle *Toby* would never offer to answer this by any other kind of argument, than that of whistling half a dozen bars of *Lillabullero*.—You must know it was the usual channel thro' which his passions got vent, when any thing shocked or surprised him;—but especially when any thing, which he deem'd very absurd, was offered (I.xxi.69).

Walter, quite by accident, has made an important comment on Toby's interest in military science, and Toby's blindness is typical of the Shandy failure to know themselves. At the same time, however, Toby's *Argumentum Fistulatorium* defeats Walter's hypothesis; and throughout the work it is clear that Toby comes to agreement with Walter never out of conviction, but only from complaisance. In Walter's complex world of theory and rhetoric, Toby's *Lillabullero* is the final argument.

Walter's mastery as a husband and brother is, therefore, a matter of theory but not of fact. Only in his third seat of authority, that of Tristram's father, does Walter achieve the success he seeks in vain as a husband and brother. Ironically, it is as a father that Walter is most aware of his failures—the diffused homunculus, the flattened nose, the misnamed Tristram; all of Walter's favorite theories concerning procreation and offspring are shattered by the

accidents which surround Tristram's life. And yet, in spite of
these disappointments, Tristram in his study is the mirrored image
of Walter in his household, and *Tristram Shandy* is a tribute to
Walter's success in educating his son in the Shandean system.
Walter's continued sway over Tristram is apparent from the beginning of the work, for though it is his theory that *"My Tristram's misfortunes began nine months before ever he came into the
world"* (I.iii.6–7), Tristram offers it primarily as his own, embracing the theory of the diffused homunculus as an important
explanation of his unfortunate life. In Tristram's opinion, his
father "was an excellent natural philosopher, and much given to
close reasoning upon the smallest matters" (I.iii.6). To be sure,
this opinion is not consistently held throughout the work; later in
Volume I Tristram accuses his father of moving both "heaven and
earth . . . to support his hypothesis" (I.xix.53), and Tristram often
demonstrates an insight into Walter's folly. But this insight can
only make the many incidents of sympathy and similarity between
father and son the more culpable—and the more dangerous. For
example, we may note that Walter's interest in public opinion and
in persuading others to his way of thinking is echoed by Tristram's
interest in worldly fame and the art of rhetoric. Walter's desire to
have Dr. Slop attend the birth, for example, is not altogether un-
selfish: "To say nothing of the natural workings of humanity and
justice,—or of the yearnings of parental and connubial love . . . he
felt himself concern'd in a particular manner, that all should go
right in the present case;—from the accumulated sorrow he lay
open to, should any evil betide his wife and child in lying-in at
Shandy-Hall.—He knew the world judged by events, and would
add to his afflictions in such a misfortune, by loading him with the
whole blame of it" (I.xviii.45). For Walter, we remember, the
"world" is four miles round. Tristram's efforts to appeal to the
world on a far grander scale are thus indicative of an important relationship between father and son: The localized folly of Walter,
seemingly harmless because it is local, assumes in Tristram's hands
universal proportions—the corruption of good taste and good sense
in a world at least large enough to include the reader. Similarly,
Walter's untutored rhetorical "genius" becomes in Tristram a self-
conscious awareness of the pedantic baggage of rhetoric. For both,
rhetoric-as-persuasiveness is the primary means by which the public can be made to mount the various Shandy hobby-horses. In

Tristram's hands, however, rhetoric is also a science; in giving to the world the label *Argumentum Fistulatorium* for Toby's *Lilla-bullero*, Tristram is obviously the learned projector, offering his efforts "That it may be said by my children's children, when my head is laid to rest,—that their learned grandfather's head had been busied to as much purpose once, as other people's:—That he had invented a name,—and generously thrown it into the TREASURY of the *Ars Logica*, for one of the most unanswerable arguments in the whole science" (I.xxi.71). While both Walter and Toby have the excuse of being "naturals," Tristram's folly partakes, as well, of a pedanticism and a pride which renders it far more culpable as a satiric target. Between the two Shandy generations lies the moral lesson that human folly, given a foothold, compounds itself; it is the lesson of the *Dunciad* and *Martinus Scriblerus* as well.

It is therefore significant that, though many of Tristram's theories are borrowed from his father, he also shows a scientific and projecting nature quite independent from Walter's. When he prepares to sell his Dedication, for example, he measures its value by the so-called painter's scale, "to speak more like a man of science" (I.ix.16). This mechanical system of art appreciation, as R. F. Brissenden recently pointed out, makes a good target for satire in the Scriblerian tradition.[15] Again, although it is Walter Shandy who loves a subtle argument, couched in subtle terms, it is Tristram's insistence upon "historical accuracy" and the origins of things that permits him to offer to us, in their entirety, the subtle legality of his mother's marriage settlement and the even more subtle argument of the doctors of the Sorbonne. Time and again, Tristram will interrupt the thread of his discourse to chase down (for he is, like his father, well mounted) the intricacies of an absurd argument, thus providing Sterne with a ready means of introducing into *Tristram Shandy* a wide range of learned folly, legal, theological, scientific, and philosophic. Much of the satire on learning in *Tristram Shandy* stems, as has long been recognized, from Walter's various theories and systems; but equally significant is the considerable quantity of pedantic nonsense brought into the work by Tristram himself.

Sterne is able to exploit the satiric possibilities of two projectors occupying the same stage, in several ways. The simplest method is

15. "Sterne and Painting," in *Of Books and Humankind* (London, 1964), pp. 93–108.

to introduce their particular hobby-horses separately, with no cross-current of any kind. More common is the use of Tristram to support and reinforce an absurd theory of Walter's, as with the homunculus. Yet another possibility is that Tristram may disengage himself from one of his father's theories; this he does with Walter's theory on names: "I Would sooner undertake to explain the hardest problem in Geometry, than pretend to account for it, that a gentleman of my father's great good sense,—knowing, as the reader must have observed him, and curious too, in philosophy,—wise also in political reasoning,—and in polemical (as he will find) no way ignorant,—could be capable of entertaining a notion in his head, so out of the common track . . ." (I.xix.49). The disengagement serves Sterne's satiric intentions as satisfactorily as when Tristram agrees with his father's absurdities. In the first place, Tristram continues his extravagant praise of Walter's "genius," reminding the reader that in many other instances Tristram gives support to theories equally "out of the common track." Second, the entire theory of names is juxtaposed, in the same chapter, with Tristram's awe at his father's untutored rhetorical genius: "And yet, 'tis strange, he had never read *Cicero* nor *Quintilian de Oratore*, nor *Isocrates* . . . ; and what is more astonishing, he had never in his whole life the least light or spark of subtilty struck into his mind, by one single lecture upon *Crackenthorp* or *Burgersdicius*, or any *Dutch* logician or commentator; . . . so that I well remember, when he went up along with me to enter my name at *Jesus College* in ****,—it was a matter of just wonder with my worthy tutor, and two or three fellows of that learned society,—that a man who knew not so much as the names of his tools, should be able to work after that fashion with 'em" (I.xix.52–53). The pedantic inclination to consider as mastered all mysteries which can be given a name is a natural target for satire. Tristram rejects his father's blatant endorsement of this mechanical operation, that is, that a proper name can influence the character of its recipient. And, yet, within three pages he marvels, along with his tutors, that his father could practice the *argumentum ad hominem* without knowing its name, as if reality resided in the word. In later passages where Sterne attacks sentimentalism, it will be this inclination to substitute the name for the feeling that will bear the brunt of the satire.

Finally, Tristram's refusal to endorse Walter's theory of names gives Sterne the opportunity to suggest that the Shandy world is, indeed, an aberration from a norm. In explaining his father's peculiar notions, Tristram suggests that they "at first enter'd upon the footing of mere whims, and of a *vive la Bagatelle*; and as such he would make merry with them for half an hour or so, and having sharpen'd his wit upon 'em, dismiss them till another day" (I.xix.53). Tristram warns us all against the "indiscreet reception of such guests" who, after some years in our brains, having entered in jest, end in "downright earnest." At the same time, Tristram also suggests that Walter's judgment "became the dupe of his wit." In any case, "he was serious;—he was all uniformity; —he was systematical, and, like all systematick reasoners, he would move both heaven and earth, and twist and torture every thing in nature to support his hypothesis. In a word, I repeat it over again;—he was serious" (I.xix.53). The emphasis on Walter's "seriousness" recalls Yorick's attack on "gravity," helping to link this normative passage to the normative complex of *Tristram Shandy*. In addition, Tristram offers us here the same insight into the nature of folly that I suggested earlier, its insidious proclivity to compound itself. All that is required to make Tristram's observations at this point a mirror of the satiric purposes of Volume I is a comment on the proselytizing instinct of folly: "What could be wanting in my father but to have wrote a book to publish this notion of his to the world? Little boots it to the subtle speculatist to stand single in his opinions,—unless he gives them proper vent: —It was the identical thing which my father did . . ." (I.xix.55). Thus Sterne presents, in capsule form, the course of a man's folly, from its first stirrings in an unguarded mind to its final triumphant emergence in a "creation" designed to propagate itself. Again and again in *Tristram Shandy*, this is the pattern of human activity against which Sterne's satire is directed. In this instance, the irony of having Tristram show cognizance of the process sharpens the satiric point, for the reader is aware that Tristram, no less than Walter, is mounted and galloping. Indeed, while the reader readily perceives that these passages should form an attack on the systematizing mind, Tristram attacks, instead, the world which refuses to be systematized: "Will not the gentle reader pity my father from his soul? . . . to look down upon the stage, and see him baffled and overthrown in all his little systems and wishes; to behold a train of events perpetually falling out against him, and in so critical and cruel a way, as if they had purposedly been plann'd and pointed against him, merely to insult his speculations" (I.xix.55–56).

There is some similarity between this lament and Tristram's earlier outcry against Fortune for denying him the "things" of the world. Like Tristram, Walter courts disaster by measuring the universe with himself as the yardstick. In both Walter's rigid systems and theories and Tristram's refusal to conform to any rules except his own one finds the same arbitrariness, the same mechanical orientation which makes the puppet and the stage important images of the Shandy personality. The seeming malevolence of the universe is no more than an assertion of the inevitable disappointment of human answers to divine questions, the defeat of human systems and theories when measured against the realities they are to explain. That Tristram fails to recognize this inevitable defeat suggests, once again, his own projecting nature and his ultimate sympathy with Walter's futile attempts to impose his mechanical mind on a flexible and organic universe. Tristram may not agree with the "letter" of Walter's theory of names, but he does agree with its "spirit"; and it is this "spirit" which bears the full force of Sterne's satiric attack.

Of primary interest in Volume II is the development of Toby's character, only broadly intimated in the first volume; Tristram has told us simply of Toby's modesty, a result of a blow in the groin at the siege of Namur. That Sterne uses Toby's modesty for its bawdy possibilities is hardly to be denied; that it perhaps mirrors, at a ludicrous extreme, the humility of Yorick may at least be suggested. Sterne, that is, offers through the character of Yorick a middle way between the pride of Walter and Tristram and the innocent naïveté of Toby. Toby's modesty is an alternative extreme to true humility, to be rejected by the discerning reader as certainly as he rejects the more obvious vice of pride.

Tristram, writing as "a man of erudition" (II.ii.85), undertakes to explain Toby's hobby-horse with the help of Locke's *Essay Concerning Human Understanding*. Significantly, Tristram offers Locke's three reasons for obscure and confused minds, only to reject them as inapplicable to Toby: "Now you must understand that not one of these was the true cause of the confusion in my uncle *Toby's* discourse; and it is for that very reason I enlarge upon them so long, after the manner of great physiologists,—to

shew the world what it did *not* arise from" (II.ii.86).[16] The true
cause, also from Locke, although Tristram does not tell us so, is
"the unsteady uses of words which have perplexed the clearest and
most exalted understandings" (II.ii.86).[17] In Volume I, we were
asked to drop a tear for Walter's defeated theory of names; we are
now asked to drop another tear for Toby's defeat by words:
"Gentle critick! when thou hast weigh'd all this . . . thou wilt drop
a tear of pity upon his scarp and his counterscarp;—his glacis and
his covered-way;—his ravelin and his half-moon: 'Twas not by
ideas,—by heaven! his life was put in jeopardy by words" (II.ii.87).
Toby's efforts to explain the siege of Namur to his many "well-
wishers" bears comparison to Walter's efforts to explain the universe to "the world." For both, failure and frustration meet their
every attempt to impose, by theory and by word, a systematic or
mechanical order on the chaotic state of their own experience. For
both, the hobby-horse is a direct result of their proselytizing zeal,
their desire to explain themselves to others. And finally, Toby, like
Walter, has a profound influence on Tristram, who is not only
proficient in military jargon, but possesses Toby's "sentiment" as
well.

It would not do to force the comparison between Walter and
Toby, however. Toby is not a *philosophus gloriosus,* not a projector or a scientist or a philosopher. In some respects—his constant stream of military talk, his complete absorption with tactics,
his persistent reduction of all subjects to one—he is in the tradition of the *miles gloriosus.* Significantly, the excessive bluster associated with this traditional character is replaced by excessive modesty; the feats of battle, told with no regard for truth, are replaced
by technical descriptions of scarps and covered-ways; and, eventually, the "Blood and Thunder" of war is turned into a back-yard
game. Like Tristram's book and like Walter's projects, Toby's
mock-battlefield is symbolic of the barrenness which mars every
Shandy effort to create. At the same time, Toby, the warrior of
the family, reverses the Shandy inclination to do combat with the
"world"; after his early frustrations, he retreats to the secrecy of
the bowling green. Most important, he embraces an attitude of
benevolence which cannot but appear ludicrous in constant juxta-

16. See Locke, *Essay Concerning Human Understanding,* II.xxix.3.
17. See *ibid.,* III.ix.

position with assaults and counterassaults. Insofar as Toby is no longer a proselytizer, he is less dangerous than Walter or Tristram. One is even tempted to suggest that Sterne offers him as an illustration of harmless folly, a true "amiable humorist," in opposition to his brother and nephew. It is also possible, however, that this tendency to accept Toby is part of Sterne's satiric design; that is to say, Sterne draws us into the folly of the Shandy world through our emotional rather than intellectual weaknesses. As Tristram has already warned us, folly enters the human mind as the slightest whim, "beginning in jest,—but ending in downright earnest." I would suggest, therefore, that Sterne's satire demands that Toby, like Tristram and Walter, be treated as an aberration from a norm of good sense and reasonableness.

Sterne signals this necessity in several ways, one of the most important being the several similarities between the two brothers. Furthermore, Sterne's echo of Swift's famous lines, "WHEN a man gives himself up to the government of a ruling passion,—or, in other words, when his HOBBY-HORSE grows head-strong,—farewell cool reason and fair discretion!" (II.v.93), is prominently positioned at the beginning of the description of Toby's flight to the country. The argument of my first and second chapters demonstrates, I believe, the importance of taking this obvious reminder of Swift as something more than an occasion to compare Sterne's good humor to Swift's savagery. The juxtaposition of Swift and Uncle Toby serves as an effective warning against an easy toleration of the follies about to be uncovered. The conclusion of this chapter is also significant, with its sexual play on the hobby-horse: "Never did lover post down to a belov'd mistress with more heat and expectation, than my uncle *Toby* did, to enjoy this self-same thing in private;—I say in private;—for it was sheltered . . . by a tall yew hedge, and was covered on the other three sides, from mortal sight, by rough holly and thickset flowering shrubs;—so that the idea of not being seen, did not a little contribute to the idea of pleasure preconceived in my uncle *Toby*'s mind" (II.v.98–99). This suggestiveness, and the lengthy play with Toby's aposiopesis ("My sister, I dare say . . . does not care to let a man come so near her ****") in chapters vi and vii, surround Toby with sexual and scatological implications that ultimately form a satiric comment on the sentimentalism of which he is the primary vehicle. Surely it is no accident that the foremost sentimentalist of *Tristram*

Shandy is sexually maimed, and, as he himself assures us, does not know the right end of a woman from the wrong.[18]

One of the important scenes in which Toby displays his sentiment occurs in chapter xii, where his entertainment of Dr. Slop with an encyclopedic discussion of fortification causes Walter to explode: ". . . I wish the whole science of fortification, with all its inventors, at the devil" (II.xii.113). This, in turn, launches Tristram's story of Toby and the fly, long a keynote for admirers of Sterne's sentimentalism. The passage demands a closer reading than it usually receives, however. It is interesting to note, for example, that before Walter's outburst, he says to Toby: ". . . But so full is your head of these confounded works, that tho' my wife is this moment in the pains of labour,—and you hear her cry out, —yet nothing will serve you but to carry off the man-midwife" (II.xii.112–13). It is also noteworthy, that immediately after wishing fortification "at the devil," Walter adds, "it has been the death of thousands,—and it will be mine, in the end." Is it merely fortuitous that Toby is accused of indifference to Mrs. Shandy's pains, and that his utter blindness to the reality of war is suggested immediately before we are told that "my uncle *Toby* had scarce a heart to retaliate upon a fly"?[19] For Tristram, the scene offers an opportunity to write in the sentimental vein: "I was but ten years old when this happened; but whether it was, that the action itself was more in unison to my nerves at that age of pity, which instantly set my whole frame into one vibration of most pleasurable sensation;—or how far the manner and expression of it might go towards it . . . this I know, that the lesson of universal good-will then taught and imprinted by my uncle *Toby*, has never since been worn out of my mind . . ." (II.xii.113–14). By expanding Toby's act to the plane of "universal good-will," Tristram draws our attention to the two instances of his emotional (and moral) failure—his insensitivity to Mrs. Shandy's "pains of labour" and to the "death of thousands" which fortifications entail. And by pointing with an index: "This is to serve for parents and governors instead of a whole volume upon the subject," Tristram

18. Cf. A. R. Towers, "Sterne's Cock and Bull Story," *ELH*, XXIV (1957), 20–24. Towers' comments on Tristram's sexual inadequacy are also quite similar to my own reading of Tristram's character; see pp. 14–20.

19. Toby's speech to the fly, "I'll not hurt a hair of thy head," also reveals Sterne's satiric design; the humor of the personification undercuts any seriousness one would like to attach to Toby's "benevolence."

signals the attitude with which we are to take his entire flight of
sentimentality. So traditional is the reading of this passage as an
indication of "universal good-will" that one feels somewhat perverse in offering another. One reason for this tradition, however, is
that the passage has been so often removed from its context and
considered as a distinct vignette—one of the "Beauties" of Sterne.
A second reason, perhaps, is that romantic irony has taught us
that a balancing of sentiment and irony offers so valid a view of
life that we like to find it wherever possible. But Tristram does
not "balance" the two; he alternates them, and the juxtaposition of
irony with sentiment seems always to be a satiric comment on the
latter. When the passage is returned to its context and when we
do not confuse the ability to balance contraries with the inability
to distinguish between them, then Sterne's purpose can be distinctly
seen.

Similarly, the second sentimental vignette of the chapter, the
reconciliation of Toby and Walter by a tender look and a warm
handshake, is juxtaposed with an immediate consideration of the
respective pleasures Toby and Walter derive from Mrs. Shandy's
begetting children for the Shandy family. The point of the scene,
as of the chapter, is not the sentiment of the passages or the emotional communication between Walter and Toby, but rather the
satiric point that when a man is astride his hobby-horse, the feelings of reasonable men, feelings of true benevolence and pity, are
not to be expected. Tristram can accept the "universal good-will"
portrayed in these scenes only because his own hobby-horse—his
skill as a writer, his subtlety as a philosopher—blinds him to the
thrust of his own commentary. Sterne's ability to imitate the sentimental style should not be taken as his endorsement of sentimentalism; and indeed, the context of such passages as that of Toby and
the fly assuredly suggests that Sterne's design is parodic. Like his
efforts to rise to intellectual brilliance, Tristram's flights of the heart
are made consistently ludicrous by his complete insensitivity to
the meaning of his own words, his inability to distinguish between
the real and its representation, the serious and the absurd. Ultimately, Tristram's endorsement of sentiment becomes more and
more pronounced and bears the brunt of the satire in the later
volumes.

In concentrating upon the main outlines of Sterne's satiric organization, I have slighted several of those obviously satirical "ele-

ments" which all critics have acknowledged. I have not made an issue, for example, of the personal and local satire which pervades the first two volumes, though this is certainly an important part of Sterne's satire. The present argument, however, is concerned not with the identification of satiric elements, but rather with the delineation of a satiric organization which can give them an organic role in *Tristram Shandy*. The critical view which finds the work informed by tolerance, amiability, and sentiment and then makes an immediate exception for the unmerciful pillorying of John Burton as Dr. Slop is not satisfactory. But, when one has demonstrated that *Tristram Shandy* is organized as a satire, positing as its norm a spirit of moderation and humility based on an acknowledgment of man's physical and intellectual limitations; and when one has demonstrated, as well, that the norm has its roots in the author's commitment to Anglican orthodoxy, then the satire against Burton, as a projector-physician and as a Roman Catholic, assumes an organic relationship to the remainder of the work. It is indicative of this relationship that Dr. Slop not only enters *Tristram Shandy* mounted, but is the victim of an actual collision with another mounted rider, Obadiah. In addition to providing Sterne with a Dr. Slop who is *"unwiped, unappointed, unanealed,* with all his stains and blotches on him" (II.x.107), the collision serves as a physical correlative to the mental and emotional conflicts which continually plague the Shandy world. Note also the similarity between Dr. Slop's accident and Toby's earlier accident which precipitated his departure to the country:

> . . . for in crossing himself he let go his whip,—and in attempting to save his whip betwixt his knee and his saddle's skirt, as it slipp'd, he lost his stirrup,—in losing which, he lost his seat;—and in a multitude of all these losses . . . the unfortunate doctor lost his presence of mind (II.ix.106).

> . . . he had the accident, in reaching over for his tobacco-box, to throw down his compasses, and in stooping to take the compasses up, with his sleeve he threw down his case of instruments and snuffers;—and as the dice took a run against him, in his endeavouring to catch the snuffers in falling,— he thrust Monsieur *Blondel* off the table and Count *de Pagan* o'top of him (II.v.94).

The similarity suggests that Sterne's vision of Toby, as in the more obvious case of Dr. Slop, was essentially a satiric one. More important, however, it demonstrates the universal (at least in the Shandy "world") nature of the accidents, the clumsinesses, the bunglings, which keep the reader constantly aware that behind the theories and the words, the volumes and the maneuvers of the Shandy world is a group of human beings quite unable to perform the rudimentary functions of their lives. In a complex pattern of metaphor and symbol, this physical awkwardness is joined to the general frustration and defeat which mars all the Shandean efforts. Like death and destiny, like impotence and the scatological, the Shandean clumsiness serves to keep the physical, indeed animal, nature of man before our eyes throughout the work.

Corporal Trim, Toby's proselyte, provides another example of Sterne's concern with the physical nature of man. Like Toby, Trim is "no mean proficient in the science" of military tactics; like Walter, "the fellow lov'd to advise,—or rather to hear himself talk . . ." (II.v.95). It is Trim, we remember, who first conceives the idea of converting the "words" which were driving Toby to distraction into the miniature imitations of the bowling green. Similarly, it is Trim who converts the natural rhetorical genius of Walter into the dramatic gestures and stances of the professional orator. In brief, Trim provides the final stroke of the Shandean system: The converting imagination which has taken a representation of reality for reality itself now returns the representation to a measure of reality again, at least insofar as the representation is given a visible, tactile manifestation. The practice is not, to be sure, limited to Trim; Walter and Toby are both masters of gesture, and Tristram's entire book, with its misplaced parts, its blank, black, marbled, and missing pages, and its typographical oddities, is a quite visible correlative for the confused and chaotic state of the Shandy mind. Trim, however, because his character operates on no other level, is the most effective representative of this aspect of Sterne's satire.[20]

Trim is also an effective vehicle for the recitation of Sterne's (Yorick's) "Abuses of Conscience Considered" sermon, which is introduced late in the second volume, after we have been quite amply exposed to the length and breadth of Shandean folly. I have already demonstrated, in Chapter I, the orthodoxy of this sermon, and need not repeat that here. But Sterne's conversion of a religious

---

20. That Sterne intended a pun on "Corporal Trim" seems rather evident.

tract into an organic part of an artistic construct, without significant alteration, warrants attention.

It is noteworthy, for example, that Sterne juxtaposes his normative statement with one aspect of the folly he is satirizing by having Trim deliver the sermon. The sense of man's corporeality, so important to the meaning of the sermon itself, is vividly communicated in Tristram's several descriptions of Corporal Trim's poses:

> He stood before them with his body swayed, and bent forwards just so far, as to make an angle of 85 degrees and a half upon the plain of the horizon;—which sound orators . . . know very well, to be the true persuasive angle of incidence. . . .
>
> .   .   .   .
>
> He stood . . . his right-leg firm under him, sustaining seven-eighths of his whole weight,—the foot of his left-leg . . . advanced a little,—not laterally, nor forwards, but in a line betwixt them . . . (II.xvii.122).

Like Walter's knowledge of rhetoric, Trim's knowledge of the proper rhetorical posture and gestures is left a mystery, though Tristram promises that it "shall be commented upon in that part of this cyclopædia of arts and sciences, where the instrumental parts of the eloquence of the senate, the pulpit, the bar . . . fall under consideration" (II.xvii.122). At the same time, one solution *is* offered, highlighted by an index: The pose is recommended "to painters:—need I add,—to orators?—I think not; for, unless they practise it,—they must fall upon their noses" (II.xvii.123). The mechanical tendency of the Shandy mind is here converted to a physical image; and the accidents and failures which accompany the Shandean efforts are reduced to a most elementary loss of balance, though, it must be noted, falling on one's nose in *Tristram Shandy* has a certain ambiguity. The reduction of man to a mechanism, a puppet, an animal—all three images are at work throughout Trim's reading—demonstrates, in concord with the sermon, the physical and mental limitations under which all men labor.

Trim also demonstrates his capacity to return the "unreal" to the world of reality, no matter how inappropriately. In this instance, Trim treats the *exemplum* of the sermon as reality itself, finding his brother in the rather overwrought description of a prisoner of the Inquisition. Far from being able to take the scene seriously, it is rather obvious that Sterne is parodying his own pulpit extravagance; Trim's tears have a Methodistical aspect to them which balances nicely the Catholic reaction of Dr. Slop who, after some mild protests, falls asleep.

Most important, however, is the sermon itself, the commentary it affords on what we have thus far seen of the Shandy world. Is not the following the gist of what we have discovered about hobby-horses, and indeed, in much the same language:

> . . . did no such thing ever happen, as that the conscience of a man, by long habits . . . might (as the scripture assures it may) insensibly become hard;—and, like some tender parts of his body, by much stress and continual hard usage, lose, by degrees, that nice sense and perception with which God and nature endow'd it:—Did this never happen;—or was it certain that self-love could never hang the least bias upon the judgment;—or that the little interests below, could rise up and perplex the faculties of our upper regions . . . : Or, lastly, were we assured, that INTEREST stood always unconcern'd whilst the cause was hearing,—and that passion never got into the judgment-seat, and pronounc'd sentence in the stead of reason . . . :—Was this truly so . . . ;—no doubt then, the religious and moral state of a man would be exactly what he himself esteem'd it . . . (II.xvii.127).

Yet Sterne is not talking about innocent "habits" of humor or folly here, but "habits of sin"; and lest one fancy that the Shandean hobby-horses are hardly sinful, it should be noted that the meaning of Sterne's sermon is that a man, weighted down by ignorance and interest, is, by himself, incompetent to judge the thin dividing line between innocence and guilt:

> If any man . . . thinks it impossible for a man to be such a bubble to himself,—I must refer him a moment to his own reflections. . . .
> Let him consider in how different a degree of detestation, numbers of wicked actions stand *there*, tho' equally bad and vicious in their own natures;—he will soon find that such of them, as strong inclination and custom have prompted him to commit, are generally dress'd out and painted with all the false beauties, which a soft and a flattering hand can give them . . . (II.xvii.131).

The answer to this incompetence is, of course, reason and religion: "So that if you would form a just judgment of what is of infinite importance to you not to be misled in,—namely, in what degree of real merit you stand either as an honest man, an useful citizen, a faithful subject to your king, or a good servant to your God,—call in religion and morality.—Look,—What is written in the law of God?—How readest thou?—Consult calm reason and the unchangeable obligations of justice and truth;—what say they?" (II.xvii.132). Taken in the context of Anglican thought, as was done in Chapter I, these lines are resoundingly orthodox, assuredly conservative. Taken in the context of *Tristram Shandy,* they are a timely and pertinent norm against which to measure the aberrations of the Shandy world. Surely Sterne says as much when he has Tristram tell us of Yorick's authorship of the sermon so that he may "give rest to *Yorick's* ghost;—which, as the country people, —and some others, believe,—*still walks*" (II.xvii.143). Those who read *Tristram Shandy* as a satire know that this is indeed the case.

V

"Tristram Shandy" as a Satire
Volumes III and IV

☞ *A dwarf who brings a standard along with him to measure his own size—take my word, is a dwarf in more articles than one . . .*

(IV.xxv.316)

Volumes III and IV

IN JANUARY, 1761, Volumes III and IV of *Tristram Shandy* were published. Sterne's letters, both during their composition and after publication, continue to suggest that both he and his correspondents thought the work a satire. The rumor that Tristram's tutor was to be the Bishop of Gloucester is protested, perhaps "too much," by Sterne; the passage does tell us something of Sterne's vision of Shandyism: "What the devil!—is there no one learned blockhead throughout the many schools of misapplied science in the Christian World, to make a *tutor* of for my Tristram? . . . Are we so run out of stock, that there is no one lumber-headed, muddle-headed, mortar-headed, pudding-headed *chap* amongst our doctors?"[1] To the Bishop, Sterne promises to keep inviolate decency and good manners, "though laugh, my lord, I will, and as loud as I can too"; and in the same letter he writes that he is "sick of this foolish humour of mine of sallying forth into this wide & wicked world to redress wrongs, &c. . . ."[2] To Stephen Croft, he defends the chapter on Noses: ". . . the principal satire throughout that part is levelled at those learned blockheads who, in all ages, have wasted their time and much learning upon points as foolish. . . ."[3] And, again to Croft, two months after publication he answers his growing number of critics by citing his pedigree: "If my enemies knew that by this rage of abuse, and ill will, they were effectually serving the interests both of myself, and works, they would be more quiet—but it has been the fate of my betters, who have found, that the way to fame, is like the way to heaven—through much tribulation—and till I shall have the honour to be as much mal-treated as Rabelais, and Swift were, I must continue humble; for I have not filled up the measure of half their *persecutions*."[4] Thus Sterne defended him-

---

1. L. P. Curtis, ed., *Letters of Laurence Sterne* (Oxford, 1935), p. 93. The letter is to Garrick.
2. *Ibid.*, pp. 115–16.   3. *Ibid.*, p. 126.   4. *Ibid.*, p. 132.

self against the increasing number of critics who found in both his publication of two volumes of sermons in May, 1760, under the name Yorick and his increasing licentiousness in Volumes III and IV cause for stern rebuke.

Tristram, too, defends himself against the critics, and his fledgling war with them adds a new dimension to the satiric activity of Tristram's study. Insofar as Sterne had a legitimate protest against his critics, Tristram becomes one with him, the flexibility of the satiric persona making this possible. Thus, the satire against critical jargon in III.xii is no different from Sterne's satire against legal cant or scientific cant, although Tristram is now a more conscious vehicle of the attack. Even here, however, Tristram's egotism suggests that personality we have come to recognize as itself an object of satire: " . . . I declare I object only to a connoisseur in swearing,—as I would do to a connoisseur in painting, &c. &c. the whole set of 'em are so hung round and *befetish'd* with the bobs and trinkets of criticism,—or to drop my metaphor, which by the bye is a pity,—for I have fetch'd it as far as from the coast of *Guinea;*—their heads, Sir, are stuck so full of rules and compasses . . . that a work of genius had better go to the devil at once, than stand to be prick'd and tortured to death by 'em" (III.xii.180). The satire is directed against arbitrary and mechanical rules, the persistent and ignorant jargon which bad critics thrust between themselves and a work of art—the acting of Garrick, the painting of Raphael, the writing of Tristram: "And what of this new book the whole world makes such a rout about?—Oh! 'tis out of all plumb, my Lord,—quite an irregular thing!—not one of the angles at the four corners was a right angle.—I had my rule and compasses, &c. my Lord, in my pocket.—Excellent critic!" (III.xii.180–81). There is no reason to believe that this is the revolt of a pre-romantic against neoclassical restrictions; Swift and Pope had both attacked the same Grub-Street activity that Sterne is attacking, and for the same reasons: "—Grant me patience, just heaven!—Of all the cants which are canted in this canting world,— though the cant of hypocrites may be the worst,—the cant of criticism is the most tormenting!" (III.xii.182).[5]

5. Pope's use of Theobald as king dunce in the *Dunciad* of 1728–29 and Swift's "A Digression Concerning Critics" (Section III) in *A Tale of a Tub* come immediately to mind. The proposed Academy in *Tale of a Tub* includes a School of Hobby-horses.

An alternative to critical cant is offered in this chapter, but Tristram's return to a "hobby-horsical" image suggests that Sterne is not quite willing to accept it: "I would go fifty miles on foot, for I have not a horse worth riding on, to kiss the hand of that man whose generous heart will give up the reins of his imagination into his author's hands,—be pleased he knows not why, and cares not wherefore" (III.xii.182). That Tristram is mounted has been apparent from the opening pages; that he rides by our permission as well as by his own volition, though often implied, is now clearly stated. At times, moreover, as in IV.xx when Tristram's galloping horse becomes an image of Sterne's indiscreet (that is, honest) satire, even the most cautious reader may give Tristram the reins:

> WHAT a rate have I gone on at, curvetting and frisking it away, two up and two down for four volumes together, without looking once behind . . . to see whom I trod upon!—I'll tread upon no one,—quoth I to myself when I mounted— I'll take a good rattling gallop; but I'll not hurt the poorest jack-ass upon the road. . . .
> Now ride at this rate with what good intention and resolution you may,—'tis a million to one you'll do some one a mischief, if not yourself— . . . see!—if he has not galloped full amongst the scaffolding of the undertaking criticks! . . . look—he's now riding like a madcap full tilt through a whole crowd of painters, fiddlers, poets, biographers, physicians, lawyers . . . —Don't fear, said I—I'll not hurt the poorest jack-ass upon the king's high-way—But your horse throws dirt; see you've splash'd a bishop . . . (IV.xx.298).[6]

The bishop was Warburton; Sterne and Tristram are both mounted at this point, although it is noteworthy that Tristram denies any satiric intent, while for Sterne the satire is pointedly intentional.[7] Sterne's ability to mount and dismount from Tristram's hobby-horse mocks our own inclinations as to when, as

6. Cf. Swift, *A Tale of a Tub*, 2nd ed. (Oxford, 1958), pp. 188–89.
7. Cf. IV.xxii.301: " . . . believe it of me [says Tristram], that in the story of my father and his christen-names,—I had no thoughts of treading upon *Francis* the First . . . —nor in the character of my uncle *Toby*—of characterizing the militating spirits of my country—the wound upon his groin, is a wound to every comparison of that kind. . . . " Tristram's recognition here of the incongruity in Toby's character supports my belief that Toby is being satirized as well as the other Shandys.

readers, Tristram should have the reins and when it is best that we keep them.

Tristram also attacks the violence of his critics, assuring them that he will not be provoked, that he will never give them a "worse word or a worse wish, than my uncle *Toby* gave the fly . . . " (III.iv.162). Tristram's argument is by analogy: "A Man's body and his mind, with the utmost reverence to both I speak it, are exactly like a jerkin, and a jerkin's lining;—rumple the one—you rumple the other. There is one certain exception however . . . and that is, when you . . . have had your jerkin made of a gum-taffeta, and the body-lining to it, of a sarcenet or thin persian" (III.iv.160). Tristram identifies himself with the encyclopedic list of Stoics who stand as proof of the exception, and perhaps in this instance we can accept his doing so. It is worth noting, however, that the intimate coincidence of body and mind, the rule rather than the exception, provides one of Sterne's principal satiric devices in *Tristram Shandy*, where the physical ineptitude and sterility of the Shandy bodies represent intellectual failure as well. Tristram's several descriptions of himself in his study all suggest how physical his intellectual activity is; for example:

> I enter upon this part of my story in the most pensive and melancholy frame of mind. . . . My nerves relax as I tell it.— Every line I write, I feel an abatement of the quickness of my pulse, and of that careless alacrity with it, which every day of my life prompts me to say and write a thousand things I should not. . . . Lord! how different from the rash jerks, and hare-brain'd squirts thou art wont, *Tristram!* to transact it with in other humours,—dropping thy pen,—spurting thy ink . . . (III.xxviii.215).

And again, in the chapter on chapters:

> . . . A sudden impulse comes across me—drop the curtain, *Shandy*—I drop it—Strike a line here across the paper, *Tristram*—I strike it—and hey for a new chapter!
> The duce of any other rule have I to govern myself by in this affair—and if I had one—as I do all things out of all rule—I would twist it and tear it to pieces, and throw it into the fire when I had done . . . (IV.x.281).

And yet again: "Instantly I snatch'd off my wig, and threw it perpendicularly, with all imaginable violence, up to the top of the room . . . " (IV.xvii.293). It is thus significant that Tristram's statement of his purpose in *Tristram Shandy* should also be defined in physical terms: " . . . If 'tis wrote against any thing,— 'tis wrote . . . against the spleen; in order, by a more frequent and a more convulsive elevation and depression of the diaphragm, and the succussations of the intercostal and abdominal muscles in laughter, to drive the *gall* and other *bitter juices* from the gall bladder, liver and sweet-bread of his majesty's subjects . . . down into their duodenums" (IV.xxii.301–2).[8] The comedy of *Tristram Shandy* cannot be denied, but even this brief passage suggests that comedy is not Sterne's total concern. Tristram here, as throughout his work, encourages us to laugh *with* him; his adoption of scientific jargon in this instance makes it equally probable that we laugh *at* him. As a writer, Tristram provides a convenient vehicle for Sterne's attacks on the critics; but, since he is also a victim of Sterne's satire, his insights are spiced by his own follies. The critics may be arbitrary and muddleheaded, but so is Tristram, and in Volumes III and IV the impression grows that his "creation" is going out of control. Between the "rule and compasses" of one extreme and the total freedom demanded by Tristram of the other extreme, the norms of order, good taste, and good sense are forgotten. Tristram's heightened physical activity mirrors his increasing difficulties, just as in later volumes his physical decline will suggest his inevitable defeat by this chaos of his own creating.

Sterne uses several other devices, in addition to Tristram's physical activity, to suggest his growing disorganization. Thus the "Author's Preface" appears in the twentieth chapter of Volume III, 445 pages into the work as it was originally published; "Slawkenbergius's Tale," some of which is also given in Latin, interrupts the Shandy affairs for 72 pages in the original edition; chapter xxiv is missing, along with ten pages; and, as a "motly emblem of my work!" Tristram offers us a marbled page, drawing our attention to its contrast with Yorick's black page in the first volume: "—Read, read, read, read, my unlearned reader! read,—or by the knowledge of the great saint *Paraleipomenon*—I tell you beforehand, you had better throw down the book at once; for without *much reading*, by which your reverence knows, I mean *much knowledge*, you will no more be able to penetrate the moral of the

8. Cf. *A Tale of a Tub*, p. 185: "The *Superficial* Reader will be strangely provoked to *Laughter*; which clears the Breast and the Lungs, is Soverain against the *Spleen*, and the most innocent of all *Diureticks*."

next marbled page (motly emblem of my work!) than the world
with all its sagacity has been able to unravel the many opinions,
transactions and truths which still lie mystically hid under the dark
veil of the black one" (III.xxxvi.226). What Tristram is urging us
to read is Rabelais; and the marbled page seems to be suggestive of
that which *Gargantua* and *Pantagruel* and *Tristram Shandy* have in
common: a satiric form, whose disorder is both a purposeful imitation of nature and an artistic creation. It is perhaps no fortuity
that "my dear Rabelais"[9] plays a large role in these two volumes,
as Sterne works to create the chaotic world in which the Shandys
are most at home.

Tristram in his study is clearly being overwhelmed by his freedom, and his work assumes more and more the chaotic form associated with satiric representations of the uncreating mind. "Ernul-
phus' curse" is a brilliant correlative of this uncreating chaos; for
five pages (and in Latin as well as English), the entire Christian
universe, the full chain of being and scope of existence is system-
atically marshaled for the sole purpose of damning Obadiah,
body and soul, for tying Dr. Slop's bag with an impossible knot
(III.x–xi). Destruction replaces creation; balance and proportion
are thrust aside, and for a brief but significant moment, the free and
happy spirit of Shandyism is revealed in all its dangerous poten-
tiality.

Tristram's efforts at inclusiveness are also beginning to overwhelm him. In III.xxiii, he debates when to tell the story of Trim
and his bridge, finally turning to the reader: "What would your
worships have me to do in this case?" For the first time Tristram
seems aware of the artistic problems of order and selectivity; and
when the readers fail him, he turns to "Powers":

> O ye POWERS! . . . which enable mortal man to tell a story
> . . . —that kindly shew him, where he is to begin it,—and
> where he is to end it,—what he is to put into it,—and what
> he is to leave out. . . .
> I beg and beseech you . . . that wherever . . . three several
> roads meet in one point . . . that at least you set up a guide-
> post, in the center of them, in mere charity to direct an uncer-
> tain devil, which of the three he is to take (III.xxiii.207).

9. Once again, the pedigree of *Tristram Shandy* is significant: "By the tomb
stone of *Lucian*—if it is in being,—if not, why then, by his ashes! by the ashes
of my dear *Rabelais*, and dearer *Cervantes* . . . " (III.xix.191).

That the "Powers" do not answer his plea is made apparent in
III.xxxviii, where the one problem is now greatly multiplied:

> My mother, you must know,—but I have fifty things more
> necessary to let you know first,—I have a hundred difficulties
> which I have promised to clear up, and a thousand distresses
> and domestic misadventures crouding in upon me thick and
> three-fold, one upon the neck of another . . . —I have left my
> father lying across his bed . . . and promised I would go
> back . . . in half an hour, and five and thirty minutes are
> laps'd already.—Of all the perplexities a mortal author was
> ever seen in,—this certainly is the greatest,—for I have *Hafen*
> *Slawkenbergius*'s folio, Sir, to finish—a dialogue between my
> father and my uncle *Toby* . . . to relate,—a tale . . . to trans-
> late, and all this in five minutes less, than no time at all . . .
> (III.xxxviii.235).

Tristram's concern that the minutes and hours are defeating his
efforts at inclusiveness is echoed by his growing awareness that the
days and years are defeating his more general effort to tell his life:
"I am this month one whole year older than I was this time twelve-
month; and having got, as you perceive, almost into the middle of
my fourth volume—and no farther than to my first day's life—'tis
demonstrative that I have three hundred and sixty-four days more
life to write just now, than when I first set out . . . " (IV.xiii.285–
86). Tristram recommends this observation to the reader for its
novelty, and he seems satisfied with his prospect—"write as I will,
and rush as I may into the middle of things, as *Horace* advises,—
I shall never overtake myself—whipp'd and driven to the last
pinch, at the worst I shall have one day the start of my pen—and
one day is enough for two volumes—and two volumes will be
enough for one year" (IV.xiii.286). Time is, in this passage, an
ally with profit, and Tristram treats it lightly; in later volumes,
when time makes clear its inevitable alliance with death, Tristram's attitude will more resemble the desperation he voices when
faced with "five minutes less, than no time at all." Like Yorick,
Time itself becomes a *memento mori*, a constant reminder that a
man's life is limited, and that it is to be lived with an eye toward
those limits.

   In addition, Tristram's struggle with time as an element of his
"creation" provides an important component of the chaos endemic
to Shandyism. In the first place, we have his ludicrous efforts to

interpret the neoclassical doctrine of the unity of time. An early example occurs in Volume II where Tristram defends himself against the "hypercritic" by proving first that Obadiah has had sufficient time (an "hour and a half's tolerable good reading") to fetch Dr. Slop; then, that if the hypercritic insists that no more time has lapsed in the Shandy world than "two minutes, thirteen seconds, and three fifths," he will remind him of Locke's idea of duration; and finally, that if the hypercritic is intractable, "I then put an end to the whole objection and controversy about it all at once,—by acquainting him, that *Obadiah* had not got above three-score yards from the stable-yard before he met with Dr. *Slop . . .* " (II.viii.104). By confusing not only clock-time with duration, but his own time in his study with time in the Shandy household, Tristram undercuts a primary means by which a reader orients himself in a narrative, and by which a man knows his place in the world. That Sterne is interested in Locke's demonstration of the relativity of time[10] is suggested by his use of various time-measures to further involve the reader in Tristram's topsy-turvy world. Sterne's interest, however, should not be confused with Tristram's interest, which is neither philosophical, nor experimental, nor even intelligent. Like his interest in other "theories," the question of time offers Tristram a chance to perform as a projector, a chance to confound us with philosophical cant and logical mazes that lead nowhere. Tristram's efforts to "control" his work with the neo-classical doctrine of the unity of time is a ludicrous failure, demon-strating both the rigid literalness of his mechanical mind and the absurdity of his quest for "freedom." Ultimately, his perverse obeisance to the unity of time produces Shandy figures frozen in the poses of caricature—Walter stretched out on his bed, Mrs. Shandy bent over the keyhole, Walter and Toby suspended on the stairs—while Tristram does business elsewhere. Far from adding realism to the Shandy history, Tristram's game with time only emphasizes the puppet-like corporeality of the people of the Shandy world.

Second, Tristram consistently orders events of the past by arbi-trary or irrelevant connections, which only adds to the work's confusion. To be sure, there is a chronological time-scheme to the events of *Tristram Shandy*; Sterne needed one to give Tristram

10. In his discussion of duration; see *Essay Concerning Human Understand-ing*, II.xiv.

an order to violate.[11] It is not, moreover, unduly difficult to keep chronological track of Tristram's story, if one desires to do so. The reader's attention, however, is directed to the violations of chronological order, to the created situations which make it *necessary* for Tristram to juxtapose his birth with events of a more distant past. The sense of confusion and chaos arises from Tristram's persistent assertions that his story is orderly, that his elaborate transitions and self-conscious digressiveness, his efforts for historical accuracy and novelistic detail are all logical and relevant. As with his plans for inclusiveness, Tristram's attempt to keep the reader fully informed of where he has been, where he is, and where he is going proves far less informative than Tristram hoped it would be. Time and the world proceed in orderly fashion; the confusion and chaos of *Tristram Shandy* come from the mind of its putative author.

Tristram shares his interest in duration with his father, who explains the theory to Toby in III.xviii, without success.[12] Walter's role as the *philosophus gloriosus* continues unabated in the third and fourth volumes; and, indeed, the primary concern of the Shandy household in these volumes is the successive formulation and defeat of one Shandy theory after another. Volume II ends with Walter's search for the seat of the soul, and his ultimate conclusion that, because it is located in the cerebellum, the many ills of the world can be traced directly to head-first births. As with Tristram's description of the weakened homunculus (I.ii.5–6), Walter describes the results of this obstetric "conspiracy," blind to its implications for both himself and Tristram: "No wonder the intellectual web is so rent and tatter'd as we see it; and that so many of our best heads are no better than a puzzled skein of silk,— all perplexity,—all confusion within side" (II.xix.151). The image of physical frailty at the moment of birth serves Sterne's satiric purposes well. From Tristram's "crushed nose," to his accidental circumcision, to his present bout with weak lungs; from Toby's wound to Walter's sciatica and suggested impotence; from

11. Cf. Theodore Baird, "The Time-Scheme of *Tristram Shandy* and a Source," *PMLA*, LI (1936), 803–20.

12. Tristram's support of his father is rather persistent. In III.xix.191, for example, he expresses deep regret that Walter petulantly breaks off his discussion of Time because of Toby's density. His doing so, Tristram writes, "was a robbery of the *Ontologic treasury*, of such a jewel, as no coalition of great occasions and great men, are ever likely to restore to it again."

Slop's cut finger to Trim's crippled leg, the Shandy world offers to the reader a collage of accidents, injuries, and illnesses which, like the more stark reality of death, provides an image of man which renders his theories and his hobby-horses, his ambitions and his pursuits at once ludicrous and culpable. The susceptibility to physical harm, in other words, comes to represent in Sterne's satiric scheme man's susceptibility to intellectual and moral harm as well.

Having set the hobby-horses of Walter and Toby in motion in the first volumes, Sterne sets about, in the present ones, to demonstrate the various confusions and collisions which result when two men, both well mounted, travel the same roads. Many of these scenes, individually taken, are simply comic, and it would be forcing the issue to insist upon a satiric design for each one. Taken together, however, the numerous collisions of Walter and Toby create the Shandy world of frustration and cross-purpose, a satiric world of misunderstanding, reconciliation, and further misunderstanding. Above all, it is the mechanical operation of the Shandy mind and spirit which creates both the comic and the satiric meaning of the Shandy household. In III.iii, for example, Walter's awkward reaching with his left hand into his right coat pocket brings the "traverses" of Namur to Toby's mind, and he reaches for the bell to summon Trim and the maps: "My father knit his brows, and as he knit them, all the blood in his body seemed to rush up into his face—my uncle *Toby* dismounted immediately" (p. 160). One moment later, however, Walter is mounted, arguing the necessity of bringing children feet-first into the world; Toby refuses to mount alongside: "Are these dangers [of birth], quoth my uncle *Toby,* laying his hand upon my father's knee . . . greater now o'days, brother, than in times past? Brother *Toby,* answered my father, if a child was but fairly begot, and born alive, and healthy . . . our forefathers never looked further.—My uncle *Toby* instantly withdrew his hand . . . and then directing the buccinatory muscles along his cheeks, and the orbicular muscles around his lips to do their duty—he whistled *Lillabullero*" (III.vi.164).

The two scenes are typical of the confrontations which characterize the Shandy household; equally typical is the confrontation between Walter and the door-hinge, which perhaps serves as the prototype for all that is at once humorous and dangerous in the Shandean system. Walter's failure to mend the doorknob, in spite of his eloquence on the subject, provides Sterne with an opportunity to suggest a normative position through his persona:

> —Inconsistent soul that man is!—languishing under wounds, which he has the power to heal!—his whole life a contradiction to his knowledge!—his reason, that precious gift of God to him . . . serving but to sharpen his sensibilities, —to multiply his pains and render him more melancholy and uneasy under them!—poor unhappy creature, that he should do so!—are not the necessary causes of misery in this life enow, but he must add voluntary ones to his stock of sorrow; —struggle against evils which cannot be avoided, and submit to others, which a tenth part of the trouble they create him, would remove from his heart for ever? (III.xxi.203)

Insofar as Tristram is talking only of door-hinges, his reaction to his father's failure to mend them is an example of satire's magnifying tendency; but, insofar as what he says proves applicable to both the Shandy household and Shandy study, the passage offers a valuable clue into the normative use of reason as a measure of Shandean folly. It is of moment that the chapter preceding this one contains the "Author's Preface," which, I shall shortly demonstrate, may be read as one of the fundamental statements of Sterne's satiric purpose in *Tristram Shandy*; and that, in the scene which follows (chapter xxii), Toby and Walter collide again, only to be reconciled in one of those passages of sentiment that are supposedly the work's raison d'être. It is hardly necessary to point out that, in this scene, Walter is bubbled by Toby's innocence, as he is by the door-hinge; that reason is again set aside, and the Shandy horses given free rein. And as with the door-hinge, one is betrayed by the innocence, the inconsequentiality of the folly: All men, we say, leave their door-hinges unoiled; all men melt at the extraordinary simplicity of Toby's "patriotism." But Sterne's normative statement has already drawn the implications of such tolerance, and the entirety of *Tristram Shandy* establishes its truth. The critics have taken no small pains to demonstrate how sentiment draws the Shandy family together.[13] It is perhaps more important to notice

13. See John Traugott, *Tristram Shandy's World* (Berkeley, 1954). A good part of Sterne's game with sentiment seems designed to reveal the transitory, inconsistent nature of sentimentalism; e.g., in III.xxiv, Walter responds to Toby's affectionate gestures by saying to himself: "May my brains be knock'd out with a battering ram . . . if ever I insult this worthy soul more" (p. 212). In chapter xxv, one page later, he proceeds to do so. See also chapter xxvi where the point is even more clearly made (p. 214).

how irrationality—particularly the willful irrationality of the hobby-horse—drives them asunder. The Shandy household is a picture of continual frustration, error, pain, and collision; and, as in the incident of the window sash, one soon realizes that the Shandys bring disaster and destiny down upon their own heads.

The full scope of Sterne's satiric design can be garnered from the fifty pages on "Noses" which end Volume III and begin Volume IV. Opening with the hobby-horsical confusion over what kind of bridge Dr. Slop is preparing and dramatically set off by Tristram's "most pensive and melancholy frame of mind" (III.xxviii.215), the meanderings of Tristram's pen take us through Walter's grief to the theory which led to it, and through "Slawkenbergius's Tale" to the theory which will hopefully compensate for it. These pages are, of course, the fulfillment of the long awaited act of creation in the Shandy household; significantly, they are filled with suggestions of impotence.

The detailed attention to posture and gesture in *Tristram Shandy* which I have argued fulfills a satiric purpose is again illustrated in Tristram's description of his father's grief. The careful distribution of each limb makes Walter something of a puppet, and the scene, a puppet show: "The moment my father got up into his chamber, he threw himself prostrate across his bed in the wildest disorder imaginable. . . . —The palm of his right hand, as he fell upon the bed, receiving his forehead, . . . sunk down with his head (his elbow giving way backwards) till his nose touch'd the quilt;—his left arm hung insensible over the side of the bed, his knuckles reclining upon the handle of the chamber pot . . . —his right leg (his left being drawn up towards his body) hung half over the side of the bed . . . " (III.xxix.215–16). The seriousness with which we are to take Walter's suffering is not indicated by Tristram's tear, but by the ludicrous detailing of the body, the chamber-pot, and the opening sally, "both man and woman bear pain or sorrow, (and, for aught I know, pleasure too) best in a horizontal position" (III.xxix.215). Toby, to be sure, sits by the bed with a ready tear ("having a tear at every one's service"), and a cambrick handkerchief. Tristram, on the contrary, forgets his tear, and returns to the lesson learned from the door-hinge: " . . . notwithstanding my father had the happiness of reading the oddest books in the universe, and had moreover, in himself, the oddest way of thinking, that ever man in it was bless'd with, yet it had this drawback upon him after all,— that it laid him open to some of the oddest and most whimsical distresses . . . '' (III.xxx.216–17). Moreover, Tristram sets about to account for "the unchristian manner he abandoned and surrender'd himself up to [his affliction]." The importance of the door-hinge in establishing a basis for the criticism of Shandean folly is thus re-emphasized, and, though briefly, made to stand a comparison with Christian ethics. Sterne's satire in this and other instances is not signaled by a direct frontal assault, but rather by the careful positing at strategic moments of alternatives to the follies Tristram both describes and embodies. In particular, Sterne often confronts the Shandean follies with the presence of Yorick, of death, of Christianity, of accident and impotence and error and failure. These numerous confrontations, which form the basis of my reading of *Tristram Shandy*, suggest the dwarf in chapter xxv who brings a standard along with him; the confrontations speak for themselves.

Tristram's appeal to our concupiscence does not at all diminish in these volumes, and indeed, reaches a climax of sorts in "Slawkenbergius's Tale." Much of the bawdiness comes from Toby's obstetrical innocence and from the general concern with birth. While such allusions keep us in mind of the painful physical process by which we come into the world, reducing, at once, our pretensions to grandeur, there is assuredly more fun than anything else in something like Toby's question to Dr. Slop: "Good God! . . . *are children brought into the world with a squirt?*" (III.xv.186). Playful exuberance also marks the chapters dedicated to "noses," although here Sterne's satiric purpose is clearly evident. The subtle devices by which Tristram ensnared our concupiscence in the first two volumes are here replaced by the most direct (and effective) device available: He tells us at the outset that "Nose" means "Nose, and nothing more, or less" (III.xxxi.218). We need not be informed of the long satiric tradition that uses noses and ears for scatological purposes to grasp immediately Sterne's similar intention, and yet, since he never reveals himself, the concupiscence must remain with us.

At the same time, Tristram seizes the opportunity to remind us of the type of book we are reading: "In books of strict morality and close reasoning, such as this I am engaged in,—the neglect [of proper definition] is inexcusable; and heaven is witness, how the world has revenged itself upon me for leaving so many openings to equivocal strictures,—and for depending so much as I have done, all along, upon the cleanliness of my reader's imaginations" (III.xxxi.218). Our imaginations were caught, Eugenius points out, by the crevice Toby stares at in II.vii; and, of course, as the work continues, Tristram will catch them again and again—with beards and buttonholes, with battering rams and *bougers*. Far from decreasing the bawdiness of his work Sterne presses home his point in answer to the critical outcry against his prurience; the story of the court of Navarre climaxes the satiric intention of these allusive passages: "Does not all the world know, said the curate *d'Estella* at the conclusion of his work [on beards], that Noses ran the same fate some centuries ago in most parts of *Europe,* which Whiskers have now done in the kingdom of *Navarre*—The evil indeed spread no further then,—but have not beds and bolsters, and night-caps and chamber-pots stood upon the brink of destruction ever since? Are not trouse, and placket-holes, and pump-handles—and spigots and faucets, in danger still, from the same association?" (V.i.347–48). The argument, Tristram tells us, was not understood—the world "ran the scent the wrong way"—they "bridled his ass at the tail." And, he adds, "when the *extreams* of DELICACY, and the *beginnings* of CONCUPISCENCE, hold their next provincial chapter together, they may decree that bawdy also." Like the other extremes in *Tristram Shandy,* delicacy and concupiscence are proved to be simply two aspects of the same unreason; an unreasonableness which stands in perpetual opposition to a reasonable center. The center need not be defined, and, in this case, is perhaps undefinable; but certainly it must be pointed out that the bawdy tales of Slawkenbergius and Navarre are introduced by Tristram in an effort to satisfy our tastes.

Tristram emphasizes the fact that the Shandy theory of noses, supported by tradition and strengthened by interest, has been in the family at least three generations before his father seized it, thus introducing an alternative to whim as an instigator of hobby-horses. To be sure, Walter does his part: "—If education planted the mistake, (in case it was one) my father watered it, and ripened it to perfection" (III.xxxiii.220). In terms of the metaphorical design of *Tristram Shandy,* it is noteworthy that Tristram describes Walter's activities with reference to Toby's hobby-horse. For example: "Accordingly he [Walter] held fast by 'em, both by teeth and claws,—would fly to whatever he could lay his hands on,—and in a word, would intrench and fortify them round with as many circumvallations and breastworks, as my uncle *Toby* would a citadel" (III.xxxiv.223). Walter's library on noses is compared to Toby's library on military science; and Toby's posting to the country like a lover after his mistress (II.v.98) is echoed now by Walter's purchase of *Bruscambille*: ". . . he solaced himself with *Bruscambille* after the manner, in which . . . your worship solaced yourself with your first mistress,——that is, from morning even unto night: which by the bye, how delightful soever it may prove to the inamorato,—is of little, or no entertainment at all, to by-standers" (III.xxxv.225). In the midst of these two-edged comparisons, Tristram suddenly turns aside, in his customary fashion, to deliver an encomium upon his uncle Toby: "—Here let me thrust my chair aside, and kneel down upon the ground, whilst I am pouring forth the warmest sentiments of love for thee, and veneration for the excellency of thy character, that ever virtue and nature kindled in a nephew's bosom" (III.xxxiv.224). Are we to join Tristram on his knees? The number of critics who have done so precludes an unqualified no, but I would at least suggest that Sterne, as opposed to Tristram, is not himself kneeling. The juxtaposition of this encomium with a direct comparison of Walter and Toby mounted; the promise of Tristram never to demolish the fortifications, immediately after they have been used metaphorically for wrong-headed opinions; and, above all, the figure of Tristram, in whose encomiastic style we have learned to recognize the irony of inversion, the Cervantic mock-seriousness—all these observations argue against sharing Tristram's enthusiasm for Toby at this point.

If Walter is to be satirized for the proselytizing sweep of his theories, should we not at least praise Toby for his peaceful nature: " . . . gently with faithful *Trim* behind thee, didst thou amble round the little circle of thy pleasures, jostling no creature in thy way;—for each one's sorrows, thou hadst a tear,—for each man's need, thou hadst a shilling" (III.xxxiv.224)? If pleasure were the end of man, perhaps we might praise Toby; if the answer to man's sorrow were merely a ready tear, and the answer to his need a ready shilling, perhaps we might again. There is, however, the continual suggestion of impotence and naïveté poised over Toby's head, and this dramatically affects his compassion and his charity, as well as his hobby-horse. Nor is it simply a question of Toby's embodying conflicting capacities, as Falstaff or Parson Adams or Leopold Bloom, all great comic characters, are able to do. Parson Adams provides a good contrast. Like Toby, the most obvious characteristics of Adams are his compassion and charity. Adams also has his weaknesses, but as Martin Battestin points out, they "are the product of his idealism and dedication to the public welfare" and of his "compassionate nature."[14] Adams's weaknesses come from his strengths, and while we sometimes laugh at him, we always acknowledge the essential unity of his personality—a man of "good nature." We cannot say the same for Toby, however. His weaknesses—his naïveté, his impotence, his hobby-horse—are not products of his virtues, but ironic comments upon them. Toby's battlefields, for example, are not a contribution to the "public welfare," not an act of a "compassionate nature," in spite of his several protestations to the contrary. Similarly, Toby's naïveté is not that of Parson Adams, shocked by the wickedness of the world, but rather a sexual ignorance which offers an implicit comment on his capacity to "love"; and his amours, the long anticipated touchstone of his feeling heart, are merely a long bawdy joke. Toby's foibles and failures argue a hollowness at his core, well signified by the red plush breeches and what they conceal. His weaknesses, in short, do not point to his strengths as in the case of Parson Adams, but rather undercut them. And this is the important distinction to be made between a comic character and a satiric victim.

Tristram, the child of Walter and Toby, figuratively speaking, exhibits both the one's intellectual waste and the other's emotional hollowness. Moreover, he makes them both constant objects of praise. Sterne's fundamental protest against eighteenth-century sentimentalism, in its broadest significations, is concealed behind the irony of Tristram's panegyrics to barrenness. Sterne attacks, with the rhetoric of the mock-encomium, the emptiness of the sentimental formula, so easily created and so readily dismissed. For Toby, sentimentalism is a way of life, but the image of that life is a mill-horse (or ass), moving through its endless round; like the hobby-horse, the image leaves us with a sense of futility.[15] For

14. *The Moral Basis of Fielding's Art: A Study of* Joseph Andrews (Middletown, Conn., 1959), pp. 108–9.

15. Cf. Arthur Cash's discussion of "mechanical benevolence" in *Sterne's Comedy of Moral Sentiments: The Ethical Dimension of the* Journey (Pittsburgh, 1966), pp. 56–59 and *passim*.

Tristram, sentimentalism is a way of writing, and one at which he is by no means unaccomplished.[16] His ready juxtaposition of the sentimental and the bawdy, his proclivity to the anticlimactic, the bathetic (as in his promise to keep the fortifications standing), and the transitory nature of even the most convincing declarations of sentiment, all suggest, however, a hollowness pervading the sentiment of *Tristram Shandy*. And it is this hollowness, a part of the Shandy world of uncreation, which is the object of Sterne's satire.

The consideration of Toby and his sentiment as satiric targets will not be immediately palatable to many readers of *Tristram Shandy*. There is, to be sure, a marked difference between the obviously satiric portrait of Walter, and the far more subtle satire on Toby; the difference, I believe, is vital to Sterne's satiric construction. In making the necessary condemnation of Walter, our immediate tendency is to seek his opposite; if Walter's absurd theories demand the rapier, we can rest comfortably with Toby's brain, so like "wet tinder" that "no spark could possibly take hold" (III.xxxix.236). If Walter's physical answers to the mysteries of creation fall obviously short, we may turn to Toby's: "—There is no cause but one, replied my uncle *Toby*,—why one man's nose is longer than another's, but because that God pleases to have it so. . . . 'Tis he . . . who makes us all, and frames and puts us together in such forms and proportions, and for such ends, as is agreeable to his infinite wisdom.—'Tis a pious account, cried my father, but not philosophical. . . . 'Twas no inconsistent part of my uncle *Toby*'s character,—that he feared God, and reverenced religion.— So the moment my father finished his remark,—my uncle *Toby* fell a whistling *Lillabullero*, with more zeal . . . than usual" (III.xli. 240–41). There is no question but that Toby's comments here are pertinent and even normative; his quick eye for absurdity, his frequent summoning of *Lillabullero* suggest an insight quite inconsistent with his simplicity, and were *Tristram Shandy* a novel, the critic could well be disturbed. The success of Sterne's satiric design, however, depends on the willingness with which we embrace Toby, the alacrity with which we leap from one extreme (analogous, in

---

16. As does any parodic writer, Sterne has mastered the idiom of the writing he satirizes. Moreover, since sentimentalism, as a literary style, works primarily by overstatement, satiric exaggeration is rendered a good deal *less* effective than it might be against other targets. Sterne's manner consists, rather, in hitting the sentimental tone with precision, and then undercutting it by the several devices suggested.

a general way, to the reason without religion of the "Abuses of Conscience Considered" sermon) to the other (religion without reason). Toby wholeheartedly endorses religion and sentiment, and if the word "zeal" is a warning, few heed it.

The conversation between the brothers is resumed after "Slaw-kenbergius's Tale"; Walter again inquires into the deep mysteries, Toby again provides the ready solution: "WHEN I reflect, brother *Toby*, upon MAN; and take a view of that dark side of him which represents his life as open to so many causes of trouble—when I consider . . . how oft we eat the bread of affliction, and that we are born to it . . . 'tis wonderful by what hidden resources the mind is enabled to stand it out, and bear itself up. . . . 'Tis by the assistance of Almighty God, cried my uncle *Toby*, looking up, and pressing the palms of his hands close together—'tis not from our own strength, brother *Shandy* . . ." (IV.vii.277). For Walter, this is not untying the knot but cutting it, and he tries once again to take Toby deeper—there is, he says, a "secret spring within us": "—Which spring, said my uncle *Toby*, I take to be Religion.—Will that set my child's nose on? cried my father . . .—It makes every thing straight for us, answered my uncle . . ." (IV.viii.278–79). The clarity of Toby's vision is refreshing, and, when weighed against Walter's idea of the "spring"—the mind's ability to coun-terbalance, as in a "well-ordered machine," the frustration of one absurd theory with another, equally absurd—we are tempted to embrace Toby completely. Sterne invites us to do so, not because Toby's faith is the final answer but because it is part of the satiric design of *Tristram Shandy* that we should dally with extremes, rejecting one for the other.

Insofar as Walter's answer to the dark side of life is to christen his son Trismegistus, we can reject it as more of his folly. But not everything that Walter utters at this point is folly; in particular, his view of man, in the passage just cited (IV.vii.277) and in that which follows, is a view fundamental to *Tristram Shandy*: "THOUGH man is of all others the most curious vehicle, said my father, yet at the same time 'tis of so slight a frame and so totteringly put together, that the sudden jerks and hard jostlings it unavoidably meets with in this rugged journey, would overset and tear it to pieces a dozen times a day—was it not . . . that there is a secret spring within us . . ." (IV.viii.278). Walter's answer to man's physical liabilities, his subservience to destiny and chance (the next chapter [ix], is the "chapter on chances") is the human reason, and if we abstract that solution from Walter's misuse, it can by no means be rejected. Toby's faith without reason is ultimately no more satisfying than Walter's reason without faith, though, like the sermon's religion without reason, it makes the greater pretense to piety and a good conscience. Toby's belief in God, like his sentimental good heart, is tempting, but it must finally be measured against his physical defect, his naïveté, and his hobby-horse—in short, against the "dark side" of life; in this regard, his views fare no better, though no worse, than his brother's.

As in the first two volumes, Sterne includes in Volumes III and IV several signposts to help the reader find his way in the mad Shandy world; more specifically, the "Author's Preface" (III.xx), Yorick's reappearance (IV.xxiii), and the death of Bobby (IV.xxxi) keep us aware of a world on the other side of the black page, against which the Shandy world may be measured and found wanting. Bobby's death is simply announced in Volume IV, Sterne saving the funeral orations of Walter and Trim for the opening of the fifth volume. Nevertheless there is little question but that he uses the dramatic entrance (or re-entrance) of death as a somehow fitting conclusion to the issues of birth and creation with which we have been primarily concerned in all four volumes. Like Yorick's death at the threshold of the Shandy world, Bobby's death marks a significant point in the satiric structure of *Tristram Shandy*, for in Volumes V and VI, and, indeed, in the remainder of the work, the basic metaphor of creation is juxtaposed with the growing importance of death in both the Shandy household and Tristram's study; "And so," he bids the reader in ending Volume IV, "I take my leave of you till this time twelve-month, when (unless this vile cough kills me in the mean time) I'll have another pluck at your beards . . ." (IV.xxxii.338).

In the same chapter, Tristram presents a list of the things left to do before he can conclude the volume, reminding us of his struggle with time in earlier passages, his desire to include everything in five minutes less than no time at all. Moreover, Tristram expresses regret over those things not yet included, promising us, in particular, the campaigns and amours of uncle Toby, who does, rather obviously, dominate the Shandy household in the later volumes as Walter has done in the first four. In terms of the satiric design of *Tristram Shandy*, the centering of attention on Toby suggests that Sterne will attempt to illuminate more fully the alternative Toby offers us, and the error we commit in embracing it. For Tristram, as opposed to Sterne, Toby's amours, the "choicest morsel of my whole story," fill him with the hope that what he has failed to achieve as a man he will be able to achieve as an author: ". . . I will answer for it the book shall make its way in the world, much better than its master has done before it—Oh *Tristram! Tristram!* can this but be once brought about—the credit, which will attend thee as an author, shall counterbalance the many evils which have befallen thee as a man . . ." (IV.xxxii.337). The distinction Tristram would draw between the man and the author is significant; the eighteenth century, from beginning to end, would admit no such distinction, and it is obvious that Sterne intends none. Tristram the author is without doubt the "heir-apparent to the *Shandy* family," and his book is precisely that which we would expect from a dispersed homunculus, whose nose was crushed at birth, who was misnamed Tristram, and who learned his wisdom at the feet of Walter Shandy and his morality at Toby's. This is not to suggest that Tristram reconciles the two extremes of his father and his uncle. In Tristram, the extremes of a linear spectrum curve towards one another to meet in their unique sameness—the irrational, however manifested; and diametrically opposed to the irrational is the rational, the middle position on the spectrum. *Tristram Shandy* is, therefore, not only a reflection of Shandean irrationality, but of the unreconciled opposites which constitute it. The brilliance of Sterne's satiric design manifests itself in the chaotic nature of Tristram's work, reflecting the chaos of unreconciled extremes in Tristram's mind.

In the "Author's Preface," Tristram characterizes his book in terms significant to this satiric design: "All I know of the matter is,—when I sat down, my intent was to write a good book; and as far as the tenuity of my understanding would hold out,—a wise, aye, and a discreet,—taking care only, as I went along, to put into it all the wit and the judgment (be it more or less) which the great author and bestower of them had thought fit originally to give me . . ." (III.xx.192–93). Tristram's argument in the Preface is that wit and judgment in *Tristram Shandy* are not only compatible, but that they proceed together; in other words, that, contrary to Locke, this particular opposition is reconciled in his work. Is it too rigid a schematization to suggest that wit is Tristram's inheritance from Walter, and judgment, his gift from Toby? Quite probably so, though Tristram encourages just such a conclusion in comparing the literature of wit to that of judgment. Wit alone, might well serve as a description of his father: ". . . we should never agree amongst ourselves, one day to an end:—there would be so much satire and sarcasm,—scoffing and flouting, with raillying and reparteeing of it,—thrusting and parrying in one corner or another. . . .—Chaste stars! what biting and scratching, and what a racket and a clatter we should make, what with breaking of heads, and rapping of knuckles, and hitting of sore places . . ." (III.xx. 195). And judgment alone, sounds much like Uncle Toby: ". . . we should make up matters as fast as ever they went wrong; and though we should abominate each other . . . we should nevertheless, my dear creatures, be all courtesy and kindness,—milk and honey, —'twould be a second land of promise,—a paradise upon earth . . ." (III.xx.195). Moreover, Tristram's reaction to a possible union of the two is quite in keeping with the character of Tristram I have suggested: "Bless us!—what noble work we should make!—how should I tickle it off!—and what spirits should I find myself in, to be writing away for such readers!—and you,—just heaven!— with what raptures would you sit and read,—but oh!—'tis too much,—I am sick,—I faint away deliciously at the thoughts of it! —'tis more than nature can bear!—lay hold of me,—I am giddy,— I am stone blind,—I'm dying,—I am gone.—Help! Help! Help!" (III.xx.194–95). Tristram's image for wit and judgment is that of liquids being poured into the brain "without stint or measure, let or hinderance . . . as each of us could bear it,—scum and sediment an' all. . . ." The brain, in turn, is divided into its "several receptacles, cells, cellules . . . and spare places . . ." each to be filled to the brim. The operation is mechanical and suggests the impossibility of any organic relationship, such as Tristram pretends to, between the elements of wit and judgment in his mind. Tristram drains one barrel after the other, thus filling his work with great quantities of wit and judgment; but any idea of reconciling the two and, in particular, of using the one to balance and control the other is lost in an ecstatic loss of all balance, all control. For Tristram, at this point, the measure of a mind is not qualitative but quantitative, and he desires for himself (and for his readers, including the doctors of the visitation dinner) a full measure of both wit and judgment.

Using the same standard of quantity, Tristram conducts a rapid geographical survey, using the traditional idea that wit and judgment are factors of climate. Thus, while in the arctic countries there is neither one nor the other, in the Scandinavian countries ". . . you may perceive some small glimmerings (as it were) of wit, with a comfortable provision of good plain *houshold* judgment, which taking the quality and quantity of it together, they make a very good shift with,—and had they more of either the one or the other, it would destroy the proper ballance betwixt them . . ." (III.xx.197). The middle position of this description, with its sense of balance and control, suggests that it is normative; Tristram, however, rushes south to the warmer climate of England, ". . . where we have more ambition, and pride, and envy, and lechery, and other whoreson passions upon our hands to govern and subject to reason,—the *height* of our wit and the *depth* of our judgment, you see, are exactly proportioned to the *length* and *breadth* of our necessities . . ." (III.xx.197). Tristram has entered upon a different argument from that with which he started the Preface; from arguing whether wit and judgment are reconciled and compatible in *Tristram Shandy,* he turns to the question of whether a man can have the abundance of both he just now wished for us. In this shift from quality to quantity, Sterne's ironic intentions are signaled by the italicized *height* and *depth, length* and *breadth.* The measuring of men's minds in physical dimensions, like Swift's similar measuring of their religious spirit, focuses attention once again on the mechanical operation of the Shandean mind.

At the same time, Tristram's discussion of the quantity of wit and judgment allowed to a man establishes an important norm for *Tristram Shandy:* ". . . so much of their irradiations are suffered from time to time to shine down upon us; as he, whose infinite wisdom which dispenses every thing in exact weight and measure, knows will just serve to light us on our way in this night of our obscurity . . ." (III.xx.198). Tristram admits that his wish for us was no more than the first "insinuating *How d'ye* of a caressing prefacer stifling his reader . . . into silence," and he proceeds to paint a satiric canvas to illustrate what would happen if "this effusion of light" could be as easily procured as he wished it. Sterne's irony is quite complex; in the learned sciences, for example, a profusion of wit and judgment would send scientists groping and blundering "on in the dark, all the nights of their lives,—running their heads against posts, and knocking out their brains without ever getting to their journies end. . . ." The point, apparently, is that wit and judgment would prevent the ready solutions of projectors and theorists, would make them more cognizant of the absurdity of their quests, of the blackness which surrounds them. A profusion of wit and judgment would set "fiddlers and painters judging by their eyes and ears," instead of measuring their arts by a quadrant; the statesman would turn the "political wheel, like a brute, the wrong way round—*against* the stream of corruption,—by heaven! —instead of *with* it"; the physician would write a book "against predestination; perhaps worse,—[would feel] his patient's pulse, instead of his apothecary's . . ."; and the lawyers would kick a "damn'd, dirty, vexatious cause" out of court, rather than in, "and with such fury in their looks, and such a degree of inveteracy in their manner of kicking it, as if the laws had been originally made for the peace and preservation of mankind . . ." (III.xx.199). In short, Tristram's pious assertion of 'infinite wisdom" is a mockery, a coming to rest in a divine dispensation that provides only enough wit and judgment to Englishmen for them to be ignorant and corrupt. A proper, not a profuse, exercise of the reason would correct the vices of Tristram's satiric portraits; but Tristram is interested only in convincing us that such an exercise of reason is beyond the portion allotted to us (and to him) by God; beyond the *"height* and *depth"* proportioned to the *"length* and *breadth"* of our necessities, our need to subject our whoreson passions to the control of reason. Tristram's idea of a brimful of wit and judgment is, to be sure, ludicrous; but his idea that God has limited the light of reason only to the extent of allowing our vices and follies to prosper is equally ludicrous. As in the other key issues of *Tristram Shandy,* the answer lies in the center: A man's reason, his wit, and his judgment are indeed measured by the divine wisdom; but the exercise of that reason, which is, without doubt, sufficient to its purpose, is in the hands of man.

Just as abruptly as before, Tristram draws a "curtain across" the page and returns to his first argument, the quality of wit and judgment. If Tristram originally intended to demonstrate that wit and judgment were reconciled in his book, he now abandons the effort to argue with "your reverences and worships" who defend judgment at the expense of wit. It is apparent that he is using wit and judgment, despite his allusions to Locke, in a non-technical sense. Judgment, which had earlier been linked to an excess of "courtesy and kindness," is now made synonymous with "gravity," illustrating once again the centripetal nature of Sterne's satire; and wit, earlier joined to an excess of "satire and sarcasm," becomes the desideratum of his writing, the answer to false gravity. Insofar as Tristram defends wit against judgment, he suggests the essential failure of his writing—the uncontrolled, unbalanced mind which pours itself forth by tapping one barrel after the other. There is a further significance to his defense of wit, however, in the disrepute into which wit had fallen in the mid-eighteenth century; and, insofar as Tristram defends wit against gravity, he perhaps speaks for Sterne's quarrel with those forces which were replacing satire with sentiment as the dominant mode of literary and social expression. In brief, Sterne is able to make the "Author's Preface" both a reflection of Tristram's folly and of his own satiric design.

That the Preface is addressed not only to the reader, but to the doctors of the visitation dinner as well, suggests, perhaps, a link in Sterne's mind between the two. In many respects, the dinner contains nothing significantly different from the many satiric strokes already delivered in *Tristram Shandy*: the Rabelaisian bawdiness and suggestiveness; the legal quibbles; the "profound" reasonings; the ultimate conclusion, amidst an abundance of legal citations and Toby's inward whistling of *Lillabullero*—all this we have encountered before, though, I might add, Sterne appears at the top of his wit in this traditional satiric setting. The special interest the scene holds is in the return of Yorick to the Shandy world. To be sure, Yorick's actions during the dinner are neither profound nor particularly moral. He cuts his sermon, just delivered to the visitation guests, into slips for lighting their pipes, and excuses the insult by declaring that a sermon from the head rather than the heart is not worth the suffering it takes to bring it forth. He possibly tosses the chestnut into Phutatorius' breeches; he certainly picks the chestnut up, which was, as Tristram says, as bad as a "plain acknowledgment . . . that the chesnut was originally his . . ." (IV.xxvii.323). And he has the last word, a bawdy joke, which is, Eugenius tells him, as good as the company deserves. Yorick is part of the Shandy community, just as surely as Tristram and Walter and Toby. Yorick changes nothing: The follies continue unabated; absurdities mount upon absurdities.

Nevertheless, like Tristram's missing chapter, Yorick's presence

is felt as a normative agent; and while Tristram is busy removing
the offending chapter, Yorick returns from the dead. Chapter xxiv,
the journey to the visitation dinner, offends, says Tristram, because
it "appears to be so much above the stile and manner of any thing
else I have been able to paint in this book, that it could not have
remained in it, without depreciating every other scene; and destroying at the same time that necessary equipoise and balance, (whether
of good or bad) betwixt chapter and chapter, from whence the
just proportions and harmony of the whole work results" (IV.xxv.
315). Tristram's opinion is that it does not matter how high or
low, good or bad, a work is, providing that it is consistent with its
own nature; the classical values of proportion and harmony are
thus made, to borrow from the Preface, "the *Magna Charta* of
stupidity." The connection of Yorick with the missing chapter is
made by having him cited in support of Tristram's opinion: "—
This is the reason, may it please your reverences, that some of the
lowest and flattest compositions pass off very well—(as *Yorick*
told my uncle *Toby* one night) by siege . . ." (IV.xxv.315). An
index points to the final moral; certainly it is as much a comment
on Yorick's role in *Tristram Shandy,* and his return at this juncture,
as upon Tristram's theory of "consistent" writing: "A dwarf who
brings a standard along with him to measure his own size—take
my word, is a dwarf in more articles than one—And so much for
tearing out of chapters" (IV.xxv.316). It would be difficult to
express the function of Yorick in *Tristram Shandy,* or the function of norms in satire, more precisely—or more delightfully. To
startle us into acquiescence with an explicit statement of righteousness is neither Sterne's way nor the way of satire. The standard
which accompanies the dwarf need not proclaim its findings; and
Yorick, persevering in simplicity, good sense, mild antagonism,
and a tone "two parts jest and one part earnest," provides a contrast
to the Shandy world simply by returning from the dead to be in it.

VI

"Tristram Shandy" as a Satire
Volumes V and VI

. . . and now, you see, I am lost myself!
(VI.xxxiii.462)

Volumes V and VI

HE DEATH of Bobby and the reappearance of Yorick in Volume IV of *Tristram Shandy* foreshadow the increasing importance of death in Volumes V and VI, published in December, 1761. Yorick is present, in much the same manner as he appears at the visitation dinner, throughout these two volumes, subtly providing a standard against which the reader may measure Shandean folly. He is there, for example, when Trim, "by the help of his forefinger, laid flat upon the table, and the edge of his hand striking a-cross it at right angles . . ." (V.xx.379), reports Tristram's accident to Toby. And when Toby and Trim, despite the accident and their responsibility for it, mount their hobby-horse, it is Yorick who returns them to the matter at hand. Yorick also makes Walter dismount by interrupting his consultation with the "polemic divines" on the issue of circumcision: ". . . I wish there was not a polemic divine, said *Yorick*, in the kingdom;—one ounce of practical divinity—is worth a painted ship load of all their reverences have imported these fifty years" (V.xxviii.387). And in order to give Toby "the best description" of polemic divines he had ever read, Yorick pulls a copy of Rabelais from his pocket to read the battle between Gymnast and Captain Tripet.

The circumcision forgotten, the conversation by the Shandy fire turns to Walter's *Tristrapædia*. Yorick's reasonableness is again available, helping us to find our way in the sustained parody of pedantry, profundity, and projection. Thus, Walter concludes that the son ought to respect his mother, referring Yorick to the "first book of the Institutes of *Justinian,* at the eleventh title and the tenth section" (an erroneous citation, as Work notes): "—I can read it as well, replied *Yorick,* in the Catechism" (V.xxxi.391–92). More subtly, Trim's inability to recite his Catechism unless he begins at the beginning calls forth a series of normative aphorisms, not from Yorick as we might expect, but from Walter; so valid, indeed, are his comments, that Yorick thinks him inspired:

> Every thing in this world . . . is big with jest,—and has wit in it, and instruction too,—if we can but find it out.
> —Here is the *scaffold work* of INSTRUCTION, its true point of folly, without the BUILDING behind it.—
> —Here is the glass for pedagogues, preceptors, tutors, governours, gerund-grinders and bear-leaders to view themselves in, in their true dimensions.— . . .
>
> .   .   .   .
>
> —SCIENCES MAY BE LEARNED BY ROTE, BUT WISDOM NOT (V.xxxii.393).

That Walter, the *philosophus gloriosus* of *Tristram Shandy*, should recognize all this and fail to see its applicability to himself is the ironic capstone to his entire career. Moreover, his condemnation of religion by rote seems reasonable, one of the few occasions when we feel authorized to accept Walter's opinion. It is left to Yorick to demonstrate otherwise. Moving beyond the demand that Trim have "one determinate idea annexed" to his Catechism, he finds it more important that he have one determinate action:

> Prythee, *Trim*, quoth my father . . . —What do'st thou mean, by *"honouring thy father and mother?"*
> Allowing them . . . three halfpence a day out of my pay, when they grew old.—And didst thou do that, *Trim*? said *Yorick*.—He did indeed, replied my uncle *Toby*.—Then, *Trim*, said *Yorick* . . . taking the corporal by the hand, thou art the best commentator upon that part of the *Decalogue* . . . (V.xxxii.393).

The passage serves as a gloss on Yorick's praise of "practical divinity" in his attack on polemic divines. At the same time, it suggests once again that in spite of what concerns Tristram Shandy, it is action not opinion that determines our moral stature.

What Yorick comes to represent in these passages, and throughout *Tristram Shandy*, is perhaps best revealed in the discussion over a qualified tutor for Tristram. Walter runs through a lengthy list of nonsensical qualifications before he lights on "wise and judicious, and learned." Toby, on the contrary, suggests "free, and generous, and bountiful, and brave." Yorick's values are sandwiched between the two, and indicate a middle way: "And why not humble, and moderate, and gentle tempered, and good?" (VI.v.415). There is nothing at all undesirable in the traits suggested by Walter and Toby; it is simply that, juxtaposed with a mean, they remind us that the brothers live on the dangerous extremities of rational behavior, inevitably flirting with the irrational. In other words, there is no balance in the Shandy household. Walter ignores Toby's values, as he does his hobby-horse, and Toby ignores Walter's values, resting content in childish simplicity. But one must be both free and wise, generous and judicious, and it is Yorick who reconciles, as Tristram is never able to do, the extremes of the Shandy family. In offering us, as moral values, humility and moderation, a gentle temper and goodness, Yorick provides an opportunity to measure the extent of Shandean deviations; and, at the same time, a catalogue of those values Sterne considers normative.

The last appearance of Yorick in these volumes is in VI.xi, where his function as a *memento mori* is recalled. Of course, in reading *Tristram Shandy* as a satire, the reader is urged by the satiric organization to associate Yorick with death whenever he appears; Yorick's black page ushers us into the Shandy world, and he returns from the dead to participate in the Shandean household. In this chapter, though, the connection is specifically drawn by a discussion of Yorick's sermons, in particular, his funeral sermon for Le Fever: "Amongst these [Yorick's sermons], there is that particular sermon which has unaccountably led me into this digression—The funeral sermon upon poor *Le Fever*, wrote out very fairly, as if from a hasty copy.—I take notice of it the more, because it seems to have been his favourite composition—It is upon mortality . . ." (VI.xi.428). What attracts Tristram's attention, however, is not the content of the sermon but the word "Bravo!" which appears at its conclusion, "though not very offensively."[1] Yorick's habit of judging his own sermons has been the subject of the chapter up to this point; and we recall that Yorick is seen at the visitation dinner cutting a "bad" sermon into strips. In a world in which Walter can condemn pedagogues and Toby can weep over both a fly and the Treaty of Utrecht, Yorick serves to suggest the necessity of self-examination and self-knowledge. Self-examination must not be mere self-approval, however, as the "Abuses of

1. It is located where the thumb would usually cover it and is written with a crow's quill, in a "small *Italian* hand." Moreover, the ink is "very pale . . . diluted almost to nothing," and, finally, there is a line drawn through it (VI.xi.429).

Conscience Considered" sermon demonstrated was too often the case. Thus Yorick's habit of evaluating his sermons is juxtaposed with an emphasis on his humility. Of all the sermons in Tristram's hands, only half a dozen have so favorable a comment as *"So, so"*; and only two have *"Moderato,"* which may mean the same as *"So, so,"* though in Tristram's judgment the sermons so marked "are five times better than the *so, so's*;—shew ten times more knowledge of the human heart;—have seventy times more wit and spirit in them;—(and, to rise properly in my climax)—discover a thousand times more genius . . ." (VI.xi.428). Tristram's exaggerations contrast sharply with Yorick's very modest expressions of self-approval, while at the same time, they perhaps make a necessary distinction between mediocrity (*"so, so"*) and moderation (*"moderato"*). The use of *"moderato"* also suggests an important relationship between humility and moderation; and, when tied to Yorick's preoccupation with mortality, they quite possibly form an essential moral triad against which the Shandy study and the Shandy household are to be measured and found wanting.

Yorick's presence in Volumes V and VI is only one aspect of a dramatic shift from birth to death as the central subject of concern in the Shandy world. The death of Bobby at the end of Volume IV presages this change, and after an opening chapter in Tristram's study, we return to hear Walter's and Trim's funeral orations. Volume VI moves quickly into the story of Le Fever, also concerned with death. The link between the two deaths, the primary biographical "event" of these volumes, is Tristram's circumcision, which, with its obvious suggestion of castration, bespeaks yet another death. Interwoven between these incidents of mortality are Walter's theories for educating Tristram; the pattern formed by the two threads is assuredly satiric. And finally, after delaying for a volume and a half, Tristram begins the amours of Toby, "the choicest morsel of my whole story." Again, the structural design which uses Toby's hobby-horse to culminate two volumes on education and mortality seems satiric in both form and function.

Walter's encyclopedic reaction to Bobby's death continues Sterne's satiric attack on the follies of philosophy and learning— common enough targets throughout the satiric tradition. Unlike the rebuffs to his several theories in earlier volumes, the death of Bobby does not incapacitate Walter, even for a moment; rather, he embraces the opportunity it offers: "My father was as proud of his eloquence as . . . CICERO . . . : it was indeed his strength . . . for he was by nature eloquent,—and his weakness—for he was hourly a dupe to it; and provided an occasion in life would but permit him to shew his talents, or say either a wise thing, a witty, or a shrewd one—(bating the case of a systematick misfortune)—he had all he wanted" (V.iii.352). Philosophy, says Tristram, "has a fine saying for every thing.—For *Death* it has an entire set. . . ." The set, to be sure, is Burton's; the situation, however, is Sterne's. Not stopping to arrange his consolations, Walter mounts; striving for the pathetic he achieves the bathetic instead. The ludicrous juxtaposition of the classical world with the Shandy household; the heaping of aphorisms; the perceptive inanity of Toby's remarks (Walter is moved to call him "Simpleton!" at one point) ; and the ultimate finale in bawdiness, all demonstrate Walter's failure to meet the situation. Moreover, he has forgotten the situation; galloping headlong, he had, says Tristram, "absolutely forgot my brother *Bobby*."

At the same time, in the kitchen, Trim also delivers a funeral oration. Tristram's metaphor to explain how this comes about is interesting: "THOUGH in one sense, our family was certainly a simple machine, as it consisted of a few wheels; yet there was thus much to be said for it, that these wheels were set in motion by so many different springs, and acted one upon the other from such a variety of strange principles and impulses,—that though it was a simple machine, it had all the honour and advantages of a complex one" (V.vi.358). The reduction of individual members of the Shandy household to machines and puppets has already been pointed out. Now the entire family is reduced to a simple machine, the word "simple" surely carrying an ambivalent meaning. Tristram's own mechanical nature is again suggested by his effort to achieve chronological accuracy; Mrs. Shandy is kept bent over the keyhole for five minutes, while Tristram descends to the kitchen. Again, the realism of time is defeated by the puppet-like disposition of the characters.

Tristram draws a comparison between his father, "a man of deep reading—prompt memory—with *Cato*, and *Seneca*, and *Epictetus*, at his fingers ends," and the corporal, "with nothing— to remember—of no deeper reading than his muster-roll . . ." (V.vi.359), and sides with Trim: ". . . going strait forwards as nature could lead him, to the heart. O *Trim*! would to heaven

thou had'st a better historian!—would!—thy historian had a better pair of breeches!—O ye criticks! will nothing melt you?"
(V.vi.359). If Sterne is really recommending Trim's oration, he
certainly takes an ironic tone in doing so. I would suggest, instead,
the need to remain aware of the ironic persona and wary of any
alternatives Tristram offers. We must reject as bathetic and mean-
ingless Walter's oration; whether we should accept Trim's, however, remains to be seen.

Like Walter, the servants all translate death as best they can—or
will. For Susannah, Bobby's death means Mrs. Shandy's mourning
and thus Mrs. Shandy's wardrobe; for Obadiah it means having
to work in the ox-moor; and for the "foolish scullion," who is
perhaps not so foolish, it is what she is not. Trim's first effort is
much like the scullion's reaction, and is perhaps his best: "Are we
not here now, continued the corporal, (striking the end of his
stick perpendicularly upon the floor, so as to give an idea of health
and stability)—and are we not—(dropping his hat upon the
ground) gone! in a moment!—'Twas infinitely striking! *Susannah*
burst into a flood of tears.—We are not stocks and stones" (V.vii.
361). Tristram breaks into the oration thus begun in order to call
our attention to the rhetorical brilliance of this gesture, this "stroke
of the corporal's eloquence" on which, he plainly perceives, "the
preservation of our constitution in church and state . . ." depends
(V.vii.361). He then returns to his phrase "We are not stocks and
stones" and continues: ". . . nor are we angels, I wish we were,—
but men cloathed with bodies, and governed by our imaginations;
—and what a junketting piece of work of it there is, betwixt these
and our seven senses, especially some of them, for my own part, I
own it, I am ashamed to confess" (V.vii.361). Tristram here expresses the traditional view of man's middle estate which I have
suggested is normative throughout *Tristram Shandy*; but for him
the middle estate is of rhetorical significance only, an indication of
the susceptibility of man to the pathetic appeal. Trim's thought,
Tristram says, was nothing; the gesture was everything: "—There
was nothing in the sentence—'twas one of your self-evident truths
we have the advantage of hearing every day; and if *Trim* had not
trusted more to his hat than his head—he had made nothing at
all of it" (V.vii.362). Tristram runs through the entire gesture
again, praises it again, and recommends it to us all—"meditate,"
he beseeches us, "upon *Trim*'s hat." In this manner, we are made

to shift our attention from the meaning of words to the shape of things, from the subject to the object with which it is compared, as we have to do so frequently in *Tristram Shandy*. Nevertheless, like the words of the scullion, Trim's sentence, self-evident though it is, expresses the single truth most ignored in the Shandy world thus far: the ubiquity of death and the regard for morality and religion which this ubiquity needs produce in every Christian. Man's middle position, defined by Tristram as his susceptibility to his imagination, suggests far more than a weakness for a rhetorical gesture; it indicates human susceptibility to both a life poorly lived and a death poorly prepared for; a life in which imagination (passion) gets astride reason and a man, even a lover of "mankind" like Toby, can be caught galloping—"gone! in a moment!" Tristram, busy melting the critics, does not comprehend this; the reader, if not melted, recognizes that he had best meditate on the mortality Trim's hat represents and not on the hat itself.

The remainder of Trim's speech is much like Walter's in that Trim mounts his hobby-horse to speak of death in battle, with the obvious intention of impressing (or seducing) Susannah. It might be noted that in this regard Trim is quite unlike his master, and, indeed, is the only successful lover in *Tristram Shandy*. Tristram glances at Trim's constant preoccupation with seduction by including his hat in a comment on chapter vii: " . . . I pray the chapter upon chamber-maids and button-holes may be forgiven me,—and that they will accept of the last chapter in lieu of it; which is nothing, an't please your reverences, but a chapter on *chamber-maids, green-gowns, and old hats*" (v.viii.363). In the Shandy world of failure and frustration, Trim reminds the reader, in a most persistent manner, of the possibilities of successful courtship. As with his idea of the bowling green and his complete repertory of rhetorical gestures, Trim's successes in love return the various Shandean follies to a measure of reality, objectifying what to Walter and Toby and Tristram is primarily a subjective, even fantastical, affair.

Trim's funeral oration finally leads him to other deaths that the Shandy household has known, and he is about to launch into the story of Le Fever when Tristram breaks in to remind himself that his mother is still in her awkward crouch by the door. When the story of Le Fever is finally told in VI.v, it is Tristram who narrates it, and he begins by reminding us of Trim's earlier, abortive attempt. This self-conscious linking of the two scenes suggests not only Sterne's desire to emphasize the prevalence of death in these volumes, but, in addition, the manner in which death accompanies, though unseen, all the Shandean activities.

The story of Le Fever's illness and death is a tour de force of sentimental writing. The "cold and rainy night"; the poor gentle-man-soldier, dying in an inn; the son, "poor creature," bringing to the sickbed the thin toast and the Bible, and receiving his mother's ring from his father's bosom; the prayers, the sighs, the tears—all the elements of sentimentalism are carefully marshaled and paraded before us. To some degree, it is difficult to avoid taking the story seriously, and it is perhaps Sterne's intention that we do so. Like the death of Yorick, Le Fever's passing dramatically reminds us of mortality, an essential element in Sterne's satiric design; and, at the same time, this death of *one* soldier may reflect ironically on Toby's campaigns. To a much larger degree, however, it is impossible to accept the story of Le Fever as completely serious. Tristram sets the tone at the outset: " . . . But this is neither here nor there— why do I mention it?—Ask my pen,—it governs me,—I govern not it" (VI.vi.416). The truth of this statement is readily demonstrated: Le Fever's story is rendered absurd by Tristram's blindness to the meaning of his own words. Were it possible to divorce the story from its telling, we might sympathize with the dying captain. As it is, the story serves primarily to demonstrate the emotional sterility, the artistic hypocrisy of Tristram's study.

Most important, we are still dealing with the Shandys: Toby cannot go out to see Le Fever that night for fear the damp will "bring on your honour's torment in your groin." Trim goes instead and Toby waits by the fire: "My uncle *Toby* filled his second pipe; and had it not been, that he now and then wandered from the point, with considering whether it was not full as well to have the curtain of the tennaile a straight line, as a crooked one,—he might be said to have thought of nothing else but poor *Le Fever* and his boy the whole time he smoaked it" (VI.vi.418). Similarly, Le Fever's death occurs just at the time when Toby was engaged in the siege of Dendermond; and, in order to turn his attention solely to Le Fever, he first orders the garden gate to be bolted, turning the siege, says Tristram, into a blockade. These and similar reminders of Toby's hobby-horse, wholly unnecessary to the narrative of Le Fever, serve to undercut the pathetic heights Tristram strives for. The undercutting is, to be sure, slight; but it is present, and it serves as a warning that Sterne's intentions here are more complex than we might first suppose.

In addition, the death of Le Fever's wife in his arms is rendered less than pathetic by Toby's hint of a "circumstance" Le Fever's modesty omitted. Having encountered in Walter's funeral oration the untimely death of Cornelius Gallus (v.iv.357), such a "circumstance" brings only one thing to our minds, again proving, incidentally, our lascivious natures. And again, what is the reader to do with a name like Le Fever? Unlike Walter (and some critics) we hesitate to change the text at will;[2] but it is clear that a dying hero with such a name is, at best, the victim of some ironic intention. It is the ending of the story of Le Fever, however, which most reveals Sterne's satiric purposes:

> The blood and spirits of *Le Fever* . . . rallied back,—the film forsook his eyes for a moment,—he looked up wishfully in my uncle *Toby*'s face,—then cast a look upon his boy,—and that *ligament*, fine as it was,—was never broken.—
>
> Nature instantly ebb'd again,—the film returned to its place,—the pulse fluttered—stopp'd—went on—throb'd—stopp'd again—moved—stopp'd—shall I go on?—No (VI.x. 426).

Tristram's exposure as a "sentimental artist" as opposed, say, to a simply sensitive human being, is thus made complete. Indifferent to the honest emotion his scene might have generated, and blind to the meaning of death, Tristram is equally blind to the incongruity of his abrupt conclusion. Tristram's facetious question does far more than prevent the passage from becoming too maudlin; it comments on the honesty of the sentiment being displayed, by demonstrating the ease with which Tristram can withdraw his feelings from the scene. The story of Le Fever is suddenly rendered theatrical and

2. The spelling of *Le Fever* as *Le Fevre* appears early in editions of *Tristram Shandy* and in critical commentaries on the work. It is justified, perhaps, by the first edition of Vol. IX, where it twice appears as *Le Fevre* (chap. ii, p. 11; chap. v, p. 22). In some nineteenth-century editions, the forty other spellings of *Le Fever* in *Tristram Shandy* are changed to *Le Fevre* and among the early critics the latter spelling becomes commonplace; see Alan B. Howes, *Yorick and the Critics* (New Haven, 1958), pp. 59, 64, 72, 79, 85, 109, 118, 167. If Sterne did indeed have second thoughts about the spelling of *Le Fever*, it argues the satiric intentions of the original spelling; and that the critics rather obviously preferred the innocuous *Le Fevre* suggests the difficulty of writing ironic satire in an unsatirical age.

artificial as Tristram is revealed to be a great distance from the participants, a puppeteer among his puppets. Tristram is an artist, shaping his scene to achieve effects, his eyes always on his audience and too infrequently on his subject. Because of this, he is a bad artist, particularly unable to distinguish between ideas which conflict with and even destroy one another: "For my own part I never wonder at any thing;—and so often has my judgment deceived me in my life, that I always suspect it, right or wrong . . . " (V.xi.367). Sterne's attack on literary sentimentalism, I would suggest, stems from the hypocrisy involved; the author pretends to deeper and deeper emotional involvement while at the same time he turns more and more from his subject to play to his audience. The attack on sentiment such as Toby displays has a broader base and is ultimately condemned only within the satiric pattern of alternatives and oppositions that is part of *Tristram Shandy's* design. The attack on sentimentalism as a literary phenomenon is more direct. Sterne perceives the hypocrisy and parodies it using Tristram as his vehicle. Having learned his morality from Toby and the fly, Tristram serves the purpose well.

Coming between the death of Bobby and the death of Le Fever, the circumcision of Tristram can be said to be surrounded by death. Nor is this as pretentious as it might sound. Sterne's innuendo clearly suggests a castration of sorts, rather than the clean circumcision Tristram assures us of; "the threat," as A. R. Towers puts it, "has been made and withdrawn."[3] In terms of the central symbol of creation, the accident is clearly destructive, the shadows of impotence and sterility growing darker over the Shandy household and Tristram's study.

The cause of the accident, Toby's hobby-horse, is particularly significant. Tristram describes what happened and tempts us with a moral:

> He [Trim] had dismantled every sash window in my uncle *Toby's* house long before, in the very same way,—though not always in the same order; for sometimes the pullies had been wanted, and not the lead,—so then he began with the pullies,—and the pullies being picked out, then the lead became useless,—and so the lead went to pot too.

3. "Sterne's Cock and Bull Story," *ELH*, XXIV (1957), 16. Towers calls attention to the "modern anthropologists and psychoanalysts who regard circumcision as a ritualistic substitute for the graver deprivation" (p. 16).

—A great MORAL might be picked handsomly out of this, but I have not time—'tis enough to say, wherever the demolition began, 'twas equally fatal to the sash window (V.xix.378).

Since Tristram leaves the "great MORAL" undefined, it would not do for the critic categorically to state it. In terms of the satiric design of *Tristram Shandy,* however, one possible lesson seems evident: The process of destruction which begins on the day of Tristram's conception operates from both ends of the spectrum, from Walter on the one hand and Toby on the other. I have already suggested that Toby's function as a vehicle for sentiment is satirically undercut by his impotence and his hobby-horse. That this impotence is passed on to Tristram is now intimated. Toby's hobby-horse is supposedly harmless, but it maims Tristram, the physical blow reflecting the emotional impotence demonstrated by Tristram in his study. That is to say, the emotional sterility of Tristram's narration of Le Fever's story, the hypocrisy of his sentimentalism, has its roots in Trim's dismantling of sash windows, just as the intellectual sterility of Tristram's efforts to tell his life has its roots in the educational system laid out by Walter. It does not matter which one we begin with: The damage to Tristram's body reflects the damage to his mind—and the converse is equally true.

That this is the case helps explain Walter's indifference to this accident in contrast to his excesses of grief over the smashed nose and the misnaming.[4] "I thought as much," he replies to Obadiah's explanation of the accident and retires to study the available writings on circumcision: ". . . if the EGYPTIANS,—the SYRIANS, —the PHOENICIANS,—the ARABIANS,—the CAPADOCIANS,—if the COLCHI, and TROGLODYTES did it—if SOLON and PYTHAGORAS submitted,—what is TRISTRAM?—Who am I, that I should fret or fume one moment about the matter?" (V.xxvii.385). The connection between the circumcision and Tristram's education is also indicated by the smooth transition Walter makes from the one topic to the other. Yorick interrupts Walter's discussion of circum-

4. Insofar as noses do not mean noses in *Tristram Shandy,* Tristram's "nose" has already been damaged once by Walter's hobby-horse, and Toby's hobby-horse merely repeats the damage. The centripetal nature of Sterne's metaphoric design, in which different subjects and different objects ultimately represent the same satiric target, is again apparent.

cision with his Rabelaisian attack on polemic divines (V.xxix.387–89), and the subject is never returned to, chapter xxx beginning, "—No,—I think I have advanced nothing, replied my father, making answer to a question which *Yorick* had taken the liberty to put to him,—I have advanced nothing in the *Tristrapœdia* . . ." (V.xxx.389). Moreover, the *Tristrapœdia* had already been introduced in chapter xvi, only to be suddenly broken off by the circumcision in chapter xvii. Here, as throughout the work, Tristram develops one brother's mount by reference to the other's. In *Tristram Shandy* the satiric paraphernalia which attaches itself to any one folly is constantly being transferred to other follies, Sterne achieving both an economy of design and an intensification of attack by so doing. The practice is, I believe, one of the fundamental devices of satire that Sterne learned from his reading of Swift. At the same time, of course, the continual linking of Walter's folly to Toby's suggests the essential sameness of their unreason. A distinction does arise, however: ". . . my father gave himself up to it with as much devotion as ever my uncle *Toby* had done to his doctrine of projectils.—The difference between them was, that my uncle *Toby* drew his whole knowledge . . . from *Nicholas Tartaglia*—My father spun his, every thread of it, out of his own brain,—or reeled and cross-twisted what all other spinners and spinsters had spun before him, that 'twas pretty near the same torture to him" (V.xvi.372–73). The metaphor of the spider may well be borrowed from Swift's use of it in *The Battle of the Books*. It suggests much of what both satirists attack in man's intellectual endeavors, the weaving of great intellectual webs out of oneself; the offering, with great pride, of one's own waste materials in extravagant and intricate ("closely reasoned") patterns designed as universal answers to universal questions. Even when Walter dips into his vast library, it is only to read another "spinner," who, once digested, is woven into Walter's triumphant designs.

A comparison between the *Tristrapœdia* and *Tristram Shandy* itself is also suggested by Tristram, though he shows no awareness of having done so. Surely Sterne is aware that Walter's struggle with time and selection is precisely the struggle Tristram is engaged in: "In about three years . . . my father had got advanced almost into the middle of his work. . . . —He imagined he should be able to bring whatever he had to say, into so small a compass, that when it was finished . . . it might be rolled up in my mother's hussive.—

Matter grows under our hands.—Let no man say,—'Come—I'll write a *duodecimo*' " (v.xvi.373). As Tristram in his study gains 364 days every two volumes, Walter falls further and further behind in his attempt to govern his son's education: ". . . the misfortune was, that I was all that time totally neglected and abandoned to my mother; and what was almost as bad, by the very delay, the first part of the work, upon which my father had spent the most of his pains, was rendered entirely useless,—every day a page or two became of no consequence" (v.xvi.375). Walter's defeat at the hands of time (he draws a sun-dial, Tristram says, "for no better purpose than to be buried under ground") is the result of a theory of selection different from Tristram's. Tristram simply wants to include everything; Walter, on the contrary, bases his view on the view of the Archbishop of Benevento, who believed that "when a personage of venerable character and high station . . . once turned author . . . all the devils in hell broke out of their holes to cajole him. . . . So that the life of a writer, whatever he might fancy to the contrary, was not so much a state of *composition*, as a state of *warfare*; and his probation in it, precisely that of any other man militant upon earth,—both depending alike, not half so much upon the degrees of his WIT—as his RESIST-ANCE" (v.xvi.374). There is no small value in the Archbishop's theory, particularly in view of Tristram's theory of inclusiveness. "Resistance," with its contrast to "wit," is obviously suggestive of the faculty of judgment, so dramatically lacking in both Tristram's theory and practice of composition. At the same time, however, the Bishop's forty years to produce a hundred "tiny pages" is obviously another extreme. Walter, unable to accept the Bishop's devils on religious principles, takes them allegorically and strives to filter out of his *Tristrapædia* all the "prejudice of education." In doing so, he proceeds so slowly that the book daily becomes more useless. Tristram draws the moral, sharply and perceptively, failing only to feel the sting himself: "—Certainly it was ordained as a scourge upon the pride of human wisdom, That the wisest of us all, should thus outwit ourselves, and eternally forego our purposes in the intemperate act of pursuing them" (v.xvi.375). No better statement than this is available, to my mind, of Sterne's fundamental quarrel with the philosophy of life and art which his ironic persona brings to the task of writing his biography. That Tristram can deliver this condemnation of himself, wholly blind to its implications, serves only to reinforce the legitimacy of Sterne's satiric campaign and the brilliance of his choice of an ironic persona to wage it.

In returning to the *Tristrapœdia* after the circumcision, Walter offers to Toby and Yorick the contents of two chapters, one on health, the other on his theory of auxiliary verbs. For a change, Walter cuts through, rather than builds upon, the writings of the past; health depending, he says, upon the "contention for mastery betwixt the *radical heat* and the *radical moisture*" (V.xxxiii.394), he takes us in and out of Bacon's web, to his own final conclusion: "—So that if a child, as he grows up, can but be taught to avoid running into fire or water, as either of 'em threaten his destruction,—'twill be all that is needful to be done upon that head" (V.xxxvi.397–98).[5] Walter has taken his hobby-horse the long way around to this sensible advice; but no sooner is his conclusion spoken than Trim and Toby take it for another ride, concluding by way of the siege of Limerick that the radical heat is brandy for the wealthy and a dram of geneva for the poor, and the radical moisture is ditch-water for both. As so often happens in *Tristram Shandy*, Sterne mounts an attack on several targets at once: against philosophers, against physicians, against the literalness of Trim and the hobby-horse of Toby. In addition, the entire subject of health must be seen as ancillary to the role of illness, injury, and death in Sterne's satiric design, the shaping of our awareness of man's frailty and susceptibility.

If Tristram's health is not significantly advanced by Walter's *Tristrapœdia*, his intellect falls even further behind. The theory of auxiliary verbs is the *reductio ad absurdum* (and yet is also borrowed from a real source[6]) of the fate of words in *Tristram Shandy*. It has already been noted that much of the confusion in both the Shandy household and Tristram's study is caused by words—their capacity to confound and betray the speaker, their tendency to take on hobby-horsical and bawdy connotations, their frequent irrelevance to the reality they are intended to represent.

5. Yorick provides the attitude with which we are to take Walter's rare moments of insight: "*Yorick* listened to my father with great attention; there was a seasoning of wisdom unaccountably mixed up with his strangest whims, and he had sometimes such illuminations in the darkest of his eclipses, as almost attoned for them:—be wary, Sir, when you imitate him" (V.xlii.404).
6. Obadiah Walker's *Of Education*, 1699. See John M. Turnbull, "The Prototype of Walter Shandy's 'Tristrapaedia,'" *RES*, II (1926), 212–15.

Walter's theory would free words completely from any responsibility to meaning; rather than *express* ideas, Walter would have words *create* them. The process is significantly mechanical: "Now the use of the *Auxiliaries* is, at once to set the soul a going by herself upon the materials as they are brought her; and by the versability of this great engine, round which they are twisted, to open new tracks of enquiry, and make every idea engender millions" (v.xlii.405). This is Walter's "North-west passage to the intellectual world," dramatically demonstrated in the concluding chapter of Volume V. It is, indeed, a fitting close to a volume in which the Shandean hopes for perpetuation are twice cut off; the Shandy efforts at creation, both of an heir and of a book, have reached an ignominious impasse of uncreating chaos in the shaping of one million ideas about a white bear. The implications of death—physical, emotional, and intellectual—suddenly pervade and overwhelm the Shandy household.

For Tristram in his study, the creative process is also marked by increasing dissolution and chaos in these two volumes. Volume V opens with Tristram's swift flight from imitators, ironically followed by an imitation of Robert Burton's attack on plagiarizers. The image of speed has been sufficiently established in earlier volumes to warn us not to sympathize too long with Tristram. That Sterne was being profusely imitated is a historical fact, but that Sterne and Tristram are one in this opening chapter is hardly demonstrable. Surely Sterne's intention is ironic when he has Tristram write of plagiarists: "Who made MAN, with powers which dart him from earth to heaven in a moment—that great, that most excellent, and most noble creature of the world—the *miracle* of nature, as Zoroaster . . . called him . . . —the *image* of God, as Moses—the *ray* of divinity, as Plato—the *marvel* of *marvels*, as Aristotle—to go sneaking on at this pitiful—pimping—pettifogging rate?" (v.i.343). Tristram's pride in mankind and in himself as an author is a primary target of Sterne's satire against his persona. In this instance, such pride is contrasted to an image of sluggish movement which, in turn, contrasts sharply with Tristram's swift flight: "He flew like lightning— . . . we scarce touched the ground—the motion was most rapid—most impetuous—'twas communicated to my brain—my heart partook of it . . . " (v.i.342). Sterne seems intent upon opening the volume with a picture of Tristram well mounted and galloping; no other reason exists, for example, that can justify the inclusion in chapter i of the "chapter on whiskers," a bawdy fragment which complements, though feebly, "Slawkenbergius's Tale." There is defiance in Tristram's tone as he offers it "as a legacy in *mort main* to Prudes and Tartufs, to enjoy and make the most of," and a certain bad taste not to be found in the earlier play on noses. In the first place, the entire issue of "noses" arises out of the Shandy household, unlike "beards" which merely fulfills a self-imposed debt to the reader. Second, because our concupiscence has already been implicated once by this particular device, it is no longer effective in proving the point. Insofar as Tristram as an author provides only what we want, a repetition of "Slawkenbergius's Tale" does, perhaps, prove a point; my own opinion, however, is that the "Fragment" does not even please our concupiscence this second time, and therefore proves nothing but Tristram's own licentiousness. It is such a weak reflection of Slawkenbergius that it suggests a conscious disparity between the two, as if Sterne were foreshadowing Tristram's coming decline at the very outset of these two volumes.

We return to Tristram's study in chapter xi and again in chapter xv. In both, Tristram offers a puzzling, almost surrealistic flow of ideas, indicative, I believe, not of Sterne's psychological insight, but of Tristram's mental dissolution. We have already glanced at V.xi, in which Tristram, remembering his mother by the door, interrupts Trim before he can start Le Fever's story. He has, he tells us, "forgot my mother, as if Nature had plaistered me up, and set me down naked upon the banks of the river *Nile*, without one." The idea leads Tristram to an apostrophe to the river and an interesting reduction of himself to a piece of damaged mud: "—Your most obedient servant, Madam—I've cost you a great deal of trouble,—I wish it may answer;—but you have left a crack in my back,—and here's a great piece fallen off here before,—and what must I do with this foot?—I shall never reach *England* with it" (V.xi.367). As with Tristram's most far-fetched digressions and meanderings thus far, the paragraph makes associational sense, though, as always, we question the lack of Tristram's artistic selectivity. But the next paragraph begins, "For my own part I never wonder at any thing;—and so often has my judgment deceived me in my life, that I always suspect it, right or wrong,—at least I am seldom hot upon cold subjects" (V.xi.367), and no link—psychological, rhetorical, grammatical—is to be found.

Were this an isolated occurrence, I would hesitate to give it any significance; but it marks, I believe, an ever increasing tendency on Tristram's part to lose what little control he has over his runaway book. At the same time, some of his self-assuredness, his easy faith in his own intellectual and creative abilities, seems to be shaken.

Between the brazen and defiant opening of Volume V with the fragment on beards and this chapter have come the funeral orations of Toby and Trim. The writing of them seems to have affected Tristram's exuberance, opened his eyes to other possibilities. He takes, for example, a noticeably moderate position now on man's quest for truth: "For all this, I reverence truth as much as any body; and when it has slipped us, if a man will but take me by the hand, and go quietly and search for it, as for a thing we have both lost, and can neither of us do well without,—I'll go to the world's end with him . . ." (v.xi.367). This is a far cry from the galloping madness in which Tristram overthrew Horace and predicted, in Volume I, a final end to all learning, so far have we advanced in the "last seven years." Moreover, Tristram's next assertion, that to avoid a dispute he would "almost subscribe to any thing which does not choak me in the first passage . . ." suggests an unwillingness on his part to mount a hobby-horse, to have an opinion. To paraphrase Sterne, we did not know he ever dismounted. There is rich irony in Tristram's resolve, "from the beginning, That if ever the army of martyrs was to be augmented, —or a new one raised,—I would have no hand in it, one way or t'other." Tristram is as much a martyr to his book as Walter to his theories and Toby to the military life. His insistence on following no rules causes him to suffer continually the anxieties of promised chapters, misplaced scenes, and his mother stranded by the keyhole; his desire for inclusiveness and historicity subjects him to the indignities of five minutes less than no time at all and indecent self-exposures; and, most important, his theory of two volumes a year until he finishes his autobiography assures us that Tristram will be carrying his cross to the grave. Walter, suffering constant defeat at the hands of his theories, and Toby, carrying on his mock battles for the good of the country (having been wounded in the groin by the real thing), are certainly enlisted in the army of martyrs. And Tristram, offspring of them both, has, until this moment, been keeping step.

A sense of acute disorientation and dissolution is evident much more vividly in chapter xv where Tristram suddenly finds himself in an orchestra pit, tuning his violin:

> HAD this volume been a farce, which, unless every one's life and opinions are to be looked upon as a farce as well as mine, I see no reason to suppose—the last chapter, Sir, had finished the first act of it, and then this chapter must have set off thus.
> Ptr . . r . . r . . ing—twing—twang—prut—trut——'tis a cursed bad fiddle (V.xv.371).

Tristram's play on the word "farce" provides both an ironic self-appraisal of his efforts thus far and the signal which sets him fiddling. The conversation in the pit, punctuated by onomato-poetic attempts to imitate "musical" sounds, is disjointed, somewhat mad—Tristram plays "three hundred and fifty leagues out of tune," in order to demonstrate that some of the audience are totally deaf to a bad note. He would, he says, "rather play a *Caprichio* to *Calliope* herself," than play for them, and he stakes his "*Cremona* to a *Jew*'s trump" ("which is the greatest musical odds that ever were laid") that "the grave man in black.—'Sdeath! not the gentleman with the sword on" will, in particular, be unaffected by his "krish—krash—krush." Tristram thus renews the attack on gravity, Yorick's favorite target, and suggests at the same time that his fit audience is the cavalier. But while this is the obvious meaning of the conversation, it is also possible that the "grave man in black" is representative of Death, a possibility reinforced by the oath which immediately follows and by the fact that this scene follows the funeral orations for Bobby. Tristram's hyperbolic style in this passage is, I believe, a warning against too ready an acceptance of his point of view.[7] That "gravity" cannot hear his music is one thing; that Death is deaf to it is another. Tristram's creation is an effort to undo Death—"but you see he is no worse." As with the Shandy household, Tristram in his study begins to face the reality of death, though at present, death is no more to him than gravity, the stolidity so unlike his own sensibilities: "O! there is—whom I could sit and hear whole days,—whose talents lie in making what he fiddles to be felt,—who inspires me with

7. In addition to the "three hundred and fifty leagues," "the greatest musical odds," and playing a "*Caprichio* to *Calliope*," Tristram's violin plays "a mile too high," and he would, in the end, surrender it to Apollo. All this, within one paragraph, indicates a conscious overreaching on Sterne's part.

his joys and hopes, and puts the most hidden springs of my heart into motion" (V.xv.372). The reader's inclination is to accept as valid the alternatives Tristram offers—deaf gravity on the one hand, the sentimental cavalier on the other. But Tristram's idea of gravity is not Yorick's idea; Tristram's gravity is tainted with the seriousness of death, which Yorick not only understands but also represents. As always, the choosing of a proper alternative in *Tristram Shandy* is no simple task.

It would be an error to suggest that Tristram drops out of sight for the rest of Volume V, since his presence is often felt in the chapters dedicated to the Shandy household. It is true, however, that we do not return to his study in any notable way until he delivers the story of Le Fever in VI.vi. To be sure, Walter's discovery in V.xvi that his *Tristrapædia* is being defeated by time is, as already suggested, an important comment on Tristram in his study. The circumcision is also important to Tristram's study; Tristram tells us that on "this day (*August* the 10th, 1761)" he is still paying part of the price of Dr. Slop's reputation. This is explained more fully in Volume VI, when Tristram writes:

> WHAT a jovial and a merry world would this be, may it please your worships, but for that inextricable labyrinth of debts, cares, woes, want, grief, discontent, melancholy, large jointures, impositions, and lies!
> Doctor *Slop*, like a son of a w—, as my father called him for it,—to exalt himself,—debased me to death,—and made ten thousand times more of *Susannah's* accident, than there was any grounds for . . . (VI.xiv.432–33).

The "world," Walter's principal concern, becomes convinced that Tristram has been castrated (or so we assume from the aposiopesis). Toby would show him publicly in the marketplace; Walter, knowing the world better, knows it would have no effect; he will put him in breeches, "let the world say what it will." The suggestion of castration, of impotence, continues to hover about Tristram forty years later; in particular, it produces an inevitable skepticism concerning his creative efforts. Tristram has finally uncovered himself in the marketplace; and, as Walter predicted, it has no effect.

Walter's *beds of justice* provide Tristram with a significant opportunity for self-analysis in VI.xvii. Noting that Walter holds court before and after the activity of the first Sunday night in the

month, Tristram praises the middle way: " . . . for from the two
different counsels taken in these two different humours, a middle
one was generally found out, which touched the point of wisdom . . . " (VI.xvii.435). Tristram finds the "middle way"
answers literary discussions as well as conjugal, and he adopts a
somewhat altered version for his own use: "In all nice and ticklish
discussions . . . where I find I cannot take a step without the
danger of having either their worships or their reverences upon my
back—I write one half *full*,—and t'other *fasting*;—or write it all
full,—and correct it fasting;—or write it fasting,—and correct it
full, for they all come to the same thing . . . " (VI.xvii.436). The
possibility that Tristram has reconciled the extremes of Walter and
Toby, of wit and judgment, of intellect and sympathy, is here
finally laid to rest. Not reconciliation, but merely alternation is
Tristram's philosophy, and he is most correct when he admits
"they all come to the same thing." The result is not an organic
view of life and art, but a mechanical one: "These different and
almost irreconcileable effects, flow uniformly from the wise and
wonderful mechanism of nature,—of which,—be her's the honour.—All that we can do, is to turn and work the machine to the
improvement and better manufactury of the arts and sciences"
(VI.xvii.436). Tristram writes now from the fullness of his heart
(and of his stomach), now with an eye toward the world, toward
the virtue of discretion; he appeals now to our hearts, now to our
heads. The image of the machine makes clear Sterne's ironic attitude toward Tristram's "creation." His own book, as opposed to
Tristram's, reconciles the extremes of emotion and intellect by a
consistent satiric undercutting of Tristram's pretensions to both.
Unlike his ironic persona, Sterne knows that the middle way lies
not in alternations of eating and fasting, but in a moderate diet.
When measured against this norm, Tristram's "middle way" is an
absurdity.

In chapter xx of Book VI, Tristram changes the direction of his
work with a sharply defined transition. "We are now going to
enter upon a new scene of events," he writes, and he takes formal
leave of Walter, Mrs. Shandy, Slop, Le Fever's son, and almost of
himself: "Let us leave, if possible, *myself*:—But 'tis impossible,—
I must go along with you to the end of the work" (p. 442). As
Wayne Booth has illustrated, Tristram all along promises us
Toby's campaigns and amours, and they thus provide a fitting con-

clusion to a work which seems to have none.[8] But why Sterne
should have Tristram alter the method of six volumes, of inter-
weaving Toby's history with his own (we know a great deal
about Toby already), and why he should indicate so emphatically
this change are questions demanding further inquiry. It is noteworthy, for example, that Tristram abandons all pretense of
getting on with his autobiography, since Toby's campaign and
amours take place before his birth. The growing disorganization
and dissolution of Tristram in his study is here dramatically epit-
omized in the structure of the work; retreating further and further
into the past, Tristram is turned completely around and, to the end
of Volume IX, never regains his bearings.

It is also noteworthy that in spite of his leave-takings, the
Shandy household continues to function as a unit, and continues
to be played against Tristram's study. Only the center of attention
changes—from Walter to Toby, from Walter's house to Toby's
garden. The satiric pattern of opposites and alternatives is still
very much operative, though we are now given a much closer view
of Toby's side of the spectrum. It has been apparent throughout
my discussion that the alternatives are unbalanced: Few, if any, can
accept Walter; few can deny Toby. Thus we leap from one to the
other, and are continually caught in Sterne's satiric trap. The *philosophus gloriosus* is so traditional a target of satire that almost the
entire burden of Sterne's satiric attack thus far has fallen on
Walter's head. Whether it is an absurd theory, a legal or theological
quibble, a bawdy play on words, a scientific investigation, all these
traditional devices reflect the follies of the systematizing mind.
Toby, however, represents a new threat to reasonable men, a mid-
eighteenth-century threat, which, while reflected in many traditional targets, is basically new. Its principal danger is its seeming
innocence, its benevolence, good will, harmlessness—hardly qualities that a satirist readily sets his pen against. To have greatly
exaggerated these qualities in Toby, to have made him obviously
hypocritical, blatantly false, is not the satirist's way. Walter's
theories, though absurd, possess satiric validity because Sterne is
able to authenticate them with citations from the world's library.
To pretend that the Roman Catholic church argued over "une
petite canulle" is fantasy; to present the document in which the
argument occurs is satire. Tristram's sentimentalism in the story of

8. "Did Sterne Complete *Tristram Shandy?*" MP, XLVIII (1951), 172–83.

Le Fever can be satirized as hypocrisy because, as a literary phenomenon, Sterne saw sentimentalism as such. But the attack against
sentimentalism as a mode of thought had to proceed more subtly.
In particular, Sterne had to demonstrate its dangerous insidiousness
by trapping the reader into sympathy with its great practitioner,
Toby. To attack the excesses of sentimentalism, the literary hypocrisies, was relatively simple work; to attack sentimentalism as it
was practiced by the most innocent hearts was the task Sterne cut
out for himself.

Is it possible that anyone could find anything satirical in Toby's
bowling-green turned battlefield? Walter, for one, assures Yorick
that it is impossible: "My father would often say to *Yorick,* that
if any mortal in the whole universe had done such a thing, except
his brother *Toby,* it would have been looked upon by the world
as one of the most refined satyrs upon the parade and prancing
manner, in which *Lewis* XIV . . . had taken the field—But 'tis
not my brother *Toby*'s nature, kind soul! . . . to insult any one"
(VI.xxii.446–47). The possibility that the bowling-green is a
satire of Toby himself would not occur to Walter, but Sterne has
offered us, indirectly, one clue to his attack. Certainly some
part of his satire is directed toward the idea of war itself, the pomp
and the posturing, the science and the slaughter. Toby and Trim
are totally committed to the forms of war—Trim with his spade
on his shoulder, Toby marching the ramparts, both raising
the colors—the elements never "compounded so intoxicating a
draught" (VI.xxii.445). In addition, much like Walter's researches,
Toby and Trim (and Tristram, I might add) are astute students
of the cant and deepest delvings of military science. This is, we
remember, the hobby-horse that gallops Toby out of sickbed into
the country; once there, the movement is toward a more and more
precise and realistic model of the real thing. The *Gazette* is read ten
times over "lest, peradventure, he [Trim] should make the breach
an inch too wide,—or leave it an inch too narrow . . . "
(VI.xxii.445). In the second year, bridges are added; then a gate;
then a sentry box; then a town and a church for the town; in the
fourth year, field pieces— " . . . and so on—(as must always be
the case in hobby-horsical affairs) from pieces of half an inch
bore, till it came at last to my father's jack boots" (VI.xxiii.448).
The area of the bowling-green is much smaller than that of
Walter's vast "learning"; it is apparent, nevertheless, that Toby's

hobby-horse has a great deal of room to romp in, and to press into its service whatever it comes in contact with. The leaden weights from Tristram's window, we remember, serve the cause. Trim's most brilliant stroke, however, the converting of his Turkish pipes into smoke-makers, occurs under memorable circumstances: "As this was the most memorable attack in the whole war,—the most gallant and obstinate on both sides,—and I must add the most bloody too, for it cost the allies themselves that morning above eleven hundred men,—my uncle *Toby* prepared himself for it with a more than ordinary solemnity" (VI.xxiv.450). Surely Sterne is recalling to our minds something Toby, with all his "goodness," seems to have forgotten about war.

With Toby and Trim mounted and charging, Tristram suddenly stops his narration to return to his study. Both men are now dead: Trim's "warm heart . . . with all its generous and open vessels, compressed into a *clod of the valley*"; Toby, at rest under a velvet pall decorated with his military ensigns (VI.xxv.452). The juxtaposition of the two scenes is ultimately more central to Sterne's satire than any of his incidental attacks on the follies and evils of war. That Toby seems oblivious to the men who die in each of the battles which give him so much pleasure is certainly worth noting; but it is his own hobby-horsical obliviousness to his own fate which is, I believe, Sterne's ultimate target. As with Walter and Tristram, Toby's activities must be measured against the inevitability of death, the frailty of man and the impermanence of all his endeavors. Toby's masterful creation of one miniature battlefield after another cannot serve, in any reasonable way, a meaningful life; when Toby is measured, he too must be found wanting. Ignoring the unpleasant ("The sentry-box was in case of rain") and the inevitable, Toby can see only one pleasure following the other, one battle and then another in his microcosm. But Toby's world, although so exact a copy in every detail, is not the real world where the unpleasant and the inevitable thrust themselves into man's awareness; the Treaty of Utrecht brings it tumbling down.

Walter does not let pass the opportunity to take a stroke at his brother's disappointment: "—Never mind, brother *Toby*, he would say,—by God's blessing we shall have another war break out again some of these days; and when it does,—the belligerent powers . . . cannot keep us out of play.—I defy 'em . . . to take

countries without taking towns,—or towns without sieges"
(VI.xxxi.458). Insofar as Sterne is attacking the military establish-
ment as he had earlier attacked the scholastic, the critical, the medi-
cal, and so forth, this is a barbed comment on the state of war
which men perpetuate in the name of God and peace. But the
satire cuts deeper, I believe, and its full intent is revealed only in
Toby's answer to his brother—his longest sustained speech in the
work. Toby would divide war into two parts—on the one hand,
the glory, on the other, the misery—and he assures us that he
knows both parts: ". . . because, brother *Shandy*, my blood flew
out into the camp, and my heart panted for war,—was it a proof
it could not ache for the distresses of war too?" (VI.xxxii.461).
Like Tristram, Toby feels that he has reconciled opposites, and he
takes issue with Yorick's view of war: "Need I be told, dear *Yorick*,
as I was by you, in *Le Fever*'s funeral sermon, *That so soft and
gentle a creature, born to love, to mercy, and kindness, as man is,
was not shaped for this?*—But why did you not add, *Yorick*,—if
not by NATURE—that he is so by NECESSITY?—For what is war?
what is it, *Yorick*, when fought as ours has been, upon principles
of *liberty*, and upon principles of *honour* . . . but the getting together of quiet and harmless people . . . to keep the ambitious and
the turbulent within bounds?" (VI.xxxii.462). I am not certain
that Yorick speaks here for Sterne's thought; a mind fully cognizant of the necessity of evil in the world might be compelled to
accept Toby's argument for the necessity of war. If, indeed, Toby
does provide Sterne's view, it is only ironic that he does so, and
equally ironic that Sterne puts into Yorick's mouth those sentiments we normally associate with Toby. Toby's absurd inflation,
immediately following, of his bowling-green activities, strongly
suggests that he does not understand the reconciliation he urges of
man's nature and war in necessity; that like Tristram he alternates
opposites, but is incapable of reconciling them: "And heaven is my
witness . . . that infinite delight . . . which has attended my sieges
in my bowling green, has arose within me . . . from the consciousness we both had, that in carrying them on, we were answering the
great ends of our creation" (VI.xxxii.462).

Toby's vaunted sympathy may well feel the miseries of war, but
his hobby-horse has carried him so far down the path of unreason
that he is unable to accept the peace which ends them. Toby does
not dismount: ". . . his horse rather flung him—and somewhat

viciously, which made my uncle *Toby* take it ten times more un-kindly" (VI.xxxiv.463). The feeling heart is no match for the mounted body. The carefully created microcosm must, with equal care, be demolished, and Toby sinks into desuetude, with silence, stillness, and listlessness for companions. The sense of uncreation is strong in these closing pages of Volume VI, the chaos in Tris-tram's study echoing the demolition of Dunkirk. In chapter xxxiii, Tristram opens "I Told the Christian reader . . ." and then breaks off to explain the troubles he is having: ". . . when a man is telling a story in the strange way I do mine, he is obliged continually to be going backwards and forwards to keep all tight together in the reader's fancy—which . . . if I did not take heed to do more than at first, there is so much unfixed and equivocal matter starting up, with so many breaks and gaps in it,—and so little service do the stars afford, which, nevertheless, I hang up in some of the darkest pas-sages, knowing that the world is apt to lose its way . . .—and now, you see, I am lost myself!——" (VI.xxxiii.462). It is, he tells us, his father's fault, and describes the errant thread in his brain; then, totally astray, he begins the chapter over again. What he really wanted to tell the Christian reader was Toby's plan for the demoli-tion of Dunkirk: ". . . we'll demolish the mole,—next fill up the harbour,—then retire into the citadel, and blow it up into the air; and having done that, corporal, we'll embark for *England.*—We are there, quoth the corporal, recollecting himself—Very true, said my uncle *Toby*—looking at the church" (VI.xxxiv.465). Tristram is lost in his book; Toby is lost on the bowling green, and somehow this is important to the Christian reader in particular. That both men have made their own wilderness is clear; that the Shandy dreams of creation are being everywhere shattered is also clear. Only the widow Wadman stands between the Shandys and total dissolution; concupiscence must accomplish what reason and sentiment could not.

 VII

"Tristram Shandy" as a Satire
Volumes VII, VIII, and IX

> *I will not argue the matter: Time
> wastes too fast: every letter I trace tells
> me with what rapidity Life follows my
> pen; the days and hours of it, more
> precious, my dear Jenny! than the rubies
> about thy neck, are flying over our heads
> like light clouds of a windy day, never
> to return more. . . .*
> *—Heaven have mercy upon us
> both!*
>
> (IX.viii.610-11)

Volumes VII, VIII, and IX

ALTHOUGH Volumes VII and VIII were published together in 1765, and Volume IX separately in 1767, a more natural division would be between Volume VII, the trip to the continent, and Volumes VIII and IX, both of which are primarily concerned with Toby's amours. For this reason, and because the three volumes are of the approximate length of the earlier two-volume sets, I shall discuss them together. It is one of the arguments of my analysis that Tristram's creative powers are fast withering, that he is caught in the chaos of his own creating, the impossibility of the task he set for himself. Sterne's own history at this time, reflected in the shortness of these volumes and the length of time he let elapse before undertaking them, suggests that he, too, was tiring of his project. How much of the general fatigue which pervades these last volumes is autobiographical and how much is part of Sterne's satiric design, while an interesting question, is perhaps never to be satisfactorily answered. The critic who persists, however, in treating the volumes solely as an autobiographical manifestation denies, in doing so, Sterne's dedication as an artist and the evidence of the first six volumes. My own contention is that Sterne from the beginning of *Tristram Shandy* in creation and birth had planned a conclusion in sickness and impotence, fatigue and death; and that, in spite of his own failing health and perhaps failing interest as well, he never abandoned his view of *Tristram Shandy* as an artistic construction.

Volume VII stands squarely in the middle of this question since it appears to be Sterne's travel notes, hastily worked into the Shandy world in order to have adequate material for publication. The history of the Shandy family, particularly of Toby's amours, is thrust aside as death pursues Tristram in a mad chase across Europe. Though written three years later, the opening chapter of Volume VII is only a page away, considering the work as an organic whole, from the discussion of curvy and straight lines which closes the sixth volume. Having lost both himself and Toby in the chaos of their respective worlds, Tristram had revived just in time to close the volume on a note of optimistic self-confidence such as he had not exhibited since the opening volumes. It is widow Wadman who brings this new hope to Tristram, the chance to "turn out one of the most compleat systems, both of the elementary and practical part of love and love-making, that ever was addressed to the world . . ." (VI.xxxvi.466). Tristram begins to see his way through his self-created mazes; diagraming his volumes in chapter xl, he perceives that in Volume V he had somewhat smoothed out his line of progression, and in VI had "done better still—for from the end of *Le Fever's* episode, to the beginning of my uncle *Toby's* campaigns,—I have scarce stepped a yard out of my way" (VI.xl.474); he feels confident that he can now proceed in a "tolerable straight line." There is irony in Tristram's straight line, however, since it is going in the wrong direction, moving further and further into the past and away from the life and opinions of Tristram Shandy. Moreover the juxtaposition of Tristram's hopefulness at the close of Volume VI and his flight in Volume VII must also be seen as ironic, suggesting the ultimate defeat of his project. Insofar as Volume VII is digressive, first, from the straight line of Toby's amours, and more importantly, from the biography Tristram is supposed to be writing, we may speak of the disorderliness, even disintegration, of the work. But insofar as Volume VII suggests the immediacy of that dissolution and death which have been gathering like storm clouds over the Shandy world, we must recognize that the disorder and disintegration are part of Tristram's study and not Sterne's. Indeed, Sterne suggests as much in the motto for Volume VII: *"Non enim excursus hic ejus, sed opus ipsum est"*: "For this is not an excursion from it, but is the work itself." A reading of *Tristram Shandy* as satire proves this to be the case.

Sterne draws together several satiric traditions in Volume VII, an understanding of which helps to define his purpose. The journey, for example, had long been in use among satirists, particularly for the advantage it offers of a dramatically different point of view. Sterne does not use the fantasy common to many imaginary voyages, but he achieves the same expansion of perspective by juxtaposing the trip to France with the narrow confines of his study and the Shandy household. At the same time, Sterne glances at the "dance of death" tradition in having Death lead Tristram (or, more accurately, pursue him) across the length of France to a final dance with Nannette in the last chapter. Like the *memento mori* tradition, the *danse macabre* is not essentially a satiric tradition. In the close relationship between sermon and satire in the fifteenth and sixteenth centuries, however, it passed freely from one to the other and became one of the satirist's methods to remind his reader of the ubiquity of death, the ultimate last journey to the grave. And finally, Sterne makes use of Tristram to ridicule the guide books and travelogues of his day, the volume having a rather clearly defined parodic purpose. Tristram is a far more active agent of parody here than elsewhere; he is aware of the follies of his fellow-travelers and both mimics and mocks their efforts with delightful results. By means of these devices Sterne incorporates Volume VII into the satiric organization of the entire work, broadening the scope of his satiric targets, dramatically revealing the nature of his satiric norms, and, in general, furthering his satiric purposes.

The arrival of Death at Tristram's door in VII.i is sudden and unexpected only to those readers who have failed to recognize the importance of death in the design of *Tristram Shandy*. To the reader who has noted death's growing dominance in Tristram's study throughout Volumes V and VI, Death's knock is a logical and dramatic consequence of Tristram's previous activity. His book, Tristram reminds us, was to continue at two volumes a year, "these forty years"; now, three years have been lost to his "vile cough," and Tristram hears Death at the door, interrupting, significantly, his telling of a "most tawdry" story to Eugenius. Good health and good spirits are what Tristram depended upon to finish his project; and against his spirits, which keep him mounted "upon a long stick, and playing the fool . . . nineteen hours out of the twenty-four . . ." (VII.i.479), he has no complaints. But Tristram's body is beginning to fail him, and the "spirits" which once could keep away the sable and sickly green, could send Death away in "so gay a tone of careless indifference" that He thought Himself mistaken, now seems less efficacious. As the physical world defeated Walter at every turn, and as it will defeat Toby in his amours, so now, Sterne's primary emphasis falls on Tristram's body—on the physical nature of man (and this includes his "tawdry" stories) which inevitably reasserts itself as part of the human condition.

Tristram's refusal to accept this inevitability, his mad dance with Death, must be seen as ironic, for his spirit, his hobby-horsical nature, has been shown to be always a manifestation of the body as well. Tristram's decision to fly is replete with clues to its importance in the satiric design of *Tristram Shandy*; for example, Eugenius offers us a brief but piercing reminder of the religious significance of Tristram's adversary:

> But there is no *living, Eugenius,* replied I, at this rate; for as this *son of a whore* has found out my lodgings—
> —You call him rightly, said *Eugenius,*—for by sin, we are told, he enter'd the world . . . (VII.i.480).

Tristram, however, has made promises in spite of death, and he must keep them in the face of it; "I care not which way he enter'd" he replies to Eugenius, "provided he be not in such a hurry to take me out with him—for I have forty volumes to write, and forty thousand things to say and do, which no body in the world will say and do for me, except thyself . . ." (VII.i.480). Death has Tristram by the throat and his voice is barely audible to Eugenius; but, depending on his "two spider legs" Tristram will "lead him a dance he little thinks of"—he will gallop and scamper to the world's end if need be. The dance of death is ironically combined with the hobby-horse, and the body of Tristram is shown in its advanced state of disintegration:

> Pray captain, quoth I, as I was going down into the cabin, is a man never overtaken by *Death* in this passage?
> Why, there is not time for a man to be sick in it, replied he—What a cursed lyar! for I am sick as a horse, quoth I, already—what a brain!—upside down!—hey dey! the cells are broke loose one into another, and the blood, and the lymph, and the nervous juices . . . are all jumbled into one mass—good g——! every thing turns round in it like a thousand whirlpools—I'd give a shilling to know if I shan't write the clearer for it—
> Sick! sick! sick! sick!—(VII.ii.481).

Yet, like the spider, Tristram will continue to spin out of himself, the vast, intricate webs of no more power to withstand physical assault than his forty books to write and forty thousand things to say can withstand the rush of time and death. As the increasing dissolution of his book in Volumes V and VI presaged his present physi-

cal dissolution, so now his sickness of body portends the ever increasing confusion and chaos of his literary endeavors. One need
not, by the way, ignore the comic proportions of Tristram's sea-
sickness in order to see its significance to the satiric design.

The primary device used by Sterne in parodying the travel-books
of his day is to juxtapose their pedantic, pompous, and pontifical
pretensions with what Tristram calls "the visionary brain." If the
typical traveler tells us that Calais was once a village and is now
a city—"it must have grown up by little and little, I suppose, to
it's present size" (VII.v.484)—Tristram simply informs us that
"it was dusky in the evening when I landed, and dark as pitch in
the morning when I set out," and so he knows nothing at all
about Calais. In both cases, whether one *"wrote and gallop'd"* or
"gallop'd and wrote" or, again, *"wrote-galloping,"* the traveler is
well mounted, proceeding with extraordinary speed through a
land which he does not see. While the pedantry of the travel-book
writers forms an interesting backdrop, it is, of course, Tristram's
"visionary brain" which is in the forefront of our attention. At
Boulogne, only a young girl catches his eye; at Montreuil, he
notices only the inn-keeper's daughter. He races to Abbeville to
see how they card and spin—"but the carders and spinners were
all gone to bed" (VII.x.491); he sees Chantilly in a passion, and
states that " 'tis the best principle . . . to travel speedily upon; for
as few objects look very inviting in that mood—you have little
or nothing to stop you . . ." (VII.xvi.497).[1] Passion enables him
to pass through St. Dennis without turning his head. In Paris,
whatever he reports is qualified by the poor illumination; of
Fontainbleau, Sens, and Joigny, there is nothing to say.

Auxerre, however, stops him momentarily, as he recalls his
Grand Tour in company with Walter and Toby and their visit to
St. Optat's tomb: " 'Twas as successful a short visit as ever was
paid to the dead . . ." (VII.xxvii.515); but, as the Shandys decide
to stay another day, he leaves them: "—NOW this is the most
puzzled skein of all—for in this last chapter . . . I have been getting
forwards in two different journies together, and with the same
dash of the pen—for I have got entirely out of *Auxerre* in this
journey which I am writing now, and I am got half way out of

1. Tristram later recants this principle, saying that "it has spoiled me the
digestion of a good supper, and brought on a bilious diarrhæa . . . " (VII.
xix.502).

Auxerre in that which I shall write hereafter . . ." (VII.xxviii.515).
At Lyons he wants to see Lippius' clock, the thirty volumes of the
history of China (written in Chinese) at the Jesuit library, and,
most important, the *Tomb of the two lovers.*[2] But the clock is
broken; the Jesuits all have the cholic; only the tomb is left to be
seen:

> —I walk'd with all imaginable joy towards the place—when
> I saw the gate which intercepted the tomb, my heart glowed
> within me—
> —Tender and faithful spirits! cried I, addressing myself
> to *Amandus* and *Amanda*—long—long have I tarried to
> drop this tear upon your tomb——I come——I come——
> When I came—there was no tomb to drop it upon (VII.xl.
> 532).

And finally, Tristram finishes his journey in the "rich plains" of
Languedoc, where his "visionary brain" fastens on the "cursed slit"
in Nannette's petticoat.

In Languedoc, Tristram assures us that unlike those dull writers
who can find nothing to say about the plains, he will manage
better. The secret, he tells us, is to turn the plain into a city, by
seizing a conversation with every soul he meets. It is clear, however,
that Tristram's conversations, here and throughout France, are of
a uniform nature, almost always salacious, and seductive where possible. Except for one allusion to Jenny, we have not seen this Tristram before: *"Ah! ma chere fille!* said I, as she tripp'd by, from
her matins—you look as rosy as the morning (for the sun was
rising, and it made the compliment the more gracious)— . . .
(she made a curt'sy to me—I kiss'd my hand) . . ." (VII.vii.487).
Again in Montreuil, Tristram is smitten, this time with an inn-
keeper's daughter: "—A slut! . . . within these five minutes that I
have stood looking at her, she has let fall at least a dozen loops in
a white thread stocking—Yes, yes—I see, you cunning gipsy!—'tis
long, and taper . . ." (VII.ix.490). Both flirtations are of the
briefest duration and of no consequence, and in this, perhaps, lies
their significance. In the first instance, Tristram turns from the

2. Tristram's praise of the story of Amandus and Amanda and his ludicrous
retelling of it provide a strong indication of Sterne's attitude toward sentimentalism, e.g.: "There is a soft æra in every gentle mortal's life, where such a story
affords more *pabulum* to the brain ["the brain being tender and fibrillous, and
more like pap than any thing else"], than all the *Frusts,* and *Crusts,* and *Rusts*
of antiquity, which travellers can cook up for it" (VII.xxxi.520–21).

girl to answer the gossipmongers' charge that he is fleeing from debt; his only debt, he assures them, is the debt of Nature, "and I want but patience of her, and I will pay her every farthing I owe her——How can you be so hard-hearted, MADAM, to arrest a poor traveller . . . ? do stop that death-looking, long-striding scoundrel of a scare-sinner, who is posting after me—he never would have followed me but for you . . ." (VII.vii.487). This apostrophe to Nature is mistaken by Tristram's host, who regrets that all "this good courtship should be lost," since the young woman is out of hearing. "Simpleton!" answers Tristram; but the host has drawn a valid comparison, for Tristram's interest in young women has much to do with his physical decline, his sense of an impending conclusion which a young, willing woman could somehow forestall. In the flirtation with Janatone at Montreuil, Tristram is also concerned with time; and, weighing whether he had best draw the dimensions of an abbey or of Janatone, he decides that while the abbey will last "these fifty years" ("if the belief in *Christ* continues so long") she will not: ". . . thou carriest the principles of change within thy frame; and considering the chances of a transitory life, I would not answer for thee a moment; e'er twice twelve months are pass'd . . . thou mayest grow out like a pumkin, and lose thy shapes—or, thou mayest go off like a flower, and lose thy beauty—nay, thou mayest go off like a hussy—and lose thyself" (VII.ix.490). Tristram ultimately neither paints Janatone nor wins her, but his desire to capture the fleeting moment, to halt inexorable time, is again relevant to Sterne's satire, as is Tristram's ironic dismissal of the only Christian hope for eternal life—the belief in Christ. Tristram's "courtships" may be seen as efforts to somehow perpetuate the transient, to delay and humor the indefatigable progress of time while yet refusing to quit its sway. Tristram's game with time here takes on an entirely new dimension; enamoured always with the possibilities of the "here and now," the present moment in its countless ramifications, he is suddenly presented with the cruel rush of time, in one vignette after another. His efforts to halt it are doomed to failure.

Sterne presses home his point in one of the most dramatic scenes in *Tristram Shandy*, Tristram's moment of failure with Jenny. Discussing his ability to make the best of the disasters of life, he calls on Jenny for proof:

—Do, my dear *Jenny*, tell the world for me, how I be-
haved under one, the most oppressive of its kind which could
befall me as a man, proud, as he ought to be, of his man-
hood—

'Tis enough, said'st thou, coming close up to me, as I
stood with my garters in my hand, reflecting upon what had
not pass'd—'Tis enough, *Tristram*, and I am satisfied . . . —
any other man would have sunk down to the center—

—Every thing is good for something, quoth I.

—I'll go into *Wales* for six weeks, and drink goat's-whey
—and I'll gain seven years longer life for the accident (VII.
xxix.517–18).

The creative urge which earlier had dominated the Shandy world
has been under constant threat from every direction; nowhere,
however, is its failure more starkly revealed than here—and revealed under circumstances of self-exposure, and, indeed, of self-
immolation, which suggest that Sterne's satire is not always light
and pleasant. Tristram's public display of his sexual impotence is,
metaphorically, a reaffirmation of the intellectual and emotional
impotence which has all along been seen as part of the satiric
attack on his book. But now, the self-exposure of the one reflects
upon the self-exposure of the other; Tristram's public display of
his incompetence as both an author and a "man of feeling" is made
to bear the burden of his appearance, garters in hand. The significance of Tristram in his study receives its full measure by comparison to Tristram in his bedroom; and as the clock and the miles
measure Death's relentlessness, Tristram tries, in Boulogne, in
Montreuil, in Languedoc, to make Death dance to another tune.
But when the opportunity comes, particularly with Nannette in
Languedoc, Tristram fails again: "—Why could I not live and
end my days thus? Just disposer of our joys and sorrows, cried I,
why could not a man sit down in the lap of content here—and
dance, and sing, and say his prayers, and go to heaven with this
nut brown maid? Capriciously did she bend her head on one side,
and dance up insiduous—Then 'tis time to dance off, quoth I . . ."
(VII.xliii.538). Faced with the reality of fulfillment, Tristram
flees from it, repeating the process all along the southern coast of
France. The world of procreation (and, of course, creation) is not
Tristram's world, and with Death still leading the dance, he ends
his journey and begins the story of Toby's amours. Ironically, the

last words of Book VII are suggestive of birth—"I begun thus—";
Toby's amours will prove as sterile as Tristram's.

The primary image of Volume VII, obviously, is that of the
journey itself. From the beginning, however, Sterne makes it apparent that far from being a unique image in *Tristram Shandy*,
the "journey" must be understood in the context of the galloping
hobby-horses of the Shandy world. Speed is still of the essence,
as it is in the Shandy household and Tristram's study, but "collision" has been replaced by "breakdown" as a concomitant image.
Certainly Tristram is talking about more than the French post-
chaise, when he aphorizes: "WHEN the precipitancy of a man's
wishes hurries on his ideas ninety times faster than the vehicle he
rides in—woe be to truth! and woe be to the vehicle and its
tackling (let 'em be made of what stuff you will) upon which he
breathes forth the disappointment of his soul!" (VII.viii.488). In
several key passages in Volume VII, Tristram returns to the implications of this passage, providing, to some degree, a series of normative statements by which we may measure his precipitant flight from
death as part of the totality of Shandean folly. He tells us, for example, in chapter xi: "WHAT a vast advantage is travelling! only
it heats one; but there is a remedy for that, which you may pick
out of the next chapter" (VII.xi.491). The remedy is that one may
die at an inn where "the few cold offices . . . would be purchased
with a few guineas" instead of dying at home, where the "quiver-
ing hand of pale affection . . . will so crucify my soul, that I shall
die of a distemper which my physician is not aware of . . ." (VII.xii.
492). Tristram is hardly convinced by his own notion—he immediately rejects the inn at Abbeville for the purposes of dying; and,
in leading Death a chase across France, he will never find the suit-
able inn. Like the heat generated in riding the hobby-horse, the
heat of traveling is proof to Tristram that he is alive. Citing Bishop
Hall's opinion that "so much motion . . . is so much unquietness;
and so much of rest . . . is so much of heaven," Tristram differs:
"Now, I . . . think differently; and that so much of motion, is so
much of life, and so much of joy—and that to stand still, or get on
but slowly, is death and the devil—" (VII.xiii.493).

Tristram maintains that the Bishop's opinion is a result of his
corpulence, while his own is a result of his thinness, and he suddenly affirms his love for the Pythagorean doctrine of " *'getting out
of the body, in order to think well.'* " He goes on, in one of the

oft-quoted and often misunderstood passages of *Tristram Shandy*: "No man thinks right whilst he is in it; blinded as he must be, with his congenial humours, and drawn differently aside, as the bishop and myself have been, with too lax or too tense a fibre— REASON is, half of it, SENSE; and the measure of heaven itself is but the measure of our present appetites and concoctions—" (VII.xiii.493–94). Tristram has penetrated to the root of the Shandean problem by returning us to the lesson of "The Abuses of Conscience Considered" sermon. That "REASON is, half of it, SENSE" is not a cause of joy, but of grief; not a source of spiritual or social insight, but rather of intellectual blindness.[3] Moreover, the faster Tristram gallops, as we have seen throughout the work, the less probability there is that his opinions will be reasonable; the hobby-horse, we recall, bids farewell to "cool reason and fair discretion." We thus agree with the innkeeper at the next inn, though for a quite different reason, when Tristram asks her who is most wrong, he or Bishop Hall: "You certainly: quoth she, to disturb a whole family so early." All of Tristram's struggles, to be born, to create, to put off death, find their ultimate cause of failure in this fact, that he and the Shandy family, mounted and galloping, are unable to bring reason to bear on the reality which surrounds them. Their desires (senses) drive their reason (ideas) and their bodies (vehicles) far "faster" than they were made to go—and over the wreckage, the destruction and dissolution which we have every-where witnessed in *Tristram Shandy* "breathes forth the disappointment of the soul."

Nor is this merely metaphorical; Sterne's orthodoxy suggests the serious vision of his satire, his serious concern for man's soul at the mercy of his folly. In the next chapter, Tristram closes this discussion by returning to the prediction near its beginning, that Christianity was rapidly to decline (VII.ix.490); the soul, too, is declining:

> In *Lessius's* time . . . they were as little as can be imagined—
> —We find them less *now*—
> And next winter we shall find them less again; so that if we go on from little to less, and from less to nothing, I hesitate not one moment to affirm, that in half a century, at this rate,

3. Cf. Arthur H. Cash, "The Sermon in *Tristram Shandy*," *ELH*, XXXI (1964), 409–10.

we shall have no souls at all; which being the period beyond
which I doubt likewise of the existence of the Christian faith,
'twill be one advantage that both of 'em will be exactly worn
out together (VII.xiv.495).

To refuse to recognize Tristram as an ironic persona, speaking out
of a vision of life diametrically opposed to Sterne's, seems to me, in
the face of such passages, an untenable position. Tristram is not
yet finished: "Blessed *Jupiter*! and blessed every other heathen god
and goddess! for now ye will all come into play again, and with
Priapus at your tails—what jovial times!—but where am I? and
into what a delicious riot of things am I rushing? I—I who must
be cut short in the midst of my days..." (VII.xiv.495). Lost again,
rushing headlong, Tristram recalls death, and then thrusts it aside
again, rushing on to *Ailly au clochers* to hear the chimes. They, too,
are out of order.

The religion which will replace Christianity is never defined, but
a few clues may be found which indicate its nature. For example,
the "Tomb of the two lovers" is, for Tristram, a shrine "as
valuable as that of *Mecca*," and as worthy of a pilgrimage as the
Santa Casa (VII.xxxi.521–22). And in chapter xxxviii, he notes
that the "*French* women . . . love May-poles, *à la folie*—that is,
as much as their matins . . ." (p. 530). Significantly, the May-
pole is set up on the eighth of September, the nativity of the blessed
Virgin Mary. Tristram's worship of Priapus suggests, of course,
the same preoccupation with fornication. That Tristram is traveling through a Roman Catholic country enables Sterne to renew
his attack on that church; and it is significant that he melds the
Catholic worship of objects, the physical manifestations of spiritual
entities, with both licentiousness and sentimentalism. In the bawdy
story of the nuns of Andoüillets, it is the rigid attention to out-
ward form that creates the little humor one finds; Tristram tells the
story because his ink burns his fingers with the desire to write
bouger and *fouter* on paper. One need not insist on a precise analogy
to suggest that the story mirrors the effort of sentimentalism to disguise natural and unnatural physical facts with a façade of proper
forms. Sentiment and the worship of Priapus seem to be Tristram's
answer to failing Christianity, and the suggestion is strong that
there is no important distinction between the two.

The sisters' efforts to stir their mule by shouting *bouger* is
echoed by Tristram's later assertion: "—But with an ass, I can

commune for ever" (VII.xxxii.523). His rush to shed a tear on the "Tomb of the two lovers" is momentarily delayed by an ass block-ing his path, and Tristram, who is always disarmed by the "pa-tient endurance of sufferings, wrote . . . in his looks," takes the opportunity to talk with him: ". . . surely never is my imagination so busy as in framing his responses from the etchings of his coun-tenance—and where those carry me not deep enough—in flying from my own heart into his, and seeing what is natural for an ass to think—as well as a man, upon the occasion" (VII.xxxii.523). Tristram feeds the ass a macaroon, more he admits, for the pleas-antry of "seeing *how* an ass would eat" one than for the sake of benevolence; and when the owner returns and drives the ass away, the end of an osier from his basket catches hold of Tristram's breeches and rips them as he shouts *"Out upon it!"* We do not need Walter's theory that "ass" means passion (VIII.xxxi.584) to recognize Sterne's consistently ambivalent use of the word in *Tris-tram Shandy.* The scatological implications of the passage are somewhat obscure, but no less prurient for being so; as with the sisters of Andoüillets, the implication is that conversing with an ass,[4] in language either as crude as *bouger* or as "sweet" as a maca-roon, is far more likely to heat the speaker than to move the beast. It is noteworthy that the owner of the ass (a commissary) asks Tristram the question that enables us to see how lost Tris-tram has now become. Tristram begins:

—My good friend, quoth I—as sure as I am I—and you are you—
      —And who are you? said he.— —Don't puzzle me; said I (VII.xxxiii.525).

The dissolution of Tristram is now complete; lost in his book, lost in France, he is now lost to himself. I would not imply a meta-physical loss, however. Rather, the juxtaposition of this question and answer, with the passage on the ass, indicates a moral loss:

Out with it, *Dunciad!* let the secret pass,
That Secret to each Fool, that he's an Ass. . . .

---

4. I am not overlooking the fact that it is a mule rather than an ass in the Andoüillets story. I would maintain, in spite of Tristram's protest in Volume VIII, that the horse, the mule, and the ass are one and the same, differing only in that one man's hobby-horse is another man's ass. It is, again, one of the lessons of the "Abuses of Conscience Considered."

It is not fortuitous that in speaking further with the commissary, Tristram, a victim of Sterne's irony, finds occasion to berate the French for their serious character:

> . . . they understand no more of IRONY than this—
>   The comparison was standing close by with his panniers—
> but something seal'd up my lips—I could not pronounce the
> name (VII.xxxiv.526).

Again, it is no accident that when Tristram loses his "remarks" his grief finds a comparison in Sancho Panza, who "when he lost his ass's FURNITURE, did not exclaim more bitterly" (VII.xxxvi. 529). Sterne could not tell us any more clearly his attitude toward his ironic persona.

That Tristram will continue his book after what I have argued is his complete dissolution should not at all surprise us. Pope had captured his character thirty years before, in the lines immediately following those just quoted:

> You think this cruel? take it for a rule,
> No creature smarts so little as a Fool.
>
> .   .   .   .   .   .
>
> Who shames a Scribler? break one cobweb thro',
> He spins the slight, self-pleasing thread anew. . . .[5]

Tristram's lost remarks are "the wisest—the wittiest"; "as full of wit, as an egg is full of meat, and as well worth four hundred guineas, as the said egg is worth a penny . . ." (VII.xxxvii.529–30). In chapter xlii, he flatters himself that he has outdistanced Death; changing from his "precipitate and rattling" course to the pace of a mule, he proceeds across the plains of Languedoc to his final failure with Nannette. In short, both Tristram and his plans continue the same. His choicest morsel remains to be told. The reader, however, before the crucial consideration of Toby's "feeling heart," has been amply exposed to, and informed of, the follies and failures represented by Tristram. If he is still able to accept Tristram's version of the Shandean household as free from a controlling ironic intent, Sterne's purpose in Volume VII has been defeated.

In discussing Volumes VIII and IX together, we may best proceed by tracing, as before, the two separate worlds of the Shandy

5. "An Epistle to Dr. Arbuthnot," 11. 83–84, 89–90 (*Imitations of Horace*, ed. John Butt, 2nd ed. [Twickenham ed., 1953], pp. 101–2). The couplet quoted just previously is lines 79–80.

household and Tristram's study. As must now be apparent, such a division is arbitrary, in that the reader comes in contact with the two worlds in a random manner, Tristram shifting at will (or whim) from one to the other. By abandoning the sequential order of events within individual volumes, at least insofar as I have presented first one world and then the other, I have been able to follow Sterne's satiric design with more clarity than if I had focused, as recent critics have done, on Tristram's "psychological interpenetration" with his past. The instances of interrelationship (symbolic and metaphorical, rather than psychological) have been discussed in terms of their function to the satiric pattern. I have found no indication in *Tristram Shandy* that Sterne intended the interpenetration of past and present to be in the center of our attention.

Tristram opens Volume VIII, in the study, with several glances at his undisciplined mode of composition. Reminding us of his vow in Volume VI to proceed in a straight line, he now tells us it is impossible to do so; his study is in France where, with "every step that's taken, the judgment is surprised by the imagination," and where slits in petticoats are left unsewed. Thus, he warns us, he will be "ever and anon straddling out, or sidling into some bastardly digression . . ." for in this country of "fantasy and perspiration . . . every idea, sensible and insensible, gets vent . . ." (VIII.i.539). Tristram's playful strokes against the French ultimately return to himself; a lack of judgment, a proclivity to digressiveness, and a philosophy of inclusiveness have marked every page of his work, six volumes of which were written in England. And, indeed, in the next chapter, Tristram appeals to a far higher authority for his style than the French climate: ". . . of all the several ways of beginning a book which are now in practice throughout the known world, I am confident my own way of doing it is the best—I'm sure it is the most religious—for I begin with writing the first sentence—and trusting to Almighty God for the second" (VIII.ii.540). Tristram's view of inspiration is a physical rather than a spiritual one, and he invites us to watch him leaping from his chair to catch an idea even before it halfway reaches him, intercepting "many a thought which heaven intended for another man." At the same time, he invokes the name of Pope, claiming that "*Pope* and his Portrait are fools to me . . ." (VIII.ii.540), a significant claim, particularly if Sterne was indeed thinking of the portrait in the Warburton edition illustrating the lines from the Epilogue to the *Satires*:

> O sacred Weapon! left for Truth's defence,
> Sole Dread of Folly, Vice, and Insolence!
> To all but Heav'n-directed hands deny'd,
> The Muse may give thee, but the Gods must guide.[6]

Pope's lines indicate better than any others in the eighteenth century the divine purpose the Augustans assigned to their "savage indignation." Tristram, however, though as full of "faith or fire" as any martyr,[7] admits to a lack of "good works," for he has no

> Zeal or Anger—or
> Anger or Zeal—

And till gods and men agree together to call it by the same name—the errantest TARTUFFE, in science—in politics—or in religion, shall never kindle a spark within me, or have . . . a more unkind greeting, than what he will read in the next chapter (VIII.ii.541).

Tristram would acknowledge no distinction between "Zeal," a word linked in Augustan satire to the inspiration (enthusiasm) of dissenters, and "Anger" which, in context, may suggest the moral stance of Pope and satire in general. Tristram's tolerance, in other words, insists upon seeing any moral judgment as oppressive and obnoxious; his "greeting" in the next chapter strongly suggests that that tolerance serves a satiric vision.

Thus Tristram greets us "kindly," by affirming that " 'tis better to be well mounted, than go o' foot" and asking after our concubine—our wife—and the "little ones o' both sides." He then runs through a list of our ailments, our colds, coughs, claps, and so forth—and their cures: " . . . a vile purge—puke—poultice . . . and such a dose of opium! periclitating, pardi! the whole family of ye, from head to tail" (VIII.iii.541). Surely this is a traditional satiric attack, echoed by many similar passages in *Tristram Shandy* on man's frailty, both of body and mind. In addition, catching hold of great aunt Dinah's mask, Tristram informs us that the lack of a mask in the Shandy family since her day is the reason

6. Work's annotation points to this portrait along with two others in the Warburton edition showing Pope receiving inspiration; one prefaces *Windsor Forest*, the other, the *Satires*. The passage quoted is from "Epilogue to the Satires: Dialogue II," 11. 212–15; Butt, p. 325.

7. Cf. V.xi.367.

that "for these four generations, we count no more than one arch-bishop, a *Welch* judge, some three or four aldermen, and a single mountebank—" (VIII.iii.542). Again, this is satiric language, directed toward religion, the law, politics; and it is, I believe, the life and opinions of the one Shandy mountebank that we have all along been reading.

It is with this in mind, perhaps, that Sterne has Tristram accuse himself in chapter vi of what the reader has long recognized: that Tristram creates difficulties in order to "make fresh experiments of getting out of 'em . . . " (p. 545). Tristram's literary problems, as I have demonstrated, are all self-created and self-sustained, and result primarily from the twin follies of inclusiveness and digressiveness (or unvarying variety). Moreover, his experiments have not succeeded in ending his problems; quite the opposite, they have involved him deeper and deeper in the processes of uncreation— confusion and chaos, disruption and dissolution. Tristram berates himself: "What! are not the unavoidable distresses with which, as an author and a man, thou art hemm'd in on every side of thee— are they, *Tristram,* not sufficient, but thou must entangle thyself still more?" (VIII.vi.545). As an author, Tristram is rushing, in as straight a line as possible, away from his avowed intention of writing his life and opinions; in addition, as his debts accumulate, "ten cart-loads" of Volumes V and VI remain unsold. As a man there are his "vile asthma" and his "quarts of blood," lost, he says, in a fit of laughter. That the unsold volumes and the failing lungs were part of Sterne's life, though interesting, should not be used to argue that Sterne and Tristram are one. Sickness is a pervasive metaphor in the satiric design of the entire work; and that the "world" for whom Tristram labors rejects his work is certainly worth noting. Sterne might well *select* aspects of his own literary career, his own life, as they are appropriate to his ironic persona, particularly as here where they warn him, without effect, to dismount. He may even "Shandy it" upon occasion in society, in his letters, in his reaction to his critics. Selection must be kept distinct from identification, however; and playing at Tristram must be distinguished from being Tristram. The ironic design which I have explored through seven volumes of *Tristram Shandy* assures us that while Sterne could "Shandy it," Tristram, if I may, could never "Sterne it"; a man can, it would seem, always play the fool, but the fool finds it impossible to be anything but a fool.

As if to prove this point, our next view of Tristram in his study is one in which he plays the fool with a Rabelaisian gusto. The amours of uncle Toby have barely been started, but it is immediately apparent that they will be bawdy, directed as we are "into the middle of it" (VIII.vii.546). The "middle" for Tristram is a *double entendre* and signals a series of insinuating allusions to the sex organs, some involved with the amours, others with Tristram in his study. When his mistress is unkind, for example, he cries:

—By all that is hirsute and gashly! . . . taking off my furr'd cap, and twisting it round my finger—I would not give sixpence for a dozen such!
—But 'tis an excellent cap too (putting it upon my head, and pressing it close to my ears)—and warm—and soft;—especially if you stroke it the right way (VIII.xi.550).

He breaks his metaphor: "No; I shall never have a finger in the pye . . . " and swears that by "the great arch cook of cooks" who invents "inflammatory dishes" for us, that he "would not touch it for the world":

O *Tristram! Tristram!* cried *Jenny*.
O *Jenny! Jenny!* replied I, and so went on with the twelfth chapter (VIII.xi.550–51).

There is perhaps little more than exuberance in these passages, but such exuberance, like the acrostic on love which follows in chapter xiii, is certainly an integral part of the satiric tradition. It would be an error to assume that a view of *Tristram Shandy* as satire ignores or rejects the many passages of comic intent, though admittedly in the present analysis an appreciation of this aspect has often been subordinated to the tracing of primary satiric patterns. Even in this passage, it should be noted, the bawdiness is functional in Sterne's satiric design, for it glances not only at Tristram's failure with Jenny, but suggests as well the entire process by which, in *Tristram Shandy,* the creative urges of men are reduced to their physical desire (and need) to fornicate. It is not mere comic wit that the last two volumes of *Tristram Shandy* concentrate on *"an old hat cock'd—and a cock'd old hat"* (VIII.x.549). Walter and Tristram have already failed in their efforts to make of the creative act something more than physical copulation; only Toby remains, and the widow Wadman soon tells him where her attentions are "centered."

Our moments with Tristram in his study become briefer from this point to the end of *Tristram Shandy*, as the narration of uncle Toby's amours occupies his attention. Nevertheless, Tristram continues to provide insights into the view of life which governs his career as an author. His final word on hobby-horses is particularly significant in that it makes overt what has been suggested from the first—the intimate connection between a man's hobby-horse and his concupiscent nature. Tristram, of course, denies it; noting his father's use of the word *ass* for the *passions*, he warns us to pay heed to the

difference betwixt
                    My father's ass
                    and my hobby-horse—in order to keep
characters as separate as may be, in our fancies as we go along (VIII.xxxi.584).

Tristram's definition of the hobby-horse closely echoes his earliest discussion of them in Volume I: ". . . 'Tis the sporting little filly-folly which carries you out for the present hour—a maggot, a butterfly, a picture, a fiddle-stick—an uncle *Toby*'s siege—or an *any thing*, which a man makes a shift to get a stride on, to canter it away from the cares and solicitudes of life . . . " (VIII.xxxi.584). As in the first definition, the inability to discriminate between a maggot and a butterfly attracts our attention, and fiddle-stick also is not an innocent word in *Tristram Shandy*. But even more important, with the added clue that the hobby-horse has "scarce one hair . . . of the ass about him," the passage reminds us that Dr. Kunastrokius was at the center of the earliest description of the hobby-horse, establishing at the outset its intimate relationship to the passions. Moreover, we have been told that the hobby-horse works by heating its rider at the point of contact, and we have become convinced that the normal pace of a hobby-horse is a headlong gallop, not a frisky canter. In short, Tristram's distinction is not convincing, nor was it ever meant to be. As with his insistence that noses are nothing but noses, Tristram simply protests too much. There is, in the final analysis, a marked difference between a trifling eccentricity and a soul-destroying concupiscence; but it is a difference in degree, not in kind, and Tristram, mounted and galloping through eight volumes, is no competent judge of when the one rushes into the other.[8] In fact, his insistence on their being dis-

8. In a moment of rather superfluous self-confession in the first chapter of

tinct pinpoints that precise abuse of conscience which is the moral center of *Tristram Shandy*: the proclivity of men to call their own ass a hobby-horse, and the next man's hobby-horse, an ass.

Tristram gives us a brief picture of himself in his study to open the final volume of his book: " . . . And here am I sitting, this 12th day of *August*, 1766, in a purple jerkin and yellow pair of slippers, without either wig or cap on, a most tragicomical completion of his [Walter's] prediction, 'That I should neither think, nor act like any other man's child . . . ' " (IX.i.600). His motley contrasted sharply to his baldness, he is a subdued Tristram compared to the enthusiast of the eight preceding volumes; and the idea of "completion," therefore, seems to allude to more than Walter's prediction concerning the dispersed homunculus. The question raised by Wayne Booth, whether Sterne completed *Tristram Shandy*, seems to me to be answerable in the affirmative only if we understand that while Volume IX is indeed the concluding volume, the work could have admitted of additional materials before it. Sterne completes his satiric design with the story of Toby's amours, but I see no reason why, had he wanted Tristram to do so, the digressive strategy could not have interminably delayed it. It is also well to remember that Tristram is far from finished with his biography; in this regard, even more conclusive than Volume IX is the missing tenth volume. In one of Tristram's rare moments of insight into the nature of his impossible project, he foreshadows the significance of this omission:

> I will not argue the matter: Time wastes too fast: every letter I trace tells me with what rapidity Life follows my pen; the days and hours of it, more precious, my dear *Jenny*! than the rubies about thy neck, are flying over our heads like light clouds of a windy day, never to return more—every thing presses on—whilst thou art twisting that lock,—see! it grows grey; and every time I kiss thy hand to bid adieu, and every absence which follows it, are preludes to that eternal separation which we are shortly to make.—
> —Heaven have mercy upon us both! (IX.viii.610–11)

This stark awareness of impending death is played against Tristram's hopes for his book in the hands of Posterity; the matter he

---

Volume IX, Tristram admits his own concupiscent nature: ". . . how I happen to be so lewd myself, particularly a little before the vernal and autumnal equinoxes——Heaven above knows . . . " (p. 600).

"will not argue" is whether his work has "done more than the Legation of Moses, or the Tale of a Tub, that it may not swim down the gutter of Time along with them?" The link between Tristram's hopes and the Grub-Streeter's dedication to "Prince Posterity" is significant, and suggests, along with the mention of the *Legation* and the "gutter," the dim future of Tristram's work. At the same time, perhaps, the linking of *Tristram Shandy* to *A Tale of a Tub* may be Sterne's own suggestion to posterity that his work is to be considered as equally ironic.

Tristram does not contemplate death for very long; immediately after his melancholy moment he begins a new chapter of one sentence: "NOW, for what the world thinks of that ejaculation— I would not give a groat" (IX.ix.611). The rapid shift in moods is seen again in chapter xii, where Tristram halts his narration to write a digression. "A good quantity of heterogeneous matter" must be inserted, he argues, "to keep up that just balance betwixt wisdom and folly, without which a book would not hold together a single year . . . " (IX.xii.614). In view of the fact that he has always made an appearance of having his digressions emerge, how-ever ludicrously, from his progressions, Tristram's blatant desire for heterogeneous material indicates further disintegration in his workshop. Tristram informs the reader that the best way to raise the powers for a good digression is by prayer: "Only if it puts him in mind of his infirmities and defects as well ghostly as bodily —for that purpose, he will find himself rather worse after he has said them than before—for other purposes, better" (IX.xii.614). Tristram has tried every other way, moral and mechanical, to raise the powers; he has argued with his soul, but without success; and he has practiced "temperance, soberness and chastity"—virtues "good for happiness in this world" and in the next, but not good for the thing wanted, because they left the soul "just as heaven made it." Finally, the theological virtues of faith and hope were tried: " . . . but then that sniveling virtue of Meekness (as my father would always call it) takes it quite away again, so you are exactly where you started" (IX.xii.615). Tristram is here pro-viding the yardstick by which to measure him—the Christian vir-tues which, by his own confession, do not serve his book. His rejection of meekness (humility) this late in the work is particu-larly significant, since it was his self-assurance in the early volumes which marked him as an ironic persona. His egotism is still strong:

—Certainly . . . there must be something of true genius
about me . . . for never do I hit upon any invention or device
which tendeth to the furtherance of good writing, but I
instantly make it public; willing that all mankind should
write as well as myself.

—Which they certainly will, when they think as little
(IX.xii.615).

Tristram's "invention," in this instance, is a quite Swiftian
mechanical operation: To restore his powers of writing, he shaves
and dresses himself "from one end to the other of me, after my best
fashion" (IX.xiii.616). A rough-bearded man writes crudely
(Homer puzzles his hypothesis!) ; a man dressed as a gentleman
has his ideas "genteelized along with him"; and Tristram's
laundry bill proves his book is clean. We are in the world of Peter,
Martin, and Jack once again; and, as in *Tale of a Tub*, the absurd
correlation between physical and literary serves to highlight the
significant correlation between moral and literary which the hack-
writer and Tristram persistently ignore. The same arrogant pride
that makes Tristram undertake his biography free from any rules
and then to pretend to authority himself suffers him to reject
meekness as a moral virtue; the rattling all-inclusiveness of his
work is mirrored in his rejection of temperance and soberness; and
the rejection of chastity speaks for itself in the Shandy world.
Moreover, the same proselytizing spirit that renders Walter's
hobby-horses dangerous renders Tristram a menace to all who
would "think as little" as he does. For Tristram, the eschewing of
"thinking" is a natural concomitant to his endorsement of spon-
taneity and "genius." For the reader, however, Tristram's failure
to think must reflect on his inventions and devices. Tristram is
condemned by his own words, and at this late point, with illness
and death so close at hand, his rejection of the work's normative
values seems a final comment on his personality and his fate. I do
not think it possible that Sterne would share that personality or
embrace that fate.

Two blank pages where chapters xviii and xix are supposed to
be provide a graphic illustration of the final dissolution in Tristram's study. There has been an interesting progression to this
blankness, from Yorick's black page (I.xii.33), to the marbled
page, emblem of Tristram's work (III.xxxvi.227), to the blank
page below an invitation to paint the widow Wadman (VI.xxxviii.

470–71). Here, however, the blankness is more complete because there are no instructions to our fancy, no indication why the chapters have been omitted and blank pages inserted in their place. Tristram appears to have finally exhausted himself, and in chapter xxiv he admits this to be the truth. "Let us drop the metaphor," he ends chapter xxiii, "—AND the story too—if you please: for though I have all along been hastening towards this part of it . . . as well knowing it to be the choicest morsel of what I had to offer to the world, yet now that I am got to it, any one is welcome to take my pen, and go on with the story for me that will—I see the difficulties of the descriptions I'm going to give—and feel my want of powers" (IX.xxiv.627). In part, Tristram's fatigue is physical—he has lost "some fourscore ounces of blood this week . . ." (IX.xxiv.627). In part, it is rational, marked by his failure to ever explain the arbitrariness of having chapters xviii and xix as a part of chapter xxv. It is a lesson, he says, *"to let people tell their stories their own way,"* and he leaves it at that. Unlike Tristram's other conscious disorderings—the Preface in Volume III, the missing chapter, the digressive style—no rationale, however absurd, is offered. Rather, as with his blatant quest for "heterogeneous matter" in chapter xii, Tristram here surrenders to his own arbitrary will; and he does so with that unquestioning obedience which perhaps always accompanies an author's insistence on total aesthetic freedom. Tristram's misplaced chapters, like his putting S before R in his acrostic on Love (VIII.xiii.551), is the *reductio ad absurdum* of the literary theories under which he labors.

Finally, Tristram's fatigue is also spiritual, in a manner of speaking; he finds it necessary, at any rate, to invoke the "GENTLE Spirit of sweetest humour, who erst didst sit upon the easy pen of my beloved CERVANTES . . . (IX.xxiv.628). For Tristram, Cervantes is representative of good humor, and he recounts his own "good humor" in France and Italy, in spite of the *"ups and downs"* of traveling. Uncle Toby's amours were in his head, moreover, putting him "in the most perfect state of bounty and good will"; he felt, he tells us, "the kindliest harmony vibrating within me, with every oscillation of the chaise alike; so that whether the roads were rough or smooth, it made no difference; every thing I saw, or had to do with, touch'd upon some secret spring either of sentiment or rapture" (IX.xxiv.629). The similarity between this description and that of the hobby-horse and rider (I.xxiv.77) is too obvious to be missed. The story of Maria, intended by Tristram to show his secret spring's being touched, demonstrates, once again, that when a man is mounted only one part gets heated. The elements are again present for a typical sentimental story: A young girl, her banns forbidden by a scheming priest, plays a sad, mad song on her flute—and tends a little goat. Tristram is touched: " . . . she was beautiful; and if ever I felt the full force of an honest heartache, it was the moment I saw her. . . . " He springs from his chaise:

> . . . and found myself sitting betwixt her and her goat before I relapsed from my enthusiasm.
>   MARIA look'd wistfully for some time at me, and then at her goat—and then at me—and then at her goat again, and so on, alternately—
>   —Well, *Maria*, said I softly—What resemblance do you find? (IX.xxiv.631)

The same emotional posing that led Tristram unwittingly to "spoil" the story of Le Fever is at work again. Unlike the earlier story, however, Tristram this time is aware of the incongruity of his remark with the sentiment he is professing. He entreats the "candid reader" to believe that the question stemmed from his "humblest conviction of what a *Beast* man is. . . . " He would not, he adds, have dropped such an "unseasonable pleasantry" for all Rabelais' wit. Tristram has steadfastly refused to recognize both humility and the "beast" in man; and he is approaching the end of Toby's amours, in which Rabelaisian wit constantly makes lascivious the "secret spring" which is so readily touched in the Shandy family.[9]

If Tristram thinks of Cervantes as visited by the "gentle spirit" of sentimental writing, Sterne obviously thinks of him in another light, revealed in Tristram's self-imposed penance for the inadvertent remark: " . . . I swore I would set up for Wisdom and utter grave sentences the rest of my days—and never—never attempt again to commit mirth with man, woman, or child, the longest day I had to live" (IX.xxiv.631). The grave irony, for which Cervantes was a foremost model to the century, is here

---

9. The address to the "candid reader" is perhaps a signal of the ironic intention of the passage; see Mary Claire Randolph, " 'Candour' in XVIIIth-Century Satire," *RES*, XX (1944), 45–62.

clearly suggested;[10] that it is the controlling irony of *Tristram Shandy* is intimated in what immediately follows: "As for writing nonsense to them—I believe, there was a reserve—but that I leave to the world" (IX.xxiv.631). The gravity of the sentimentalist is in Tristram's farewell to Maria: " . . . she took her pipe and told me such a tale of woe with it, that I rose up, and with broken and irregular steps walk'd softly to my chaise." The Rabelaisian wit is in the very next line: "What an excellent inn at *Moulins*!" And taken together, with all their incongruity, they form the "nonsense" that Tristram Shandy has left to the world, written in the "grave manner" of "my beloved Cervantes."

Tristram's handling of Maria provides a convenient bridge from his study to uncle Toby's amours, for Sterne's best Rabelaisian nonsense plagues Tristram's every attempt to present the affair with gravity and sentiment. Tristram introduces the problems of love with an anatomical survey of its location: " . . . so long, as what in this vessel of the human frame, is *Love*—may be *Hatred*, in that—*Sentiment* half a yard higher—and *Nonsense*————no, Madam,—not there—I mean at the part I am now pointing to with my forefinger—how can we help ourselves?" (VIII.iv.542). Too many forefingers will be pointed in the course of Toby's amours for us to miss Tristram's meaning. While Toby tries to conduct an affair of the heart, the widow Wadman is busy conducting an affair of the groin. Resembling in some respects the Lady Wishforts and Mrs. Loveits of Restoration comedy, the widow Wadman finds a more certain presage in the frank concupiscence of the Wife of Bath. The coming of love to the Widow is, I believe, one of the most successful passages in *Tristram Shandy*, and evidence, perhaps, that while Tristram's energies are flagging, Sterne's satiric wit is as sharp as ever. The first night that Toby stays in her house, the Widow sits up until midnight; the second night, she asks for a couple of candles and reads her marriage settlement; the third night

> when *Bridget* had pull'd down the night-shift, and was assaying to stick in the corking pin—

10. See Norman Knox, *The Word Irony and its Context, 1500–1755* (Durham, N.C., 1961), p. 171, and Ronald Paulson, *The Fictions of Satire* (Baltimore, 1967), pp. 97–99. I am not arguing that Cervantes was incapable of seeing simultaneously the ludicrous and the touching, but rather that Tristram is unable to do so, and that his version of Cervantes' "gentle spirit" is undercut by this inability.

—With a kick of both heels at once . . . she kick'd the pin
out of her fingers—the *etiquette* which hung upon it, down—
down it fell to the ground. . . .
    From all which it was plain that widow *Wadman* was in
love . . . (VIII.ix.548).

The resemblance between this kick and the kick of Walter's ass
(passions) should not be disregarded; and in chapter xiii, after
Tristram's acrostic on love, we are told that "she stood . . . ready
harnessed and caparisoned at all points to watch accidents" (p.
552). This, then, is the "daughter of *Eve*" ordained to test Toby's
tender heart and universal good will.
    The Widow's approach is simple: She will mount Toby's
horse in order to make him dismount; and when he is dislodged,
she will offer another mount for his pleasure. Thus her first tactic
(and the word is well chosen) is to lay siege to the sentry-box.
Tristram's metaphor for the assault is somewhat bawdy. A man,
he says, "may be set on fire like a candle, at either end—provided
there is a sufficient wick standing out . . . " (VIII.xv.553). Whether
Toby will prove sufficient remains to be seen; but the Widow is
aware that if she lights Toby only at the bottom the flame may
easily be put out: "—And so to make sure . . . Mrs. *Wadman*
predetermined to light my uncle *Toby* neither at this end or that;
but like a prodigal's candle, to light him, if possible, at both ends
at once" (VIII.xvi.554). The scene is a parody of both the excessive detail of the novelists and the minute sensuality, under the
cover of sensibility, of the sentimentalists. Inch by inch across
Toby's maps, widow Wadman pursues his fingers with her own;
while under the table, she presses her leg against his calf:

    —So that my uncle *Toby* being thus attacked and sore
    push'd on both his wings—was it a wonder, if now and then,
    it put his centre into disorder?—
    —The duce take it! said my uncle *Toby* (VIII.xvi.556).

The persistent reduction of human love to its physical manifestations is the weapon Sterne brings to bear against the sentimental
view of man which Toby embodies. And though the widow Wadman and her "venereal" eyes are the primary battery, Trim and
Walter also press the point home to Toby. From every side, Toby's
damaged "center" is pondered, and questioned, and challenged, as
the Shandy world tests his capacity to "love."

Significantly, Toby is not ensnared until after the Treaty of Utrecht. For eleven years, in spite of the Widow's fingers and knees and eyes, he remains true to his bowling-green. That on the day he is finally forced to dismount, Mrs. Wadman should succeed in doing "uncle *Toby*'s business," suggests that rather than awakening to love, Toby merely changes mistresses. It is not, to be sure, an easy change; against the background of Trim's futile efforts to tell the story of the "King of Bohemia and his seven castles," Toby airs his hobby-horse for one last time. Like everything else in these last two volumes, however, Trim's frustration and Toby's galloping ultimately come to rest in the latter's groin. Arguing whether an injury to the knee is more painful than one in the groin, the master and servant leave the question—and Mrs. Wadman, who is listening with bated breath, an unpinned mob, and on one leg—unsettled; and Trim, abandoning his untold story, tells instead the story of his own amours.

Love means only one thing for Trim. That he wishes to divide all he has with the fair *Beguine*, and that he sickens and loses color when she leaves him are not signs of love. He explains this to Toby:

> . . . for during the three weeks she was almost constantly with me, fomenting my knee with her hand, night and day— I can honestly say . . . —that * * * * * * * *
> * * * * * * * * *   once.
> That was very odd, *Trim*, quoth my uncle *Toby*—
> I think so too—said Mrs. *Wadman*.
> It never did, said the corporal (VIII.xx.572).

Love comes only when the *Beguine*, after a long session of rubbing, begins also to rub above the knee. "I perceived, then, I was beginning to be in love," Trim tells Toby; and continues:

> The more she rubb'd, and the longer strokes she took— the more the fire kindled in my veins— . . . I seiz'd her hand—
> —And then, thou clapped'st it to thy lips, *Trim*, said my uncle *Toby*—and madest a speech.
> Whether the corporal's amour terminated precisely in the way my uncle *Toby* described it, is not material; it is enough that it contain'd in it the essence of all the love-romances which ever have been wrote . . . (VIII.xxii.574–75).

It is no wonder that after this story the widow Wadman's "venereal" eyes undo Toby. Nor is it to be wondered that he at first confuses the feelings of love with the pains of a blister on his nethermost part, got in trotting too hastily to save a wood of "singular service to him in his description of the battle of *Wynnendale* . . ." (VIII.xxvi.580). It is possible to maintain that Sterne is simply having fun at Toby's expense, yet even this assertion indicates a view of Toby not shared by Tristram. Tristram continues to praise his uncle's "milk of human nature," his "all benignity," his "sentimental heigh ho!" and his taking love "like a lamb," as opposed to Walter, who was "all abuse and foul language" when in love. Nonetheless, every moment of Toby's amours returns us to his groin. He lets "the poison [of love] work in his veins without resistance—in the sharpest exacerbations of his wound (like that on his groin) he never dropt one fretful . . . word . . ." (VIII.xxvi.579). He pensively smokes his pipe, "looking at his lame leg." Trim tells him to wear his "thin scarlet breeches"; he decides on the "red plush ones." He wants to wear his sword: " 'Twill be only in your honour's way, replied *Trim*." In short, Toby's amours may with justice be called "Toby's education," and what Toby learns about is the sexual and frankly lascivious nature of human love. In a larger application, but one which the satiric structure of *Tristram Shandy* demands, Toby's view of life, the broadly defined "sentimentalism" of my second chapter, meets its overwhelming match in the physical nature of man. Like Walter's systems, like Tristram's book, Toby's "goodness" fails when faced by the real world; in particular, the sentimental vision of man's innate goodness fades before the reality of human passion and human promiscuity. That this passion and promiscuity belong to the harmless widow Wadman suggests the universality of their existence. The Widow is a "daughter of *Eve*," "*a perfect woman*," a human being with merely the flesh that man is heir to; the flesh that the sentimentalist would like to ignore, and indeed does ignore. Toby has it forced upon him.

It is important to note that Sterne is not introducing a new yardstick by which to measure Toby. Rather, he is re-emphasizing what the satiric design has insisted upon throughout: that all men, even Toby, participate in the human condition. Toby's hobbyhorse, Tristram assures us, is not like Walter's ass. I have demonstrated above, however, the irony behind this assurance; and the fact that Toby conducts his amours in the manner of a siege further suggests Sterne's ironic intentions. To be sure, there is a difference:

. . . I declare, corporal I had rather march up to the very
edge of a trench—
     —A woman is quite a different thing—said the corporal.
     —I suppose so, quoth my uncle *Toby* (VIII.xxx.583).

Nevertheless, Toby and Trim plot their attack, their flanking
action in the kitchen, their frontal assault in the parlor; they dress
in their uniforms; and they march, more or less boldly, up to the
Widow's door. The baggage of the one folly is transferred to the
other, strongly suggesting the essential sameness of Toby's bowling-green and amours—a sameness of irrationality when they are
measured by any reasonable standard.

As with his defense of war, Toby shows a surprising grasp of
love when faced by his brother's galloping mount. There are,
Walter informs him, two distinct kinds of love, that of the Brain
and that of the Liver: "What signifies it . . . replied my uncle
Toby, which of the two it is, provided it will but make a man
marry, and love his wife, and get a few children" (VIII.xxxiii.
585–86). Yorick is present to acknowledge the "reason and plain
sense" of Toby's comment, indicating by doing so, that this is the
reasonable norm against which we are to measure Toby's amours.
Although the central metaphor of *Tristram Shandy* is creation,
not since Bobby's death at the end of Volume IV have its positive
aspects played a significant role in the satiric design. Injury, dissolution, and death have become the important metaphors in the
later books, attaching themselves to the central metaphor by their
antithetical nature; that is, they are metaphors of uncreation. It has
been suggested that Tristram's futile flirtations in Volume VII were
meant to indicate his desire to propagate himself before his impending death. His failure to do so leaves only Toby remaining to
fulfill the Shandy desire for creation. The suggestion is strong,
however, that he will not succeed; and Walter's letter on love,
filled with reminders of love's concupiscible nature, further supports this belief. Advising Toby never to "go forth upon the
enterprize . . . without first recommending thyself to the protection
of Almighty God . . ." Walter then tells him to shave his head
clean every few days to "keep ideas of baldness out of her fancy";
to wear breeches neither too tight nor too loose—"A just medium
prevents all conclusions"; to speak softly and never "throw down
the tongs and poker"; and to keep the Widow from reading
Rabelais, Scarron, or *Don Quixote*: "—They are all books which

excite laughter; and thou knowest, dear *Toby*, that there is no passion so serious, as lust" (VIII.xxxiv.591–92). In brief, Toby is to keep the widow Wadman as warm as possible. At the same time, if his own "ASSE continues still kicking," he must let blood and go on a cooling diet, derived from Burton. Toby's "milk of human nature" is being called upon to perform like the blood of a quite different, yet more probable and necessary, human nature: "I think the procreation of children as beneficial to the world, said *Yorick*, as the finding out the longitude—" (VIII.xxxiii.588). But though Toby knows that procreation is the purpose of marriage, there is no evidence either that he has yet discovered the right end of a woman, or that he can satisfy the widow's desires. Like his mock battles, Toby's amours are destined to be only a futile imitation of the real thing.

The final volume of *Tristram Shandy* confirms all these earlier intimations. Once again, a story by Trim, that of Tom and the Jew's widow, forms the background for the Shandy failure. Tom's success returns us to the center of Toby's problem:

> She made a feint however of defending herself, by snatch-
> ing up a sausage:—*Tom* instantly laid hold of another—
> But seeing *Tom*'s had more gristle in it———
> She signed the capitulation— (IX.vii.609).

The bawdiness of Tom's victory is juxtaposed with Toby's assertion that he loves mankind, a juxtaposition which reduces the assertion to cant. Moreover, Toby's vaunted humanitarianism is shown to be the cant of a hypocrite as well, for he seizes the occasion to dismount from his ASSE and gallop away on his more familiar horse: " . . . as the knowledge of arms tends so apparently to the good and quiet of the world—and particularly that branch of it which we have practised together in our bowling-green, has no object but to shorten the strides of AMBITION, and intrench the lives and fortunes of the *few,* from the plunderings of the *many*—whenever that drum beats in our ears, I trust, Corporal, we shall neither of us want so much humanity and fellow-feeling as to face about and march" (IX.viii.609–10). Sterne italicizes the key words of his ironic inversion, yet critic after critic has acquiesced in Toby's "milk of human nature." Just a few pages earlier, Toby and Trim had earnestly discussed the problem whether "A Negro has a soul?" and had decided he must, since

"It would be putting one sadly over the head of another" if he did not (IX.vi.606). Now Toby defends war as a means of protecting the *few* from the *many*. Whatever "mankind" is to Toby, it is not "the *many*"; nor is it the *one*, since Toby seizes this opportunity to face about and march away from the Widow's door, the corporal following, "shouldering his stick." Toby's "humanity and fellow-feeling," his love for mankind and for the widow Wadman, is all of a piece. The bowling-green, as an "instrument" of Toby's humanity, finds its parallel in whatever is behind his "red plush breeches." The insufficiency of the one is transferred to the other; the ludicrous pretensions of the one are also shared by the other. In war and in love, Toby plays a game in miniature; his games are, I believe, Sterne's final satiric evaluation of the sentimental vision.

The importance of these passages revealing the nature of Toby's universal benevolence is perhaps signaled by Tristram's ending the chapter with his recognition of time's flight and his pitiable "—Heaven have mercy upon us both," the significance of which has already been discussed. It remains only for Toby to be made aware of his defeat at the hands of reality. When we return to him in chapters xvi and xvii, he is at Mrs. Wadman's door, whistling *Lillabullero*; chapters xviii and xix are missing; and in chapter xx, after a lacuna, Toby tells the widow: "—You shall see the very place . . ." (IX.xx.623). Tristram never tells us why he omits the two preceding chapters, but it is apparent that Sterne wants to move as quickly as possible from the revelations we have just read to the crux of Toby's amours while still maintaining a due regard for the digressive chaos which is marking Tristram's dissolution. This, too, is a revelation, produced by the same satiric device of ironic inversion. Tristram labors *not* to explain what is obvious from the start, namely, that Mrs. Wadman wants to know the condition of Toby's groin. Using an image from Slawkenbergius, Tristram compares the choosing of a husband to the choosing of a proper ass; a woman must search all the panniers down to their bottoms, rejecting those which carry empty bottles, tripes, trunk-hose, and pantofles. But when she finds the pannier containing "it" she " . . . samples it—measures it—stretches it—wets it—dries it—then takes her teeth both to the warp and weft of it—" (IX.xxi. 624–25). What "it" is, Slawkenbergius and Tristram refuse to say, but, of course, there is no need to; and the gross lasciviousness of the passage serves as an important commentary on Toby's view of love—and life.

That a husband must be so tested is the result of Nature's eternal bungling in "making so simple a thing as a married man." This, for Tristram, is a mystery and a riddle, since Nature "seldom or never errs" when making any other beast; but whether it is "the choice of the clay," or the baking of it, a man never seems to come out right: " . . . by an excess of [baking] a husband may turn out too crusty . . . —or not enough so, through defect of heat . . . " (IX.xxii.625). The reduction of man to clay, the "world beset on all sides with mysteries and riddles," and the puzzled query as to man's consistently imperfect nature, in one extreme or the other, all suggest the religious atmosphere of Christianity, the moral atmosphere of satire. The passage is an abstraction of those main points of doctrine which make the "Abuses of Conscience Considered" an orthodox sermon. And yet, Tristram tells us all this only to dismiss it as inapplicable to his uncle Toby: " . . . she [Nature] had formed him of the best and kindliest clay—had temper'd it with her own milk, and breathed into it the sweetest spirit—she had made him all gentle, generous and humane—she had fill'd his heart with trust and confidence . . . " (IX.xxii.626). Moreover, Tristram assures us, in another lacuna, that Nature had bestowed Toby with all that Mrs. Wadman could desire and that "The DONATION was not defeated[11] by my uncle *Toby*'s wound" (IX.xxii.626). We are familiar enough with Tristram at this point to know that in passages of this nature the irony of mock-encomium is at work. Particularly foolhardy would be an acceptance of Toby as somehow exempt from the human condition of flawed clay; and we have noted as well that Toby's benevolence is beset by follies, extravagances, and hypocrisies which render it, at best, insufficient as either a moral position or a vision of life. Tristram cannot, of course, acknowledge this fact, since his nature is made up of many of the same follies; he does admit, however, that his assertion concerning Toby's wound was "somewhat apocryphal": ". . . and the Devil . . . had raised scruples in Mrs. *Wadman*'s brain about it . . . turning my uncle *Toby*'s Virtue thereupon into nothing but *empty bottles, tripes, trunk-hose,* and *pantofles*" (IX.xxii.626). Thus does Tristram

11. Work's edition incorrectly prints "defended"; "defeated" is the reading of the first edition.

finally declare what we have slowly been coming to recognize ourselves: the worthlessness of the sentimental attitude which Toby
embodies. It is hardly to be wondered at that, in the next chapter
but one, Tristram offers us his pen in surrender, and then goes on
to show the failure of his own sentimentalism in the story of
Maria. The worlds of Tristram's study and the Shandy household
are collapsing simultaneously.

Still Sterne is not finished with Toby. Though the reader can
no longer take his "humanity" seriously, Toby's naïve faith in the
humanity of others remains intact. Tristram returns once again to
Toby's amours, giving us chapters xviii and xix as part of chapter
xxv. Again the center of attention is Toby's groin, and Mrs. Wadman's curiosity over its sufficiency. The result is a clash of hobby-
horses such as we have seen before in the Shandy world; every one
of the Widow's solicitous questions concerning the wound is turned
by Toby into a lecture on the battle of Namur. For Toby, Mrs.
Wadman's constant interest in his wound is a mark of her humanity, and drawing up a list of her thousand virtues, he has Trim
write "H U M A N I T Y" at the top of the page: "Prithee, Corporal, said my uncle *Toby*, as soon as *Trim* had done it—how
often does Mrs. *Bridget* enquire after the wound on the cap of thy
knee . . ." (IX.xxxi.642). The answer is that she does not inquire,
and Toby sees this as proof of Mrs. Wadman's superiority; when
he goes on to assert that had he been wounded on the knee, the
Widow would have been equally compassionate, Trim finally sets
his master straight:

> —God bless your honour! cried the Corporal—what has
> a woman's compassion to do with a wound upon the cap of
> a man's knee? . . .
> "The knee is such a distance from the main body—whereas
> the groin, your honour knows, is upon the very *curtin* of the
> place" (IX.xxxi.643).

Toby's defeat is complete. He lays down his pipe as "gently . . .
as if it had been spun from the unravellings of a spider's web"
and marches with Trim to Walter's house, where, significantly,
Walter is already in the process of spinning his own web to Yorick.
Walter Shandy has the next-to-last words in *Tristram Shandy*,
an indictment of man's means of procreation: "—THAT provision
should be made for continuing the race of so great, so exalted and

godlike a Being as man—I am far from denying—but . . . I still think . . . it to be a pity, that it should be done by means of a passion which bends down the faculties, and turns all the wisdom, contemplations, and operations of the soul backwards . . ." (IX.xxxiii. 644–45). Why, Walter asks, do we put out the candle when "we go about to make and plant a man"; why are all the instruments of the process held unfit for a cleanly mind? And why, he asks, looking at Toby, is the "act of killing and destroying a man" considered glorious, and the weapons honourable? Yorick rises to "batter the whole hypothesis to pieces," perhaps by pointing out that only in the Shandy world (which is, of course, large enough to include every reader) are the values of creation and destruction perverted in this manner.

His answer is unnecessary, however, for those who have read *Tristram Shandy* as a satire; for those who, following the satiric pattern, have watched all the Shandean hopes of creation collapse in dissolution, destruction, and death. For this is what *Tristram Shandy* is finally about: the triumph of the uncreating spirit in man, the celebration of chaos and confusion, destruction and death, whether in Toby's bowling-green, Walter's household, or Tristram's study. Procreation and Toby's battlefield are merely metaphorical representations of the larger principles at work in Sterne's satire. In the Shandean world, all the possibilities of creation—literary, intellectual, spiritual, as well as physical—are surrounded and subverted by the passions which turn "all the wisdom, contemplations, and operations of the soul backwards." Moreover, out of this failure of the reason to control the passions arises a perverse praise for men who bid farewell to "cool reason and fair discretion" and who gallop through life, heated by the imaginings of unreasoning minds and sentimental hearts. Surely Yorick is rising to put the blame for this perversity where it belongs: upon man's insistence on obeying the call of these passions wherever it leads him; giving his mount full rein, charging headlong into the mysteries and riddles of God's universe.

Sterne's satire comes to rest here. Through a complex pattern of metaphor and symbol, all the diverse activities of the Shandy household and Tristram's study share in the fundamental movement of the satire from its beginning in birth and creation to its conclusion in dissolution and uncreation. At the same time, by offering the reader a series of oppositions and alternatives, Sterne provides a means by which we may measure the Shandean efforts. Walter, the *philosophus gloriosus*, creating out of himself systems and theories bearing no relationship to reality, is easily found wanting. Defeated by a dispersed homunculus, a crushed nose, and a misnaming, Walter's desire to create reaches the ignominious epitome of uncreating chaos in the shaping of one million ideas about a white bear. The celebration of death and destruction on Toby's mock battlefield is not significantly different from Walter's faith, echoed by Tristram, in his "North-west passage to the intellectual world." Man's mind proves not only insufficient to the task of creation, but proves amiable to processes of destruction as well.

If science and philosophy prove inadequate, would it not be better to place our trust and hope in the feeling heart, the simplicity of Toby's sentimentalism? Sterne tempts us to do so, and then in Volumes VIII and IX proves the folly of so doing. Toby's amours, like his mock battles, are futile imitations of the real thing. The insufficiency of the one is transferred to the other; the ludicrous pretensions of the one are also shared by the other. The sentimental attitude, like the red plush trousers, proves empty and sterile —a façade to cover an insufficiency which, if not simply hypocritical as in sentimental writing, is nonetheless pervaded by moral blindness, a failure of self-knowledge and self-examination. In war and in love, Toby can only reduce life to a game; the diminution is, I have suggested, Sterne's condemnation of the sentimentalism which Toby embodies.

The same spirit of uncreation pursues Tristram in his study where, unable to reconcile his inheritance from Walter with that from Toby, he simply alternates the one with the other, moving ever closer to chaos and dissolution. Filled with pride, he abandons at the outset every rule but that of his own whim. Later, caught by his own freedom, lost in the self-made maze of his inclusiveness and digressiveness, he pins all his hopes on the story of Toby's amours. The futility of the amours, however, mirrors the futility of his creative efforts. Death, from which he fled in Volume VII, is clearly felt in the physical failures of the last volumes and in the missing Volume X. As with Walter and Toby, reality, the physical nature of man and the universe, defeats Tristram. It is Sterne's persistent return to the physical—whether the hobby-horse, illness, impotence, or death—which provides throughout the work the norms against which the Shandy dreams wreck themselves. Reason is insufficient because it proves unable to control or account for the physical accidents which everywhere make havoc of the Shandean systems. Sentiment is equally insufficient because it cannot mask or compensate for the physical frailty which is also integral to the Shandy world. And Tristram, garters in hand, a sport of accident and frailty, embodies both failures. His book is, indeed, a celebration of, and an encomium to, the uncreating spirit of which he is sole heir and lifelong practitioner. As the uncreating spirit emerges triumphant in *Tristram Shandy*, it is Yorick, Sterne's symbol of Christian death, who has the final word; the Shandy bull has proved impotent:

> L--d! said my mother, what is all this story about?——
> A COCK and a BULL, said *Yorick*——And one of the best of its kind, I ever heard (IX.xxxiii.647).

Tristram did not live, nor could he have lived, to complete the work.

Index

207

DATE DUE